"Is Terry King dead?"

Sergeant Bain refused to say. "It's still too early in the investigation. All we know is a male victim has been found dead inside the home."

"Can I look at the body and identify the victim?" Chavis asked. He seemed eager to view the crime scene.

"The victim will be identified by the Medical Examiner's Office," Bain replied.

"Do you think the boys killed him?"

The deputy was stunned. "Why would you ask that question?"

Ricky replied, "Well, Terry was an abusive father." He added that he had helped Terry find the boys a couple of days earlier when they ran away from home.

Ricky Chavis's intense interest in the murder did not go unnoticed. Bain would later write in his report: *I found it odd that Chavis had not inquired about the condition or whereabouts of the boys, given the circumstances.*

Realizing investigators might want to question the man further, Bain took down Ricky's personal information. He then suggested that Chavis return home, where an investigator would contact him.

But Ricky Chavis had other plans.

A
PERVERSION
OF JUSTICE

A SOUTHERN TRAGEDY
OF MURDER, LIES, AND
INNOCENCE BETRAYED

KATHRYN MEDICO
AND MOLLYE BARROWS

AVON BOOKS
An Imprint of HarperCollinsPublishers

A Perversion of Justice is a journalistic account of the actual murder investigation of Ricky Chavis, Derek King, and Alex King for the 2001 killing of Terry King in Florida. The events recounted in this book are true. The personalities, events, actions, and conversations portrayed in this book have been constructed using court records, police reports, personal interviews, newspaper reports, and personal papers. The names Billy and Danny are fictitious, and the names of Ronnie, Randy, Mark, and Velma have been changed to protect their privacy. In any such event, the use of a name of an actual individual is entirely coincidental.

AVON BOOKS
An Imprint of HarperCollins*Publishers*
10 East 53rd Street
New York, New York 10022-5299

Copyright © 2004 by Kathryn Medico and Mollye Barrows
ISBN: 0-06-054929-7
www.avonbooks.com

First Avon Books paperback printing: June 2004

Avon Trademark Reg. U.S. Pat. Off. and in Other Countries, Marca Registrada, Hecho en U.S.A.
HarperCollins® is a registered trademark of HarperCollins Publishers Inc.

Printed in the U.S.A.

10 9 8 7 6 5 4 3 2 1

For Terry Lee King,
whose lessons of love endure beyond his short years
and
Precious Mamasan,
whose heavenly nature inspires all in her realm

Acknowledgments

The story that follows is one of heartbreak, lightened only by the wonderful people who opened their lives to us in their most difficult times. Few of us will ever know the pain of their loss or the depth of their anguish as they sat under the world's microscope of judgment. To these family members, we owe our greatest gratitude. The information they provided pushed us to look beyond the headlines to try to understand how this tragedy happened. To Herb Helton, who found the courage to face his molester so that other children might not have to, we are deeply thankful. His contribution to the book is inestimable.

We are also profoundly grateful to the people at Harper-Collins who shaped this book: Sarah Durand, who helped us find the critical elements of the story; attorney Mark Jackson, who lent his expertise; Peter Weissman, whose brilliant copyediting saved us; Jeremy Cesarec, who kept everyone on track; and publicist Diana Tynan, who brought her enthusiastic support to the project. Many thanks to Ashley and Carolyn Grayson, whose experience and finesse taught us the priceless value of agents.

Special appreciation is due Deb and Paul Truitt, who freely gave so much time to gently and painstakingly measure each word for its value. Their insight gave us the objective vision we needed to present the information fairly and honestly.

We would also like to acknowledge the valuable help of our wonderful friends—Jennifer Merritt, Charlie Swan, Dave H., and Donald Figura, for rushing to help when we called. To the Mercurio Men who educated us about law enforcement and legal defense, many thanks. Cindy, Jean, Ramona, and Melanie, you were a wonderful tag-team of cheerleaders, advisers, and comrades. And unexpressible gratitude to Grant, eternal friend, whose timely invitation to Mexico was the most perfect of rewards.

Finally, we are indebted to our wonderful families. Although the mechanics of writing were learned in school, the foundation for Christian compassion was laid by Orvid and Jean Hamrick, and Edith and BJ Barrows. They instilled in us a desire to fight for the ones who most need it. To Donna, Joy, and Billy, we cherish you. To David, Pete, Lindsey, and Katie, whose emotional support sustained us during the challenging year, we are tremendously grateful. Your patience with our obsession was the truest measure of love, and without it, this book would not have been written.

Author's Note

Although both authors interviewed and corresponded with Ricky Chavis, all meetings and letters are attributed to Mollye Barrows for the sake of continuity.

The names of four victims—Ronnie, Randy, Mark, and Billy—have been changed. They were minors when the crimes against them were committed, and their real names have not been published to date. The name of Ronnie's mother has been changed to Velma to protect her privacy. The name Danny is also fictitious.

Prologue

Ed Harris kicked off his slippers, slid into bed next to his wife and felt her cringe. You'd think after fifty-one years of marriage she'd get used to my cold feet, he thought. However, she quickly nestled against him, thankful for the added warmth on the brisk November night. The winter of 2001 was proving to be unusually chilly for the Sunshine State.

Harris soon drifted off to sleep. He slept fitfully, dreaming of fishing at his favorite spot on Perdido River. The long, murky waterway that wound through Northwest Florida's towering pines and marshy bayous often gave up a bountiful catch. In his dream he heard a loud popping sound that didn't seem to fit the peaceful scene. Like a diver surfacing for air, his mind awoke in search of an explanation. For a moment he lay disoriented, trying to shake off the dream. Hearing the noise again, he realized it was coming from outside his bedroom window. Stumbling through the darkness, he could already see the raging fire engulfing his neighbor's house and realized the mysterious popping sounds were the windows of the small, wooden home blowing out from the heat.

Harris grabbed the phone and dialed 911, quickly reporting the address of the fire. The house sat next to his, along Muscogee Road, a busy thoroughfare in the small, rural town of Cantonment. A few yards and a chain-link fence were all that stood between them. Harris explained to the dispatcher that his neighbor's house was set back from the main road, but she was having trouble understanding the location. Her calm questioning alarmed and angered Harris.

"Terry King and his two boys are in that fire!" he yelled, close to panic. "I know they're home because their car's in the driveway!"

David Jordan, a seventeen-year veteran firefighter, heard the call go out over his scanner. Muscogee Road, he thought. That's less than a mile away. He decided to drive there directly instead of reporting to the Cantonment fire station.

When he arrived, he found the small wooden house had become a blinding, orange inferno. The fire had already burned through the roof and was shooting a geyser of flames thirty feet into the air.

Ed Harris saw Jordan pull up and ran to him, calling frantically. "The family's still in there!" he screamed over the blaze. "You've got to get them out!"

Jordan hurried to the back of the house and kicked the door open. A rush of black smoke poured out. He realized that without his fire gear he couldn't breathe or see in the burning home. Instead of entering, he decided to prepare the building by cutting off the power so firefighters wouldn't get shocked when they doused the house with water.

Ed heard the fire engines coming and almost wept with relief. Only six minutes had passed since he called 911, but it seemed like an eternity. As he stood back and watched the firefighters swarm the house he wondered to himself how anyone inside could still be alive.

Firefighter Marcus Williams kicked the front door three times with his heavy boot and it burst open with a bang. Williams dropped to the ground and crawled into the house, staying low where the dark smoke was thinnest. His years of experience had taught him he must consciously control the adrenaline coursing through his veins. He knew about "squirrels"—firefighters who got so excited they used up their air tanks too quickly. Some firefighters hummed tunes to slow their breathing. Williams preferred to chew gum.

The smoke was so thick that he could see nothing but blackness. He felt his way along the wall with his hand, searching for the father and his children. He knew that in house fires, children often hid in closets or cabinets to get away from the smoke, making it even more difficult to find them.

On the other side of the house firefighter Brandon Beecher was crawling blindly through the darkened living room. There were no flames in the room but the heavy smoke prevented him from seeing anything. He stayed close to the wall so he wouldn't lose his way in the blackness. When his shoulder bumped into a sofa, he swept his hands across the cushions, groping to make sure no one was there.

By now Marcus Williams had worked his way through three rooms without a sign of the missing family. A horrible dread began to grip him—still no survivors. After twenty-five minutes in the smoldering house, he knew his air was almost gone. He reluctantly began backtracking and was almost to the front door when he heard a chilling report on his radio from Brandon Beecher: "We've got a body in here."

PART ONE
DEATH AND ASHES

*"Like as the waves make towards the pebbl'd shore,
so do our minutes, hasten to their end."*
William Shakespeare

Chapter 1

BRANDON BEECHER'S TRAINING AT THE SANTA ROSA Fire Academy had taught him that every house fire held potential victims, even if neighbors insisted that no one was home. For Beecher, the searching procedure never changed.

After all, neighbors had been wrong before. In a fire several years back, Beecher rescued a teenager in a "vacant" house. The runaway had found a safe place to hide, and in trying to keep warm, accidently set the house on fire and became trapped. Beecher found the frightened girl huddling in a corner, surrounded by flames, and he guided her outside to safety.

Now, in the early morning hours of November 26, 2001, Beecher entered Terry King's burning home and calmly began his routine search for victims. He was "patting" the sofa when his hand hit an object resting on the arm of the couch. Unable to see in the dark, smoky room, he gingerly groped what his hand had bumped, and an icy chill ran up his spine. *He was grasping a human foot.*

He jerked his hand away and then raised his heavy flashlight. Its beam fell on a gruesome sight. Terry King seemed relaxed, sitting in a chair with his hands folded across his stomach, a coffee cup next to his leg. Even the expression on the small man's face was serene and would have appeared normal except the right side of his forehead had a fist-sized hole in it. Blood had flowed down King's face, drying in streaks. The heavy smoke clung to his wounds and blackened the blood, warping the forty-year-old's features like some gruesome Halloween mask. Stifling an urge to scream, Beecher took a deep breath, pushed the button on his radio and shakily reported his finding.

It was obvious to Beecher that Terry King's injuries had nothing to do with the fire, and he had a very disturbing thought: If the dad was in this condition, what did the children look like?

Although the fire burned forty percent of the house, what remained still held clues as to what happened on that mysterious evening of November 25. After the last flames in the back bedrooms were doused, firefighters began venting the enormous accumulation of black smoke. As the cloud cleared they saw the signs of a house with children. Toys were left where small hands had dropped them, piles of kids' laundry were not yet put away. There were boxes of Christmas decorations lying open—ornaments waiting for hooks, an angel ready to ascend to the top of a tree. Strings of lights were being untangled to hang outside the humble home, all in preparation for a Christmas celebration that would never come.

The firefighters found no sign of the young boys Ed Harris had reported were home that night. Relieved there were no more bodies, their spirits lifted a bit.

"Missing children sure beat dead ones," someone commented.

At first the firefighters thought Terry King had been shot in the head. Broken bone fragments framed the gaping hole, looking like the damage left behind in the wake of a bullet, but they could find no entry wound. Behind the chair where Terry sat was a floor lamp. Blood was splattered on the lampshade, the walls, and the ceiling.

In strange contrast to the violent head wound, Terry's last moments of life appeared to have been very peaceful. His hands were folded in his lap and a full cup of coffee rested between his leg and the chair. His moccasin-clad feet were propped up on the arm of his couch as though he had fallen asleep watching his favorite television show. But Terry King didn't own a television. He didn't want his boys exposed to too much violence.

Chapter 2

THE MURDER OF TERRY KING WAS APPALLING FOR quiet, conservative Pensacola. The town is perched on the Gulf of Mexico, at the tip of Florida's Panhandle. The state's westernmost county, Escambia, borders Alabama to the west and to the north. Here, history and tradition are often valued more than progress.

Pensacola vies with St. Augustine, on Florida's east coast, for bragging rights as the oldest city in the United States. The Spanish did indeed settle Pensacola first, but disease and poor planning drove them away. They returned years later better prepared for the long haul. This time Spanish settlers bedded down in St. Augustine and stayed. Pensacola claims its place as the oldest *original* settlement.

History isn't what draws most tourists to the City of Five Flags. Pensacola is renowned for its sugar white beaches and emerald waters.

The city has managed to avoid drawing the huge influx of retirees that flood so many other Gulf Coast towns. Many of these "snowbirds" from up north take to the highways intent on trading their frigid roots for gorgeous seventy-degree winters in Florida. Most keep driving right past Pensacola and land on some sunny beach farther south. The ten-degree difference in temperature between North and Central

Florida may be responsible for keeping some outside influences to a minimum and ensuring that true Southern traditions continue to thrive in the Panhandle town that is often referred to as "L.A.," or Lower Alabama.

And *thrive* they do. Good manners are not just customary, they are enforced by community pressure. In the mid-1990s some Pensacolans became outraged when they saw their genteel way of life eroding. Traditionally, drivers would pull off the road and stop when a funeral procession passed, a token of respect for the deceased. But gradually motorists began pausing before slowly picking up speed and leaving the procession in their wake. Other cars moving in the opposite direction continued to cruise right on by, not bothering to stop, pause, or even nod in the general direction of mourners. This serious act of irreverence was an affront to right-thinking southerners, and letters poured in to the *Pensacola News Journal* for weeks, decrying the breakdown in moral values and warning of the doom sure to follow. Before long funeral processions reclaimed respect from both sides of the road and the small town breathed a sigh of relief, another disaster averted.

Though seemingly ordinary, the county of 300,000 produced more than its share of national headlines. Pensacola found itself in the limelight in 1993 when a doctor and a volunteer were gunned down as they went to work at an abortion clinic.

The eyes of the country were glued in horror when a young tourist visiting Pensacola Beach lost his arm and a chunk of his leg to a bull shark in the summer of 2001. The boy's uncle wrestled the monster to shore, where a park ranger shot and killed it. The men then pried the huge mouth open and propped it with a police baton. They reached in with forceps and tugged. The severed arm emerged torn and bloody but in good enough shape to be successfully reattached. Donations soared at area blood banks for weeks as people sought to help the unfortunate child.

The pristine vacation spot that lures so many tourists is also easy prey for nature's tropical fury. Each June when hurricane season begins, Pensacola holds its breath like other seaside cities hoping hurricanes or tropical storms will slide past their community. Sometimes they do and other times they land with a vengeance. Hurricanes Erin and Opal decimated the Northwest Florida coastline in 1995. The powerful storms ravaged the same shore twice that season.

In its early days, Pensacola's natural harbor and easy access to the Gulf quickly established the town as a thriving port city, building its economy on lumber and red snapper. Like many coastal cities with a bustling shipping industry, secondary income producers such as taverns, houses of prostitution, and gambling establishments soon flourished. Wealthy, God-fearing citizens drew an invisible line around the downtown area's red light district. They ignored the social eyesores, and protests were kept to a conscience-soothing minimum as long as participants did not flaunt their activities and the cash continued to flow.

This sort of back-scratching economy has continued to grow through the decades, creating a clash of cultures. Pensacola Beach is the gay capital of the country during Memorial Day weekend. Thousands of gays and lesbians converge on the beach, camping out and celebrating. While some in the church community still criticize, others look the other way over the three-day holiday. The controversial tourists bring an economic boom that is hard to ignore. The local Chamber of Commerce then attempts to attract family-oriented visitors for the remainder of the vacation season.

Escambia County is also home to Naval Air Station Pensacola, the home of the world famous Blue Angels flight team. There is a constant rotation of young military recruits and weather-beaten veterans to the area. In fact, thousands of military retirees call Northwest Florida home. Between the influx of military personnel and tourists who enjoy indulging in the coastal amenities, the population is rarely stagnant.

The result is a strange mixture of Southern tradition, conservative capitalism, and contemporary ideals. The right-wing roots run deep in the strongly Republican community. People discuss family values and religion freely in their workplaces, taking for granted that their Christian beliefs are a given among coworkers. This attitude causes some tour guides to describe Pensacola as the "buckle" of the Bible Belt.

This environment produced families like the Kings, who were deeply committed to their Pentecostal faith. In the mid-1950s twenty-four-year-old Wilbur King was a butcher by profession and a minister by choice. If his hands weren't carving up a cow, they might be gripping the edges of a pulpit in an impassioned sermon to his congregation.

Wilbur's seventeen-year-old wife Joyce was a tiny, thin, delicate woman with a gentle voice and modest attire. Joyce had always wanted to be a homemaker. Her love of family and devotion to God epitomized the best qualities of the Pentecostal faith. In their first five years of marriage, Wilbur and Joyce had three children whom they dedicated to the Lord and took to church regularly. During revivals, the Kings attended services as often as five times a week.

Joyce was a protective mother and felt strongly about keeping her children close to home. Rather than allowing them to spend the night with friends, she invited others to the King home. She was more comfortable when her children were nearby.

The King family loved Christian music. Patricia, the old-

est of three and the only daughter, played the keyboard, and
Mother Joyce delighted her young children by singing
gospel songs. Terry, her youngest child, loved it when she
sang the beautiful melodies in her delicate soprano voice.

As the boys got older, they were eager to join in the music
making. Wilbur and Joyce encouraged their children and
sacrificed to provide them with instruments and lessons.
Brother Greg played the guitar while Terry backed him up
on the drums. During the 1960s when most of their peers
were dancing to the Beatles, the King kids were honing their
skills on their own instruments. A decade later, when bulky
eight track tapes spreading *"disco fever"* seized a generation,
Patricia, Greg, and Terry stayed the course, playing their
own brand of Christian tunes set to a snappy beat.

In the mid-1970s, Pensacola was struggling with serious
racial conflicts. At one point in 1978, Escambia High School
became engulfed in a race riot that sent frightened parents
flying to school with guns. Fearing for her son's safety,
Joyce quickly withdrew Terry and began teaching him at
home.

When Terry was eighteen years old, his parents decided to
end their marriage. After twenty-five years, Wilbur and
Joyce had simply grown apart. Wilbur moved out and bought
a small house in neighboring Pace, a few miles east of Pensacola, where he would still be able to see his children.

Twenty-one-year-old Terry King was visiting his father's
home in 1986 when he met seventeen-year old Janet French.
He was immediately attracted to the beautiful blond southerner and admired her vivacious spirit. Janet returned
Terry's admiration and called him the next day. The two began to date.

Terry loved Janet's gregarious nature. The bubbly
teenager attracted all of the attention to herself, something
that the introverted Terry welcomed. Both of them were

small. At five-two, petite Janet was a good match for Terry's five-foot-five-inch frame, and her long golden curls looked dramatic against his jet black hair. Janet had a natural beauty, punctuated by dimples, perfect teeth, and dancing brown eyes.

Terry was known to have a good heart and a gentle nature. Before long he and Janet moved in together. Although they never married, they were delighted when Janet learned she was pregnant. On May 4, 1988, she gave birth to Derek. One year later, on July 12, 1989, she had a second son, Alex.

Terry and Janet did not transition into parenthood smoothly. The young couple was poor and couldn't afford a car, and their lack of higher education made it difficult to get ahead financially. And Terry was overwhelmed by the responsibility of taking care of his children. The result was instability when the young children most needed security. He played with them, read to them, and when they weren't feeling well, he stayed up with them at night. But as he settled into the role of family man, Janet grew more restless. She had gone straight from her parent's home into Terry's. She longed for a chance to see what the world held for her without the restrictions of parents or infants. Family life seemed to suffocate her.

At nineteen, with two babies, Janet fell into a deep depression. She was no longer in love with Terry and began to distance herself from her family. She stayed away from home, at first for hours, then overnight. She apologized each time she returned and swore not to do it again. Terry forgave her and hoped to make her happy enough to stay at home with him and their two sons. Meanwhile, he began recording his thoughts in a journal, venting his sadness and frustration. Penning his feelings seemed to be a much needed salve for his emotional wounds.

After one episode when Janet was gone for a while, she found herself pregnant by another man. Terry was by her side when she delivered the twin boys, but Janet didn't tell him the babies were fathered by someone else.

Terry struggled to meet the daily needs of the family, which now included four children. Early each morning he caught a ride to Mobile, Alabama, with other laborers who did construction work. It was a long, hot trip from Pensacola, and Terry was consigned to ride in the back of the truck to make room for the other workers in the cab.

Before long the strain of supporting a family of six on a minimum wage job took its toll. One weekend, Terry and Janet decided to search the want ads for better work. Flipping through page after page, Terry was discouraged to find little work that he was qualified to do. Then the couple noticed an advertisement promising BIG MONEY FAST! It read: "Dancers: Earn $1,000 a week!" Terry and Janet stared at each other. With that kind of money, they would be able to pay off several checks they had bounced and still cover their bills. They could stock the cabinets with groceries and perhaps eventually buy a car. But to Janet it felt like a deal with the devil. Both she and Terry had been raised as strict Pentecostals, and working as an "exotic dancer," which was what the ad meant, was unthinkable. *Almost.* Putting her conscience on the back burner, she applied for a job at Benny's Doll House and was immediately hired.

The attractive mother began working nights, dancing seductively before glassy-eyed men who stuffed dollar bills into her sequined G-string. Although the advertisement had boasted $1,000 per week, Janet found she could only earn $200 to $300 a week. But this was far more than Terry was making, so he agreed to stay home with the children while she worked.

The party environment of the topless bar was new to Janet and the potent enticement pulled her away from her family even more. The club's manager soon became her new boyfriend, and made no effort to hide it from Terry. In spite of four children waiting at home, she stayed away for days at a time. Terry found himself desperate, with no money, no food, and four hungry little boys. At the peak of his despair, he poured out his anguish in his journal: *All four children were there with me wondering when she was going to come home. I called her at work and she said she would be home that night. She didn't show. I went to see her at work the next night. She didn't show. The third time I sent someone else to tell her. Two days later she finally came home. She claimed that staying gone those periods of time was such a relief from being a "mommy."*

In spite of the excellent money her dancing paid, her new boyfriend didn't like it. He jealously demanded that she stop, so after a few weeks Janet traded her high income position as a dancer for the more modest one of a waitress. Her earnings immediately began to drop.

Terry realized he would have to support his four boys. Janet returned to the house during the days to watch the children while Terry worked, but when she wasn't there, he turned to relatives for help. Linda and Jimmy Walker, Janet's mother and stepfather, agreed to take five-year-old Derek into their home. Terry placed four-year-old Alex with Jimmy and Lisa French, Janet's father and stepmother.

Janet finally told Terry that the twins were not his, and although the news shocked and saddened him, he told her that he loved them like his own. When Janet moved in with her boyfriend, she agreed to keep the two-year-old twins with her so Terry could work. After packing up the children's clothing, favorite stuffed animals, and blankets, Terry King found himself alone for the first time in five years.

Terry breathed deeply and focused on earning an income to support his scattered family, but his moment of calm was short-lived. Two days after leaving with the twins, Janet abruptly returned, saying she needed to leave the toddlers with him. She said they made too much noise and were getting into her boyfriend's things. She stayed with them during the day at Terry's house, then returned to her boyfriend's apartment after they went to bed. The father's journal entry spoke volumes about his frustration: *A lot of times people mistake children for objects of personal property. They are not objects, they are little people with feelings and emotions and those feelings and emotions are very fragile and should be protected and considered.*

The year 1994 found the King family fragmented. Terry kept the twin boys; Alex remained with Janet's father, Jimmy French; and Derek, now in kindergarten, was still living with his maternal grandmother, Linda Walker.

Linda and her second husband, Jimmy, had a good marriage and worked at making each other happy. She collected teddy bears, and Jimmy often surprised her with new ones. The Walkers preferred the rural life, and their looks reflected it. Jimmy was usually dressed simply in jeans and a plaid shirt, his full head of light-colored hair peeking out from under a cap. His outdoor activities kept him fit, despite the beer he enjoyed after a hard day of work as an electrician. Like her daughter, Linda had long hair well down her back, with thick bangs. She wore little makeup, and she too preferred jeans. The Walkers hunted, fished, and spent much time camping on the banks of the Styx River, enjoying the outdoors.

Linda and Jimmy had always been active in Derek's life; they had witnessed his first steps and given him his first haircut. While others may have labeled Derek "hyper," Linda thought "lively" was a better description. To her, Derek was just a very loving little boy who always wanted to give hugs.

After keeping him for six months, Linda asked Janet to sign over temporary custody of Derek. She agreed and composed an informal handwritten note on a page torn from a spiral notebook. The agreement granted Linda and Jimmy temporary custody of Derek, but allowed Janet and Terry to visit their son whenever they wished. The parents could also cancel the agreement at any time, for any reason.

Linda was delighted with the arrangement. She had been worried about her grandchildren for years. She was a devoted grandmother, collecting baby pictures, tiny T-shirts, and locks of hair in a shoe box. But more important, she amassed an impressive collection of the Power Ranger figures that Derek loved so much. With Derek now under her roof, Linda could relax, knowing he was safe and happy.

While Derek lived with Janet's mother, Alex moved in with Janet's father and his second wife. Lisa and Jimmy French realized that Alex was troubled as soon as he arrived at their home. Like Derek, Alex had a difficult time adjusting to his mother's absence. He seemed comfortable and affectionate with his grandfather but kept his distance from Lisa during the first few weeks of his stay. He didn't want her to touch him or to hug him. She believed her temporary role as a mother figure in Alex's life caused him to identify her with Janet.

One day as he was walking by, Lisa reached out, pulling the child to her and hugging him, hoping to break through the barrier. Instead of warming to his grandmother's embrace, Alex slapped her. Lisa was shocked. She held his tiny shoulders and looked him in the eyes. "I will not tolerate that behavior," she told him. "In this house, we love and hug each other, morning, noon, and night."

Alex shared a room with the French's son, Jonathan. The boys were nearly the same age and often played together. Lisa kept a treasured collection of board games she'd had since childhood in the top of her son's closet. The games were in mint condition, and she gave the boys strict orders that they weren't to play with them. One afternoon their play turned destructive. While Lisa was away, they climbed into the high reaches of the closet and pulled the games down. The boys scribbled on the boards with a permanent marker and broke all the pieces. Lisa was extremely upset. She realized that the idea had been Alex's and believed he was taking out the anger he felt toward his mother on her.

Lisa enrolled Alex in a nearby day-care center owned by Marie Boone, who had taught children for more than fifty years. Learning of Alex's family history, Marie thought Alex was starved for attention and took extra care with him. Over time he became one of her favorite students. He obeyed his teachers, played well with others, and was eager to please. He loved to study and everyone noticed his good manners. Alex never finished a sentence without adding "ma'am" or "sir." The stability of the French home and the nurturing day care was having a positive effect on the boy and he was settling in nicely.

Derek was also blossoming under the Walkers' care. He was now enrolled in kindergarten and his report card reflected the positive change. While living with his parents, Derek had been tardy to school twenty out of forty days and received failing marks in all but one category. The teacher noted Derek's difficulty with even the simplest tasks, including hopping and skipping. Two grading periods later he received passing grades in all areas and had zero days tardy.

Linda and Jimmy adored Derek and taught him the pleasures of a rural life. The active five-year-old loved to fish with his grandfather and felt special when his "Paw Paw" assigned him the all-important task of throwing the casting net off the pier into the Gulf water.

Terry, however, didn't want his kids to grow up to be "rednecks." He was very concerned when he learned that Jimmy Walker used profanity and kept loaded guns in his house. Jimmy also drank beer, and Terry feared that Jimmy might give Derek sips. Terry strongly disapproved of the environment, so after a year, and to the heartbreak of the Walkers, he began looking for a more conservative home for his son.

Terry wanted his children to stay together in a safe, Christian environment until he could get on his feet, but his financial situation had not improved. Not only was he burdened with debt, but he also faced another challenge: he had narcolepsy, a physical ailment that caused him to fall asleep without warning. He lost consciousness at work, behind the wheel of his car, and while caring for his children.

Lisa realized she could not keep Alex indefinitely and told Terry about Heritage Youth Academy, a small refuge that housed boys in crisis, surviving only on contributions from a handful of churches. Terry liked the idea of keeping the four brothers together. He poured out his heart to the home's director, telling of his struggle to support the boys and his desire that they be raised in a Christian atmosphere. In spite of tight finances, the small home quickly agreed to take in all four King boys, and immediately issued a cry to the community for financial help.

Page four of the October 13, 1994, edition of the *Santa Rosa Free Press* displayed photographs of the darling boys, arms around each other in a snug little group. Four angelic faces smiled sweetly under the headline, I HAVE NO ONE TO CARE FOR MY BOYS. The article that followed gave a few details of Terry King's plight and described their tearful separation.

At that time, Heritage Home sheltered thirteen boys. Some of the children were abused and some were abandoned. It required $130,000 a year to house, clothe, and feed them all, an amount that grew increasingly difficult to raise. The home survived month-to-month with no assistance from the government, relying entirely on charity from the community.

Jimmy and Linda Walker went to visit the children during their stay at Heritage Youth Academy. Each time they said their good-byes, Derek would hang onto their legs and cry. He wanted to go home.

Chapter 3

FRANK LAY WAS TALL AND TRIM WITH A HANDSOME face and a deep, confident voice. As the principal of Pace High School, Frank inspired warmth and respect, commanding the attention of wayward and stellar students alike. His office was adorned with elegant cherry furnishings, family photos, and whatnots in the school colors of red-white-blue. The neat and orderly room was indicative of the man, an efficient, no-nonsense molder of young minds.

His wife Nancy was a petite woman with an unaffected attitude. Her blond hair was cut in a short, modern style. She preferred casual clam diggers to dress suits and wore little makeup. Her all-American good looks complemented those of her husband.

The Lays made their home in Pace, a bedroom community in neighboring Santa Rosa County about twenty minutes east of Pensacola. The once small, rural town was one of the fastest growing areas in Northwest Florida. Its new sprawling subdivisions and cozy established neighborhoods were nestled among towering pines. There were also acres of undeveloped property. The affordable tranquility lured many away from the convenience and expense of the nearby cities where they worked. Although Pace now offered all the shopping and living amenities of a suburban haven, it still

managed to provide the comforting atmosphere of a nurturing country town. The Lays enjoyed a spacious two-story
home a stone's throw from the high school.

The Lays had one child in college and two others in high
school, and they believed God had blessed them with the financial resources to help others. They contributed time and
money to Heritage Home, taking a special interest in the
plight of the King brothers. They had first seen the small
faces smiling shyly from the pages of the newspaper. The
Lays wanted to give them a brief respite from the orphanage
and made arrangements for Alex and Derek to visit their
home on weekends.

When Nancy arrived to pick them up, they looked like or-
phans; their clothes didn't match and their shoes didn't fit.
Derek's were so big he walked out of them. Nancy decided
to take them to the mall to get each boy a new pair, but she
had no idea how challenging that task would prove. The little boys were bubbling over with excitement and lacked the
discipline to control it. Derek and Alex were thrilled with
the outing and fascinated with the Lays' roomy passenger
van. "It's like a house car. We could live here!" exclaimed
Derek with delight. He and Alex took their seat belts off and
began climbing around. They tugged on cords for the blinds,
flipped open ashtrays, and clicked light switches. To the deprived youngsters the ride was much more than transportation—it was a rolling field trip. Nancy strapped them back in
and instructed them to sit still, but it wasn't long before they
had once again removed their seat belts and renewed their
exploration. Nancy had to stop the van several times on the
way to the mall.

When they finally arrived at the shopping center, she
firmly clutched their little hands. Alex and Derek had never
been to a mall before. They were entering a new world and
their faces reflected their awe. They wanted to see every-

thing, touch everything, and quickly squirmed free from Nancy's hands. Each swiftly moved in a different direction and Nancy began to panic. She had to run to gather one and then the other.

Once back in hand, she scolded them about the dangers of becoming separated. As she lectured she moved onto an escalator and didn't notice the wide, frightened eyes. The boys had never seen such a contraption and had no idea where it would take them. Alex and Derek began to scream and tried to crawl over her to escape the mechanical monster. It had not occurred to Nancy how frightening the experience might be to an unprepared child. She battled to gain control and reassure them. As they stepped off, she breathed a sign of relief and made a mental note to use the elevator next time.

At the shoe store, the boys bounced excitedly as the salesman measured their feet and found each one a new pair of "light-ups," popular sneakers with flashing lights in the soles. They were fascinated to see that each step they took caused the lights to flash, and they were so focused on their feet that the rest of the shopping trip was much easier. When the long day ended and Nancy returned the boys to Heritage Home, she was ready to collapse.

The King boys spent just eight months at Heritage Home before its funding ran out and the children were on the move again. They packed their meager belongings and waited to see where they would land next. With little money and no permanent place to live, Terry could not afford to support the four children and watched in utter despair as they went to live with strangers.

The twins were permanently adopted by a well-to-do local family. Five-year-old Alex was too despondent to bond with his new family. He grieved openly, crying almost non-stop for a month. Unable to console the anguished child, the foster family called Terry and told him Alex had to go. When the boy returned to his father, Terry clung to him. He was determined to keep his son.

Frank and Nancy Lay agreed to take Derek, who was six years old. The boy was tiny when he arrived at the Lay's home. Although he was almost seven years old, he still wore a toddler size four. He was always hungry, as if he hadn't been able to get enough to eat over the years. His fragile spirit was also hungering for love.

Derek's nightly prayers all revolved around his family. He would plead, "God, please let my mom and daddy get back together with all my brothers." The boy was more interested in reuniting with his biological family than he was in bonding with his foster parents. He seemed unable to face the possibility that he would remain with the Lays permanently. Frank suggested to the boy that praying for a reunion with his family was hopeless.

During Derek's years with the Lays, tensions grew between the families. Terry King told the Lays that he did not want Linda and Jimmy Walker to have contact with his son. Janet felt the Lays wanted the boy isolated from all of them. For the first several years, the Walkers had no idea where Derek was. According to Janet, when she or Terry phoned to talk with their son, they were frequently told that he wasn't there, was doing homework, or was at the ballpark. Janet says she once asked if she could take Derek for the weekend, but Nancy told her it wasn't a good time and suggested she call back in a few months. Janet hung up the phone in tears. "This wasn't part of the deal," she cried.

According to Janet, Nancy said their calls upset and confused Derek. His behavior then made their job more difficult. Janet decided to stop trying to contact her son since she believed he was in a happy, loving home. Derek, however, clung to the hope that his mother would reach out to him. He remembered her last words, "I'll write to you," and every day he went to the mailbox for a letter that never arrived.

One afternoon Derek became suspicious when he saw Nancy sifting through the mail. He thought she may have hidden a letter from his mother. "Do you think that I would keep mail from your mother?" Nancy asked him. "I would never do that. Never would I lie to you. You have been lied to and abandoned all your life." Apparently it was easier for Derek to think that his foster mother would hide mail than to accept that his real mother was gone forever.

Soon after Derek arrived at the Lays, the family joined Olive Baptist Church, the largest Baptist congregation in Pensacola. They took Derek and their other children to church three times each week. The lonely boy responded to his youth group with enthusiasm, eager to make friends and learn Bible verses. He was usually the first to volunteer to pray aloud. His Sunday school teacher was deeply saddened to hear the six-year-old's pleas for his parents.

"God, my parents are not Christians," the downhearted child prayed. "I want them to get back together and bring me and my brothers home." He was convinced it would happen.

The teacher lovingly embraced the troubled boy and implored the entire group to pray for the broken family. Derek seemed greatly comforted when the small group lifted up his wayward parents to the Lord in prayer each week.

One day when the teacher saw Frank and Nancy Lay, Bible in hand, sitting in the church pew with Derek, he assumed they were the child's problematic parents. He immediately thought the faithful prayers had been answered and the miracle of salvation had been performed on them. The teacher threw himself upon the surprised Lays with tears in his eyes. He described how he and the youth group had diligently prayed for their redemption, beseeching God to reunite them with their son and free their lives of drugs. Frank and Nancy were mortified. They looked at each other with horror and quickly broke the news of mistaken identity to the stricken teacher. He was embarrassed, and Nancy laughingly declared she was getting a T-shirt that said, "Derek is not my biological son!"

While Derek settled in with the Lays, Terry and Alex moved from place to place, often relying on the generosity of friends and family. At times Alex was enrolled in school; other times, Terry taught him at home. With no curriculum, Terry relied on a variety of reading materials. Books became Alex's constant companions.

In January 1997, Terry asked his mother, Joyce, to consider moving back to Pensacola. Since divorcing Terry's dad, she had remarried and moved to Texas with her new husband. He had recently passed away, leaving Joyce alone and far from family. Terry was working the night shift at a print shop and wanted her to help him care for Alex. He had been taking the child to work but the hours were hard.

Joyce agreed and soon returned to Pensacola. They visited Derek, and Terry shared with her his hopes of regaining custody. Although Janet still had custody, Frank and Nancy Lay thought it was in Derek's best interests to remain with them. Joyce and Terry contacted an attorney, and Terry was disappointed to discover that a fight in court would require money he couldn't raise.

Meanwhile, Terry concentrated on building a stable life for Alex. In addition to his job at the print shop, he worked weekends at the T & W Flea Market where he sold odds and ends for various vendors. Alex was always with him, enjoying the bustling activity of the swap meet.

When Joyce arrived from Texas, she was determined to expand the boy's social life. She began taking Alex to church on Sunday mornings, while Terry worked at the flea market. Alex became an active member of the congregation, joining the youth choir and playing a wise man in the children's Christmas musical. He even won third place for learning the most Bible verses. Alex seemed to enjoy his newfound social life.

Terry also yearned to see his eldest son, but over the years his financial situation did not improve. He often found himself without transportation. Despite the expense, he once took a taxicab from Pensacola to Pace to see Derek. The cab driver sat outside the Lays' home for three hours while they visited.

By the time Derek was nine, he had not seen his parents in two years. He was shocked and unprepared for an unexpected meeting with Janet. Nancy had taken him to the mall after an ordeal at the dentist's office. Derek's baby teeth were badly decayed and he had to have eight teeth pulled. While they were there, someone called out. Nancy did not immediately recognize Janet. Her long blond hair, once a cloud of gravity-defying curls, was now short and straight.

"Come here and give me a hug," Janet said to her child. Derek refused and shyly moved behind his foster mother. Janet was clearly hurt. She had not seen her child in years and complained to Nancy, "He won't hug me."

"Derek had a tooth pulled and he's not feeling well," Nancy said in an attempt to soothe her feelings. "And boys this age don't really like to hug," she added. While that might have been true for some, Derek was an exception. He often hugged perfect strangers.

After a few more minutes of chitchat, Janet left. Derek asked Nancy, "Who was that?"

Nancy replied with her own question. "Who did you think that was?"

"Well, the way that you're acting, you'd think she was my mother or something," he said, hoping in his heart that she wasn't.

Nancy confirmed his suspicions. "That was your mother, Derek."

He shook his head. "My mother is taller than that," he insisted.

"Your mother stayed the same size," Nancy explained. "You've grown taller."

He pondered that a moment. "Why is she at the mall?"

Nancy knew what he was thinking, and replied, "She has a job here. She drove."

"She has a car?" Derek asked. The pain in the question was obvious. The child had convinced himself Janet did not have a vehicle and couldn't visit him. The mistaken belief had helped him maintain the illusion that his mother would see him if she could.

"Derek, you've known all along that your mother has a car," Nancy said. "I told you she had a car. She knows she's welcome to come see you anytime she wants. She *chose* not to. You're going to have to deal with that."

Dealing with his parents' rejection was a heartbreaking task for Derek. There was no closure. While he obsessed about getting his family back together, they went on without him. Derek's heartache and insecurity surfaced as a desperate need for attention. Always an active child, his behavior in school challenged even his most patient teachers. His pediatrician diagnosed him with attention deficit hyperactive disorder and prescribed medication to keep him calm and focused in school. The medication helped Derek better control his conduct but the wounds of rejection went untreated.

The Lays had Derek tested by school psychologists and

learned that he possessed an impressive IQ. He was quickly admitted into the gifted program, but was still unable to curb his impulses. Derek spent much of his time standing in the corner, both at school and at home. The child who yearned for acceptance became a source of frustration to his foster family, teachers, and sometimes his peers.

Frequently he would come home from school and tell his foster parents excitedly, "Today I got a best friend!" The pride was evident on his smiling face.

Nancy would ask, "Well, what's his last name?"

"I don't know," Derek would admit.

"If you don't know his last name, he's *not* your best friend," Nancy would inform him.

The Lays made an effort to be truthful with Derek and instill honesty in his character. "If you lie, I'll spank you," Nancy told Derek. "I will never lie to you. If I say we're going to have chicken for supper, I will kill the chicken if necessary to make that happen."

Derek's foster parents took him to a Christian counselor who sought to pinpoint the root of his trouble. She found that he talked longingly of his family, focusing great attention on the happy time he had spent with Linda and Jimmy Walker. The counselor called the Walkers and suggested it would be good for Derek to see them. They were ecstatic and quickly arranged to take Derek to a family reunion. They offered to pick him up at the Lay home, but the Lays declined, opting instead to meet the Walkers in the parking lot of a local restaurant. When Jimmy Walker finally saw his grandson, he was overcome with joy. The burly man cried when he embraced the child he had missed so much.

Arriving at the reunion, Derek was thrilled to see Alex and his parents. He spent a blissful day hugging family, eating fried catfish, and playing darts. After the party, the

Walkers took Derek to their house to show him where they lived. Then they called the Lays and told them they were on their way to bring Derek home. When they arrived, Nancy was waiting in the front yard and did not invite them in. The grandparents were not supposed to have taken Derek to their house.

The Lays kept Derek heavily involved in the many youth activities offered by Olive Baptist Church. He seemed to thrive in the nurturing Christian environment. His Sunday school teacher, Steve Ackerman, thought Derek was a delightful child. Instead of discouraging Derek's high spirits, Steve enjoyed laughing and having fun with the boy. Derek also got along with the other students and was generally well-liked.

The teacher discovered Derek was a quick learner and very knowledgeable about the Bible. He always participated, volunteering to read aloud. He memorized scripture and would excitedly finish a story before the teacher could. Steve recognized Derek's true need was for attention and approval, and the youth leader made a special attempt to be kind and patient with him.

During his seventh grade year, Steve noticed that in addition to being lively, Derek also had a gentle side. When the Sunday school students met at Steve's house for a devotional, Derek was drawn to his water garden. He loved the beautiful fountains and waterfalls, and was fascinated by the exotic Japanese koi fish.

The good-natured boy was also small, a combination that often made him a target for bullies. He once complained to Nancy that some boys at school had pushed him around and called him "faggot."

"You should fight back and defend yourself," she advised. But he couldn't do it; he just wasn't a fighter.

Although his nature was gentle and passive, Derek also had a mischievous side. During a visit to Pace High School, he snuck into a secretary's office and hacked into her computer. He searched through confidential records until he found what he wanted. When caught, he admitted that he had been searching the files to learn the date of a girl's birthday.

On another occasion at the high school, he rifled through a dean's desk and stuffed some items confiscated from other students into his pockets. Nancy Lay found the small collection of pocketknives and cigarette lighters in Derek's room. She confronted him, but he denied knowing how they got there.

Frank and Nancy Lay were pulling out their hair in frustration. When a student accused Derek of stealing a wallet carrying twenty-five dollars, Nancy paid the child back. Derek insisted he didn't take the wallet or the money, but his foster mother knew he was lying.

"Your character stands for everything," Nancy admonished. "You don't have good standing. You're going to have to work it off in the yard to repay it." He completed the required chores and later admitted that he had taken the money. The Lays believed he wanted to impress the kids at school with his rebellious behavior.

Derek's exploits became progressively worse as he approached his teenage years. Like many boys, he liked to play with matches and lighters. The Lays were concerned his pranks would become dangerous and possibly harm their young grandchildren, who often visited.

They sought more counseling for their foster son. A psychologist told them that Derek's problems probably weren't as serious as they thought. He was just making bad decisions and needed to be redirected. Adjusting his medication and regular counseling would go a long way to improve his behavior, the counselor advised. But with the private foster arrangement providing no money, additional therapy was prohibitively expensive.

Chapter 4

ALEX ALSO SEEMED TO SUFFER FROM DEEP EMOTIONAL wounds. His grandmother, Joyce, felt he needed counseling, but Terry had other views. Like his brother, Alex would not abandon the hope of a traditional family. He dreamed of having a mother and planned for the day that Terry would remarry. He encouraged his father to date and was thrilled when Terry agreed to do so as soon as his car was in good repair. Unfortunately, it needed a new motor and he was short on both time and money.

The quest for reliable transportation would eventually destroy the life Terry King hoped to build. When an acquaintance suggested he could help ease Terry's car trouble, the struggling father could not have known the price that friendship would cost him.

Ricky Chavis, in his late thirties at the time, had transformed his yard into a mechanic's workshop and offered Terry full use of it. He worked on his car until late into the night and occasionally stayed over. Terry remained close to Ricky over the next couple of years, often relying on his generosity to help pay bills or watch Alex while he worked.

Before Alex's twelfth birthday, Joyce noticed changes in her grandson's behavior. Alex became quiet and withdrawn and began pulling away from church. The child who had once enjoyed Sunday school now refused to attend services. Joyce was concerned because she felt Alex needed the spiritual connection and the interaction with children his own age.

She became increasingly alarmed when she noticed marks on Alex's neck that looked like small hickeys. When she questioned him, Alex seemed unaware of the problem.

Joyce wasn't the only one who saw changes in the boy. Terry's longtime friend Kevin Bailey noticed them as well. Kevin was a successful businessman who helped Terry establish a booth at the flea market where he could make some extra cash. Kevin appreciated the caring relationship he saw between Terry and Alex and wanted to help the struggling father. In February 2001, Kevin leased him a home in Cantonment. The deal was a dream come true for Terry and Alex, who had been living in a travel trailer.

Father and son were ecstatic to have a place of their own. The small wooden house was built in the 1940s and had been moved from Pensacola to the Cantonment lot. Although it was older, the place was clean and in good repair, and Terry and his son took pride in making improvements like painting and gardening. Kevin talked with Terry every week. Alex proudly showed him the room he was glad to call his own and the flower beds he and his father had planted around the house. Kevin adored Alex, who often visited the Bailey home with his father to fish or enjoy their hospitality. He thought so highly of him, he was willing to adopt the child if the need ever arose.

Kevin was concerned when Alex became subdued several months after they moved into their new home. Although he was still polite, Kevin noted Alex wasn't smiling as much, a sharp contrast to the happy child he knew. He attributed the problems to Alex's lack of interaction with other children. He tried to convince Terry to enroll the boy in school, but Terry was determined to home-school his son.

* * *

In the meantime the Lays were struggling with Derek. He was in seventh grade and desperate to impress his peers regardless of the consequences. For most of the year he was not allowed to eat in the lunchroom because of his continual disruptions. He was relegated to in-school suspension and ate lunch alone in a supervised classroom. During one of his lunch periods, the teacher caught Derek putting pressure on the large veins in his neck, trying to catch the "buzz" that came along with passing out. When Derek was later caught sniffing lighter fluid on the school bus, his foster parents said, "No more."

The Lays soon discovered there would be no simple solution. They phoned Terry and asked if he would agree to send Derek to a military-type school. As foster parents, they had no legal right to make the decision. Terry refused and jumped at the chance to reunite his family. The Lays, however, were reluctant to hand Derek over to him. In their opinion, the boy's father was incapable of giving him the care he needed.

Nancy and Frank were frustrated and turned to their last resort, Janet. Finding her was a struggle. Nancy spent several days calling relatives before tracking her down in Kentucky. Frank returned from work to find Nancy at wit's end.

"I told Janet that Derek needs help," she told her husband. "That he's not going to make it if she doesn't get him help. I told her, 'If you take Derek, at least he'll know you love him.'"

"And what did she say?" Frank asked.

"She said, 'Oh, I can't do that. My husband doesn't like children and we have two cats.'" Frank was disgusted and quickly realized that Terry would probably be taking Derek home.

After talking to Nancy, Janet phoned her mother, Linda

Walker, who eagerly agreed to take her grandson. But Terry told Janet that he wanted Derek back home. She respected his wish to raise his son and agreed to mail the boys' birth certificates so Terry could have custody transferred under his name. The Walkers begged Frank and Nancy to let Derek live with them, but the Lays told them that Terry wished to keep him, and they had to abide by that.

The Lays warned Terry that Derek would be more than he could handle, but after nearly seven years, Terry was only focused on reuniting with his eldest son. Derek, however, did not welcome the move. With the Lays, at least he had stability.

Nancy tried to prepare him. 'Derek, it looks like your dad is going to take you," she told him. She waited for a response but he said nothing. "Is there anything you want to ask?"

"What's for supper?" he said, skirting the issue.

By the end of September 2001 the troubled boy could no longer ignore the pending move. He came home from school and found Nancy packing his things. He sat on his couch and watched but still refused to talk about it. Nancy told him, "You will always be my greatest disappointment," and then he wept.

The following afternoon Nancy picked him up from school, and when they arrived home he found his belongings in the foyer. It was all there: his clothes, photo albums, the decorations from his room, even the cover from his light switch. The Lays had bought a scooter for him and another one for Alex. He went into Nancy's room, laid down on the floor, and sobbed. Although they'd had difficult times, the Lays were the only family he'd ever really known and he was losing them.

The move did not go smoothly. Terry was due to arrive at

any moment, but it wasn't his vehicle that first turned into the driveway. Linda and Jimmy Walker had somehow learned about the move. Nancy told Derek to wait in the bedroom while she answered the door.

"We want to see Derek," Linda stated.

"This is not a good time for you to visit," Nancy told them. "Derek is upset and this is only going to complicate things."

Linda turned to her husband and said, "He's in the bedroom." Nancy felt the beginnings of panic when it occurred to her they might try to take him. She also feared a fight would ensue if she didn't get rid of them before Terry arrived. As if on cue, Terry drove up. Nancy welcomed him into the hallway. The grandparents waited outside the open door. Although reserved, Terry seemed upbeat about seeing his son. Nancy tried to impress on him how difficult Derek could be, but the message was lost on the determined father.

After giving him instructions on Derek's ADHD medication, Nancy, more tense than ever, said, "Terry, the Walkers want to see Derek. Is that okay?"

He was silent, then finally answered, "Not at this time."

Nancy turned to them. "You heard the man. He doesn't want to have you see him right now."

To Nancy's relief, Frank arrived home then and escorted the Walkers farther from the house. Linda stood on the front lawn staring up at the bedroom window. In frustration, she yelled, "Derek, Granny loves you!" She knew they had to leave but she desperately wanted the child to understand how much they cared.

When Terry, who'd gone into the house, stepped outside, Jimmy Walker approached him. "How you doing, Terry?" he asked, trying to break the ice.

"Okay," Terry replied.

"Are you going to let us see the boys?" he asked.

"Not at this time," Terry said, avoiding Jimmy's eyes. "Maybe later."

"Where are you living now?" Jimmy asked, wanting to know where his grandchildren would be staying.

"Out on Muscogee Road."

"What's the address?" Jimmy pressed.

"It's 1101 Muscogee," Terry said, giving him the wrong house number. He did not want the Walkers dropping in for a visit.

But Jimmy wasn't finished. "I want you to tell me straight up what you have against us. We never did anything but help you," he said, blinking back tears. "Tell me right now what you have against us."

"Well, I have to think about that," Terry replied, trying to avoid a confrontation.

"Terry, when I have something against a person, I don't have to think about it. I can look him in the eye and tell him what it is." But Terry refused to respond, and the frustrated grandfather turned and left.

Frank talked with Derek as he gathered his things. "You call me, whenever you need us. Whatever you need us to do," he said reassuringly. "We're here, still a family, still a team."

Before walking out the door, the Lays' youngest son appeared to say his good-byes. He asked Derek if he had his Bible. Derek nodded, indicating he had all four that belonged to him.

"Good," the teenager said. "Because you're going to need them."

PART TWO
UNRAVELING THE MYSTERY

*"All truths are easy to understand
once they are discovered;
the point is to discover them."*
Galileo

Chapter 5

WHILE THE FIRE STILL RAGED AT TERRY KING'S HOUSE, a roadblock was set up and a sheriff's deputy diverted traffic away from the scene. The fire was extinguished around two in the morning, and Ricky Chavis arrived at the roadblock shortly afterward. He attempted to pull off the road and drive around but the deputy stepped in front of his car and blocked it. Ricky got out to speak with the officer, insisting he was a friend of the King family and needed to get to the house.

Ricky was just over six feet tall and weighed 185 pounds. He wore jeans, sneakers, and a gray sweatshirt. He had thick brown hair that was slowly working its way back from his forehead, emphasizing his wide, hazel eyes. He smiled a lot, revealing a mouth full of teeth in various stages of decay. He anxiously began asking questions.

The deputy politely declined to give him any answers. "If you want to park across the street in the church parking lot," he said, "I'll see if a supervisor will speak to you."

Chavis waited across the street from Terry's charred home for more than an hour until Sergeant Tony Bain approached him. Ricky took a long, last drag on his cigarette, tossed the butt to the ground and crushed it under his toe. Then he shook hands with the officer and introduced himself.

"I'm Ricky Chavis, a friend of Terry's," Chavis said. "Is Terry King dead?" he asked anxiously.

Sergeant Bain refused to say. "It's still too early in the investigation. All we know is a male victim has been found dead inside the home."

"Can I look at the body and identify the victim?" Chavis asked. He seemed eager to view the crime scene.

"The victim will be identified by the Medical Examiner's Office," Bain replied.

"Can I tell Terry's mom he's been killed?" Ricky persisted.

The sergeant eyed him suspiciously. "When positive identification is made, Sheriff's Office investigators will notify next of kin."

"Do you think Terry committed suicide?" Ricky asked, pressing for clues as to what the officers had uncovered inside.

The deputy refused to rise to the bait. He repeated that the cause of death had yet to be determined.

Ricky didn't give up. "Do you think the boys killed him?"

The deputy was stunned. "Why would you ask that question?"

Ricky replied, "Well, Terry was an abusive father." He added that he had helped Terry find the boys a couple of days earlier when they ran away from home.

Ricky Chavis's intense interest in the murder did not go unnoticed. Bain would later write in his report: *I found it odd that Chavis had not inquired about the condition or whereabouts of the boys, given the circumstances.*

Realizing investigators might want to question him further, Bain took down Ricky's personal information. He then suggested that Chavis return home, where an investigator would contact him. But Ricky Chavis had other plans.

Investigator John Sanderson shook off sleep as he arrived at the crime scene shortly after five that morning. The deputy was approaching forty. He was tall, with blue eyes, a thin mustache, and short, sandy hair. His quick smile and wit epitomized Southern charm. He walked into the smoldering house to survey the damage.

Investigator Terry Kilgore was already there. He was shorter than Sanderson, with a stocky build. His brown hair was occasionally dyed blond and often bristled in a short buzz cut. His brown eyes could appear warm or threatening in an instant.

Kilgore and Sanderson made detailed notes of the crime scene as analysts snapped photographs and gathered evidence around Terry's body. Then Sanderson began searching the victim's ruined home.

He noted sparse furniture and the open boxes of Christmas ornaments in the living room. The rooms were dark and smoky as the investigators walked through the small house. The fire had spread from the back bedroom into the adjoining hallway and then to the attic. Debris covered the floor; water-soaked insulation dripped from what had been the ceiling. The acrid smell of smoke permeated the house.

An investigator with the State Fire Marshal's Office briefed him on what they had found. An accelerant had been used, and a crushed can of what could have been lighter fluid was in the master bedroom doorway.

The fire investigators easily spotted the pour patterns where the accelerant had burned with intense heat through piles of clothes and the floor itself. Nothing but springs was left of the bed.

The room at the front of the house obviously belonged to the children. Officers found boys' clothes, games, and toys. A short time later Sanderson's search was interrupted by a deputy.

"There's a Jimmy Walker outside. Says he's the boys' grandfather. Wants to talk to you. You want to see him?"

Sanderson nodded and glanced at his watch. It was a few minutes before seven. He stepped out of the smoldering house, smelling of smoke and wet ashes.

Like so many of the rustic folks who lived in rural Cantonment, Jimmy was dressed simply in jeans, boots, and a plaid shirt. He immediately asked about the boys. Sanderson shook his head sympathetically, introduced himself, and informed him the children were still missing.

Walker gave a firm handshake and explained his relationship to the children. He told Sanderson he was the boys' step-grandfather. His wife, Linda, was their grandmother, and her daughter, Janet, was their mother. Sanderson took a moment to follow the family tree before asking Janet's whereabouts. Walker sighed wearily. He told the deputy she was living in Kentucky with her new husband and that she rarely had contact with her children. Sanderson made a note to get in touch with Janet soon, but for the moment he asked Jimmy if he had any thoughts about where the boys might have gone.

Walker shrugged his broad shoulders. "They were missing all last week, until Terry found them in Pace. Ricky called last night to tell us that they were back home with Terry."

Sanderson raised an eyebrow and questioned Jimmy more closely about who Ricky was and why he felt compelled to call the Walkers about the children.

"Ricky Chavis is Terry's friend," Walker told him. "He was worried about the boys—you know, with Terry abusing them and all." He made the statement as though it was common knowledge.

Sanderson nodded but continued making notes. He asked Jimmy for the specifics of his conversation with Ricky Chavis. Walker said Ricky had called them around nine last night, worried that Terry was planning to have a long session with them in the therapy room.

Sanderson looked up from his notebook. Therapy room? He took a mental inventory of the charred home and tried to recall anything that could remotely be described as a "therapy room."

Jimmy explained. "Ricky told us about it. Have you been inside? You saw that room with the green walls? Ricky said Terry makes the boys sit in there for hours, staring at each other, and sometimes he stares at them. Ricky said Terry told him he was going to have a long therapy session with them last night. He's the one who told us Terry was dead."

Sanderson wanted to know exactly what Ricky had told the grandfather. Walker stared at the ruined home. "He called us about a quarter to six this morning. He said Terry's house had caught fire, the boys were gone, and Terry was the only one in there when the firefighters showed up. I asked him how he knew about the fire, and he said he heard the call go out over the scanner he has at his house. That's when he left and came over here."

Jimmy dragged his gaze away from the charred house. "He said Terry was so burned he couldn't recognize him. Is that true?"

Sanderson asked Jimmy how Ricky could have known that.

Walker shrugged. "Said he saw the body. He told me he knew some of the firemen and they let him go in there." He nodded toward the house. "Said he recognized Terry's pants, the same ones he had on the day before."

Sanderson knew that Chavis had not been allowed inside and could not have seen the dead man's body.

Although the King brothers weren't his own grandchildren, Jimmy Walker was as protective of the boys as he was of his wife's happiness. He realized their disappearance must look suspicious to investigators, and remembering Ricky's words on the phone earlier that morning, he asked Sanderson if the boys were in trouble. The deputy assured him that at this point they were only concerned about their safety.

"Rick told me if there's a criminal investigation I would have to go to court and testify that Terry abused the boys," Walker said.

Sanderson wondered briefly why Ricky was already talking about a criminal investigation and court testimony, but he knew there were many more witnesses to interview while the crime scene was still fresh. He asked if Jimmy had ever seen Terry drink or use drugs.

"I never knew him to do either. My wife and I, we ain't been around the boys a lot lately, but we heard the abuse was pretty bad. Rick said they took all the knives in the house when they ran away last week."

Sanderson spent the rest of the morning tracking down the murdered man's family. He had the unenviable task of breaking the grim news of Terry King's death to his mother, Joyce Tracy. The homicide investigator drove to the assisted living facility in Pensacola where Joyce lived. She was a tiny, frail, blue-eyed woman, well under five feet tall. Her long gray hair was pulled back in a bun, and a conservative dress hung loosely on her thin frame.

Sanderson gently told Joyce there had been a fire and Terry was dead. She stared at the investigator in disbelief as the blood drained from her face. Afraid that she was about to faint, he took her elbow and helped her to a chair. The one part of his job he had always hated was notifying people of a loved one's death, especially when the victim had been so brutally murdered. He hoped to give Joyce the grim facts later, but she immediately wanted to know how her son had died. Reluctant to reveal the gruesome details to the devastated woman, he told her victims of house fires usually died from smoke inhalation. Despite her grief, Joyce realized the investigator was being evasive, and she demanded to know the specifics. John briefly described Terry's injuries. The words were painful to them both, but John needed to continue his questioning. He asked Joyce about her missing grandsons.

She told him she had no idea where they were, but that the boys had also disappeared last week, making her son sick with worry. He could hardly sleep until both children had been returned. She told the investigator they found the boys in Pace, where they claimed to be hiding in the woods near a subdivision where Derek had friends. When Sanderson asked what reason the boys gave for running away, Joyce told him the only thing she knew was they said they wanted more freedom.

Joyce described her son as a caring, concerned father who didn't drink or use drugs. Remembering Terry, she began to cry. Sanderson spotted a box of tissue on a nearby desk and took it to her. The seasoned investigator gave her a moment before continuing.

Sanderson was not surprised to learn that Terry had no enemies and that Ricky Chavis had been a close friend. Sympathetic and concerned for Joyce, he phoned a victim's advocate who he hoped could provide some comfort until Joyce's family could be with her. Not wanting to leave her alone, the investigator waited with the heartbroken mother until the advocate arrived.

Sanderson left Joyce's apartment intent on talking to Terry's brother, Greg King, a computer analyst for Pensacola Junior College.

Where Terry's hair was dark, Greg's was thick and white.

He had pale blue eyes like his mother, framed by glasses. Greg was articulate and as soft spoken as his mother. When Sanderson told him about Terry's death, he was visibly shaken. He had last seen his brother the day before, when he helped him search for Alex and Derek.

Overwhelmed, Greg stared at his desk in silence before rising to his feet. He insisted he needed to go to his mother and offered to talk with the investigator later. Sanderson understood, he gave his card to Greg and headed back to his unmarked cruiser, flipping back through his notes as he walked. Scanning the pages, he noticed one name was consistently there: *Ricky Chavis*.

An hour later Sanderson was interviewing Chavis at the Escambia Sheriff's Office.

"I really care about those boys," Ricky told Sanderson. "Terry was abusing them, a lot of it psychological. Like the way he looked at Alex; I got on to him about it." Ricky's voice tightened. "That's bad for a kid's self-esteem. Last I saw them was around two or two-thirty Sunday afternoon. Then I called Jimmy Walker to tell him they were back home."

Sanderson nodded and asked Ricky if he had any idea where they might be now. Rick thought for a moment. "They may be back out in the woods. That's where they stayed when they ran away last week. I helped Terry look for them."

Sanderson pressed on about how their father had found them, and Ricky's eyes grew wide. "He found Derek in Pace on Saturday. I went back there Sunday with Terry and his mom, Joyce, to help look for Alex. Then Alex called me. He was hiding behind a convenience store. I turned him over to Joyce, but he didn't want to go back with Terry. Neither boy wanted to be with Terry. There was hard friction between them. You really need to talk to Deputy Reggie Jernigan,"

Ricky pushed. "He knows what's been going on with the Kings."

Sanderson nodded, and listened with a trained ear as Ricky talked about the fire call he heard over his police scanner at home. "I was sitting in my house watching TV and I heard the call go out over my scanner, heard there was a fire at Terry's address. I was real scared and worried. Terry and the boys were supposed to come by my house that night, but they never showed up. I drove over there, afraid something bad had happened, but I didn't go inside."

Sanderson carefully confronted him with what Jimmy Walker had said—that Ricky had told him he'd seen the body and identified Terry by his clothing since he'd been burned beyond recognition.

Ricky gazed over Sanderson's shoulder as if thinking. "No, no. I told Jimmy I was *trying* to get inside but no one would let me."

Seeing the investigator's reaction, Ricky dropped his head sadly. "I don't know what happened to Terry, how he died, I mean." He stared at the deputy and lamented, "If it was a *homicide*, those boys had something to do with it.

"Terry was real worried after they ran away the first time," Ricky continued. "He told me they had taken a lot of knives from the house when they left. Derek was very cool toward his father. Terry had been pulling away from me lately too."

The homicide investigator, focused on what Chavis had to say about the children, ignored Ricky's reference to his deteriorating relationship with their father. Sanderson asked for details about the alleged abuse.

"Alex told me once that on weekends they go through therapy and can't talk. Terry makes them just stare at each other for hours."

Sanderson asked him about Terry's other relationships,

and Chavis shrugged. "Terry didn't have friends," he said, "and I didn't know of any problems. I was the closest friend he had, but he could be weird." He realized he had the deputy's interest, and continued. "When the boys would get done with school, he made them go in the house and lock the doors. He just put a new lock on the front door. They couldn't talk to *nobody*," Ricky emphasized, "until Terry picked them up and took them to work with him. He worked at a print shop, Pace Printing."

Sanderson nodded, encouraging Ricky to continue.

Chavis said Terry had moved to Cantonment within the past year and recently enrolled his children in school. Although Terry's family insisted he did not drink or use drugs, Sanderson knew it was possible the single father hid some habits from his loved ones. Ricky confirmed that Terry didn't drink, but admitted they both occasionally smoked marijuana, although not around the boys. "I smoked with him about a year ago, but I only smoked pot a couple of times in the past year," he added quickly. "I don't drink neither, gave it up a few years back."

Ricky hoped the small confession would increase his credibility with the homicide detective. In fact, he felt so comfortable with the interview that he could no longer contain himself. "I never saw any *physical* abuse between Terry and the boys," he said. "But Alex told me that his dad had hit him before." Ricky leaned toward the detective and spoke confidentially: "You know, Alex didn't like his dad." His tone dropped as he said slowly, "And Derek told me he wished his dad was dead."

Sanderson gave Ricky his full attention, demanding to know when the boy's comment was made.

"Must have been a couple of weeks ago, before the kids ran away the first time. We were in my front yard, talking about Terry, and that's when Derek said it. And a couple of months ago, Alex told me that he wished someone would kill his dad." He added quickly, "I told him don't ever wish death on nobody." The deputy agreed.

Ricky sighed heavily. "I haven't been around the kids much lately because I had gotten too close to them. Terry and I weren't very close," he said sadly. "I tried to be his friend." He paused as if trying to decide if he should go on. "There's something else," he said slowly, as if he couldn't bear to say it. "Derek likes to play with fire. Terry got on to him about that."

The statement intrigued the investigator, along with Ricky's revelation that the boys had left a message on his answering machine during the week they first ran away. Sanderson suspected Ricky might know more about Alex and Derek than he was revealing. He asked Ricky if he and Kilgore could accompany him back to his trailer in case the brothers had called again.

Ricky became flustered, inhaling deeply. He informed Sanderson that he needed to use the bathroom as soon as he returned home. Sanderson watched him carefully, and politely offered him the use of deputies' facilities. Rick shook his head, saying that he could only use his own bathroom.

Sanderson and Kilgore pulled up to Ricky's property a short time later, immediately noting the privacy fence, electric wire, and security cameras. The officers waited while Ricky opened the locked gates.

There was a working junkyard inside the fence. The clutter competed for space. A lawn chair teetered on the top of a car piled with mechanical parts and tools. Metal tanks leaned against the fence and garage. Ash poured from the bottom of a large burn barrel, commonly known as a "poor man's incinerator." An engine dangled from the end of a thick chain that hung from the limb of an oak tree, and there were close to a dozen shabby cars in various stages of repair or disintegration.

Sanderson and Kilgore walked inside his trailer, where the thick smell of cigarette smoke hung in the air. The inside was as cluttered as the yard. The furniture was a mismatched collection of high-backed armchairs, a worn-out orange recliner, and a stained couch. Stacks of books and manuals perched on top of boxes, bookcases were filled to overflowing with pictures and knickknacks, and the tables were topped with fans, stereo equipment, pillows, and ashtrays laden with cigarette butts. Piles of paper and software were scattered across Ricky's computer station, which was tucked into a cubbyhole off the kitchen, and there wasn't one inch of available counter space. Every wall in the small living room was mirrored, and the cops could see themselves at every turn. A full-size traffic signal hung in the corner. It was no novelty item, but the investigators had more on their minds than a stolen light.

Ricky's brother, Mike Chavis, sat on the couch. He was tall, with dark, receding hair. His thin frame and the numerous discolorations on his arm gave him the appearance of battling AIDS. That wasn't the cause, however. Mike's frailty stemmed from his weekly trips to the blood bank where he sold his plasma, his only source of income. Ricky hurried to the back of the trailer, leaving the investigators to wait with his brother. The deputies chatted with Mike while Ricky remained preoccupied in the back. After fifteen minutes passed, he finally emerged and made nervous conversation.

"I put those up myself," Ricky said proudly, following Sanderson's gaze around the mirrored walls. "I pulled every one from a Dumpster. Somebody had thrown them away."

Sanderson nodded. A variety of neon and fluorescent beer signs hung on the walls, along with dusty strings of Christmas lights. An entertainment center swallowed an entire wall, stacked with a forty-inch television set, stereo speakers, and a video-game player. The high-tech equipment seemed completely out of place in the slovenly trailer. Several small monitors, connected to security cameras outside, were situated under the television. They offered black and white images of the front, back, and sides of the trailer.

A floor lamp hovered over one of the armchairs and an end table, illuminating a legion of antennas. They were attached to several police scanners and a CB radio transmitter.

There were no recent calls from the missing brothers, but Ricky replayed the message Alex had left when he ran away the week before his father's death. The young boy's voice briefly crackled to life as he asked Ricky to tell his father they weren't coming home. Sanderson thought the small, childish voice belonged to a boy younger than twelve. The investigators recorded the message and scanned the trailer carefully as they turned for the door.

"I'll do everything I can to help find the boys," Ricky called out after them.

Ricky watched the investigators on the monitors in his living room until they left. When he was sure they had driven away, he quickly headed for the small laundry room off the kitchen. Sliding a piece of worn carpet out of the way, he pulled open a hatch in the floor and peered down.

"Okay, boys," he said. "You can come out now."

Derek and Alex crawled up from the small room hidden beneath Ricky's trailer. They were accustomed to this routine. They had slid through the trapdoor several times over the past week, hiding from their father. Ricky had made the crawl space comfortable for the boys by putting down carpet and providing a lamp, pillows, and blankets. As Terry begged Ricky to help him find his missing sons, they were literally right under his feet.

The phone rang as the brothers scampered out of the laundry room. Ricky's longtime friend Reggie Jernigan was on the other end of the line.

The Escambia sheriff's deputy was a familiar sight at Chavis's trailer, and Ricky's friends and neighbors recognized the heavyset officer easily. At fifty, Jernigan carried more than 200 pounds on his five-foot-eight frame and his brown hair was thinning. The deputy had known Ricky for most of his twenty-one years in law enforcement. The officer was also no stranger to the King brothers, as he had often seen them and their father visiting at Ricky's.

The two talked for a few minutes when Ricky realized someone else was calling. Glancing at his caller ID, he recognized Joyce Tracy's number. He quickly hung up with Jernigan and answered the call from the boys' grandmother.

Worried about her grandsons, Joyce hoped Ricky could help find them. After all, she believed Ricky and Reggie had done all they could to help find Alex and Derek previously. She was relieved when Ricky didn't seem to share her concern about the boys. In fact, instead of expressing his condolences to the grief-stricken woman, he demanded the return of a digital camera he had loaned Terry. The desperate father had used pictures of his sons, stored on the camera, to make "missing" posters of them. Joyce assured Ricky the investigators would return his camera, but he continued to pressure her about it.

She was surprised at his insistence, and his seeming lack of concern about Terry's death. Her son had been killed only hours earlier, and his so-called friend had yet to express any sadness. Still worried about the plight of her grandsons, she asked if he knew where they might be found.

Ricky speculated that it was unlikely the children were hiding in Pace again, since they would expect family and friends to look there. Only hours earlier he had told the investigators the exact opposite, pointing them toward the neighboring county and away from his own backyard.

Joyce suggested that perhaps Reggie Jernigan could help find her grandsons. Ricky offered to call him, and soon they were on a three-way call. The deputy was polite but hung up after telling the grandmother that he too was stumped over their disappearance. Ricky wrapped up his conversation with Joyce, then immediately dialed the deputy's number again. The two talked briefly before Ricky returned to the two children playing video games in his living room.

Meanwhile, Sanderson finally reached the boys' mother, Janet, to discover that she already knew about Terry's death and her missing children. The news had been shocking and surreal, but she was even more devastated to hear what the investigator told her next: he suspected the boys had killed their father.

While the investigators tried to track down the King brothers, the media scrambled for information. Not much happened in Cantonment. The rural community a few miles north of Pensacola was mostly known for deadly car accidents, the occasional train wreck, and the stench of the massive paper mill. Reporters from the local television stations and newspapers began combing the Cantonment community, interviewing neighbors and family members, who were horrified to learn Terry was murdered and his sons had vanished.

Local WEAR-TV 3 news reporter Mollye Barrows received the assignment to cover Terry King's murder. At twenty-nine, she was the darling of the local media, with her Sherlock Holmes brain and Charlie's Angel's body. At five-five and 110 pounds, she could have chosen a career as a bikini model instead of the news reporter's job that landed her in the trenches. She had a blond pixie haircut and a girl-next-door quality that prompted people to bare their souls to her without a second thought. Mollye was well-established as the TV 3 crime reporter. Aggressive, even possessive, about her beat, she had every intention of finding the truth about the King murder.

The TV 3 newsroom buzzed with the shocking story, speculating about the brothers' disappearance along with the rest of the community. Had they been kidnapped? Were they dead? As reporters and producers discussed avenues of information, someone remembered a strange visitor knocking frantically at the back door of the newsroom days before Terry King's death. He was desperate for help to find his missing sons. *That man had been Terry King.*

He was turned away like so many frustrated parents before him. The newsroom stuck to a strict policy about missing persons cases. Unless law enforcement officials called to say the disappearance was suspicious, people were turned away. Otherwise, there just wouldn't be enough time in the newscast to talk about all the angry runaways, teenage delinquents, or spouses who may have wanted to disappear. Only this time Terry King had been right. There was foul play.

And within a week he had joined the list of victims.

Chapter 6

THE AFTERNOON OF THE MURDER, INVESTIGATOR JOHN Sanderson was busy putting the complicated pieces of the puzzle together. At three o'clock he and Terry Kilgore went to see Frank Lay at Pace High School. They flashed their identification to Derek's foster father and began interviewing him.

Lay explained the King boys' background to the investigators and how Derek had come to live with his family. He revealed that they had sent Derek back to live with Terry over a month ago because he'd become a problem for them.

The investigators learned that Frank had received a call about a week before, telling him that Derek and Alex had run away. Then, on Saturday night, November 25, a neighbor several doors down from the Lays called to let them know that Derek was at their house. Frank and Nancy went to pick him up, but the boy ran away from them.

Frank said Derek was very upset, that he'd told him that he and Alex had been living with Ricky Chavis during the week they ran from their father. Frank also revealed to Sanderson and Kilgore that Alex hated Terry and wanted to kill him, that Derek described his father as a "control freak" who wouldn't let them go anywhere and kept them locked in the house. Derek had told him, he said, that Chavis helped them plan their escape and protected them by hiding them from their father.

Sanderson thanked Frank Lay and left to look up the neighbor whose daughter Derek had visited. Ten minutes later the deputies were interviewing the young friend. She told them that on the day before the murder, Ricky Chavis had dropped Derek off to visit friends in Pace. Derek told her that he was living with Ricky. He had only stayed half an hour when her parents called the Lays and they promptly came to get him. When Ricky arrived later to pick him up, the runaway had already been caught and turned over to the police.

The following day, November 27, Sanderson continued tracking down potential witnesses in the case. He learned more about Terry's relationship with Ricky Chavis from Debbie Alltop, an administrative assistant at Ransom Middle School. Debbie said that Ricky had special permission from Terry to pick up the boys after school. However, about two weeks before the murder, he angrily revoked that privilege without explanation.

Terry's longtime friend Lewis Tyson said Terry and the boys were visiting his West Pensacola home the evening he was killed. Lewis told Sanderson that Terry jokingly said, "They look like they're plotting something," as the two men watched Alex and Derek talking outside his house. Hours later someone smashed Terry's skull with enough force to splatter his blood twelve feet away on the walls and ceiling.

Tyson had known Terry and Alex for about eight years. This was Sanderson's second interview with Terry's friend in as many days, and the ex-biker seemed to be warming to his involvement in the highly publicized murder case. Sanderson listened patiently. Diplomacy was one of his assets.

In fact, Sanderson got along well with almost everyone at

the investigations office, not an easy task for a department steeped in politics. Investigators were rotated in and out of their departments as soon as a new sheriff took office. Those who supported the incoming administration were often rewarded with the coveted positions, replacing those who were politically aligned with the losing campaign. While some of Sanderson's colleagues found themselves back on patrol, Sanderson himself managed to tiptoe through the political quagmire. His solid investigative track record and easy demeanor helped make it possible.

Lewis Tyson told him the boys were "acting very strange" that evening. Derek was unusually affectionate, but Alex called his father "Terry" instead of "Dad."

"I know Alex well enough to know he only does that when he's angry with his father," Lewis said confidently.

Listening to the ex-biker elaborate on that last night with his murdered friend, Sanderson asked if Terry seemed suspicious.

Lewis remembered back. "He said he was going to sleep on the couch because he didn't trust the boys. He thought they might run away." Lewis had also revealed to the investigator that the boys told him they stayed with a friend when they were gone.

"I talked to those boys before they left that night. While Terry was inside, I told them I wanted to know where they had been when they ran away." Lewis sternly crossed his arms across his broad chest as if reliving the scene. "I said, 'I know you're lying. You two didn't stay in the woods. Derek, you're afraid of spiders, and Alex, you're afraid of the dark.' That's when they just kinda looked at the ground and told me about their friend."

Lewis said the boys liked the man a lot and enjoyed spending time at his home because he had a good computer system and a big house. They said his place was surrounded by a gate that was topped with wire and security cameras. Sanderson recognized the description of Ricky Chavis's trailer.

A time line of the events that led up to Terry King's murder began to take shape for the deputy. He realized Ricky Chavis had kept the brothers from their father the week before his death and likely knew more about their whereabouts now than he had revealed. As he probed for more details, his cell phone rang. Another investigator had called to tell him the search for Alex and Derek King was over. The brothers were on their way to the Sheriff's Office with Deputy Reggie Jernigan and Ricky Chavis.

Sanderson and Kilgore were casually questioning Ricky at the department, not far from where another officer sat with Alex and Derek. Like Sanderson, Terry Kilgore was a seasoned cop with years of experience in most facets of police work, but homicide was where he intended to stay until retirement. That was another goal that didn't seem to be far from the investigator's mind. Kilgore kept an elaborate timer on his desk that ticked down the hours, minutes, and seconds he had left until police work would only be a memory. In the meantime, he was assessing the man who claimed to have found the King brothers.

Ricky was obliging and humble as Kilgore thanked him for bringing in the children. The deputies were anxious to interview the boys, but they first needed to know how Ricky had "found them." They found his story as bizarre as his home.

Ricky told the deputies he received a phone call from an anonymous woman who insisted he should come to a certain convenience store in Pace. Without another word, he jumped in his car. Thirty minutes later he arrived at the store and the boys materialized out of the woods and got in his vehicle.

Ricky tearfully described Derek's gruesome confession in the car, that he beat his father to death with a baseball bat. He was quick to point out that he was devastated by the crime and that he had demanded that the boys turn themselves into the police whether or not they were willing. Ricky said that's when he called his friend, Reggie Jernigan, to pick the brothers up.

Since Sanderson had begun digging into Terry's death, Ricky had been right there, hovering like a fly over a rotting corpse. But in spite of his obvious entanglement, investigators looked in the opposite direction. They believed the faces of Terry King's killers belonged to the children who called him Dad.

Sanderson and Kilgore walked into the interrogation room where Derek and Alex King waited and introduced themselves. They asked the boys if they needed to use the facilities, and Derek took them up on an offer for soda.

Both boys were small for their age. They looked like vagabonds, with bushy hair and mismatched, oversized clothes. Derek was four feet ten inches tall, with a slightly stocky build, dark hair, and big blue eyes. Alex had blue eyes like his brother, but the resemblance stopped there. He was blond and even shorter than Derek, but with a slight frame that belonged more to a child than a boy on the verge of adolescence.

The investigators easily developed a good rapport with Derek. Although subdued, he had an eager smile and watched them with wide eyes. Sanderson noted that Alex was more direct and matter-of-fact with them. They questioned each boy separately before recording their statements.

Voluntary statements to police could be tricky. Investigators needed to ensure that they were properly recorded and followed the letter of the law. Overlooking one step in the legal process could give a good defense attorney the foothold to have hours of investigative work thrown out of court. Sanderson and Kilgore had no intention of making a mistake, but they needed to nail these interviews while the opportunity was available.

Before they began recording the boys' statements, the deputies called Assistant State Attorney David Rimmer, a homicide prosecutor with the State Attorney's Office. The deputies explained to him that the boys' legal guardian was dead, their mother was out-of-state, and there was a lot of turmoil between family members. The investigators also told Rimmer they had asked the children if they wanted anyone in the room with them during the interview. Derek requested Ricky, but the officers told him Ricky's involvement in the case meant he couldn't be there. Derek then asked for Deputy Reggie Jernigan. Rimmer told them to proceed with the interrogations.

They spoke to Derek first. The investigators read him his Miranda rights and told him that he could stop answering questions at any time. Then Kilgore and Sanderson fell into the same question and answer routine they used with countless criminals. Only this time the suspects were the age of Sanderson's children. He had four of his own, two daughters in their late teens and two sons thirteen and fifteen. The comparison almost made him shudder.

Kilgore began the interview lightly, asking Derek simple, basic questions about his age and grade in school.

Sanderson, wanting to make sure Derek understood the gravity of the situation, asked, "Do you know the difference between right and wrong?"

"Yes, sir."

"And we've been told and we talked earlier before the tape came on that you have a very high IQ. Is that correct?"

"Yes, sir."

"Okay. And you at one time, or here recently, you possibly should be or have been in the gifted program at school?"

"Yes, sir."

"Okay. So do you understand what's going on?"

"Yes, sir."

"Okay. What we'd like to do is start and talk about what happened at your house over on Muscogee Road. Now, that would have been late Sunday night or early Monday morning. You can say anything you want to on tape, and what we want you to do is just kind of start from the beginning and let us know what happened, okay?"

"Okay." But Derek stopped there.

"All right, go ahead," Sanderson encouraged.

"I caught my dad throwing my brother around, my twelve-year-old brother, and—" Derek began, but Sanderson interrupted with another question.

"If you would, start a little bit ahead of that, okay? Just go back a little bit further, when we were talking about when you were at this guy's house and where y'all went from there. If you don't mind."

"Okay. We were sitting on the swing and I told Alex, if anything—if it gets real serious—that I would get physical with Dad, and so . . ." Derek paused again.

"Whose house were y'all at?" Sanderson asked.

"Lewis."

"Lewis. Do you know Lewis very well, or where do you know him from?" Sanderson continued.

"The flea market."

Sanderson remembered Lewis told him the boys kept pestering him about the time as if anxious to get home.

"Did anybody ask Lewis what time it was or did Lewis say anything about what time it was before y'all left?"

"I saw his watch," Derek answered. "I saw the time on his watch when his hands were crossed."

"Do you know about what time it was then?"

"Twelve midnight."

The interrogation was interrupted as Deputy Reggie Jernigan entered the room. Kilgore noted the officer's arrival for the tape recording.

"Just entering the room now—the time is 1708 hours—is Deputy Reggie Jernigan. Okay, go ahead," he said to Derek.

"Okay," Sanderson said. "Where had you been earlier in the day? Do you remember that?"

Derek told the officers they were at the flea market, where they took down all the missing persons flyers his father had tacked up during the week they disappeared. They then went to Lewis's house, where Terry and his friend spent much of the time talking privately.

"They were kind of being secretive about it," Derek elaborated, "and then me and Alex were playing with his cats and his dog and just playing games and stuff. Having fun."

"Okay."

"And then we just sat down on the swing. I told Alex if— if stuff gets serious, I will—I will defend you."

"Okay. What would make you say that? Why would you say that?"

" 'Cause Alex told me he was weak and he didn't have enough—he didn't have strength to fight him off, fight my father off."

Sanderson asked the boy to clarify his answer. "Did you feel like something might happen? I mean that's why y'all were having that conversation?"

"Why, because we—we were scared that something might, since . . . That was the day he got both of us back. I was—I was just afraid that once he got both of us back, he would get physical with both of us at once."

"Okay," Kilgore pressed. "Is that because you ran away?"

"Yes."

"Okay. Well, let me ask you this: you were brought back home on Saturday."

"Yes, sir."

"And Saturday would have been the twenty-fourth. Okay, did your dad get physical with you then?"

"Mm-mm." Derek shook his head no.

"Okay, I need you to speak up," Kilgore said.

"No, sir," Derek repeated.

"Okay, did he threaten you in any way?"

"No, sir," Derek mumbled. "Not like verbally."

"What do you mean?"

"Like he was—he was staring me down some," Derek tried to explain.

"Okay," Kilgore said.

"Let me ask you something about that," Sanderson pressed. "Has your dad ever hit y'all?"

"Not punched us or nothing, but he has thrown us around."

"Has he ever used any kind of—I don't know what word you'd use—I was going to say weapons on you or anything?"

"No."

"Did he ever spank you with a belt or a switch or—"

"No," Derek interrupted.

"Or anything like that?" Sanderson continued.

"No, sir," Derek repeated.

"As far as pushing you around, how serious has that ever gotten? I mean is it something that leaves physical marks on you or anything?"

"Barely," Derek replied.

"Anything like that or—"

"I might trip over something and fall down."

"Okay, okay, okay," Sanderson said. "Now most of what

we've been talking about—we talked about some pushing around—is that a frequent event, pushing, or was it mostly something else that he would do?"

"Disciplinary action," Derek stated.

"What kind of disciplinary action?"

"If we did something wrong, like . . ." Derek hesitated.

"Give me a for instance," Kilgore said.

"Mmm, we talked back to him."

"Okay," Kilgore continued. "What would he do if you talked back?"

"He would, he'd be like, he . . ." Derek faltered.

"That's all right. Take your time," Kilgore said.

"I don't want to waste tape," Derek explained.

"Oh, don't worry about wasting the tape. We've got plenty of tape."

"Okay," Derek said.

"We've got plenty of tape," Kilgore repeated.

"All right."

"Don't be afraid of the tape," Sanderson insisted.

"Okay," Derek agreed.

"I'm just trying to hear so we make sure we got everything on tape," Kilgore said.

"Okay."

"That's all that is," Kilgore explained.

"I forgot the question now," Derek said.

"The question is, give me a for instance," Kilgore repeated. "What would he do to you, if you talked back to him?"

"He'd be like, 'When I say something, my answer's final,' and he'd be pushing us while he said that."

"Okay."

"And he said, 'When I say yes, I mean yes. When I say no, I mean no. No questions about it.' "

"Okay."

" 'Do you understand?' " Derek tried to repeat his dad's words. "He'd be pushing us around while he's saying that."

"Let me ask you something on the same grounds too," Sanderson said. "As far as food, did he feed y'all good?"

"Yes, sir."

"Okay," Sanderson said.

"He made us dress the way he felt was right."

"Sure," Kilgore agreed. "All right, so you're at Lewis's house? You're sitting on the bench. You talk about that."

"Did y'all specifically say anything when you were sitting there?" Sanderson asked.

"Not specifically. I said—I said," Derek stammered, "I will—I will fight him off and if it gets serious enough, I will kill him, 'cause I know that you are not physically strong, you're not strong enough to fight him off. And so when we got home—'cause he stared me down pretty good one time while they were there, while we were at Lewis's house—and so when we got home, he dealt with Alex. Then I—I tried to get on his good side and cool him down, like hugging him. Stuff like that."

"Okay, now you said he dealt with Alex. What do you mean by that? What happened?" Kilgore asked.

"He shoved him around. He didn't really yell that much and, um . . ."

"Do you remember what he was saying?"

"No."

"Okay. And so he pushed him around, and he pushed him and Alex fell on the table and started crying and then I was—I was in—I was out of the room and I walked by and I caught him as soon as, when he was pushing Alex, and then, uh, I—I was like . . ."

"Do you know what that was all about?" Sanderson asked.

"No. Not really."

"Okay," Sanderson said.

"Go ahead," Kilgore prodded.

"And so . . . it—well actually it was about running away. He didn't . . . He was mad 'cause we ran away."

"But he didn't say anything to you about it at that time. He was just . . ." Sanderson trailed off.

"Mm-hm," Derek answered. "And so we like started playing and stuff with toys and I said don't worry about him, I'll—I'll deal with him. So when he went to sleep, I got—I made sure he was asleep. I got the bat and I hit him over the head."

"Now you had told us earlier when you . . ." Kilgore began. "Where was your dad at when you hit him?"

"In the green room."

"And the green room is just a part of the house? Is that correct?"

"Mm-hm."

"Okay. Where was your dad asleep at?"

"On a recliner."

"And you talked about earlier how your dad was . . ." Kilgore continued.

"Feet propped on the couch. He had a coffee cup in his hand."

"And you're showing us a coffee cup and you've got it down almost on your inseam in your groin area. Is that correct?"

"Yes."

"And you're showing . . ."

"I can't remember. It was either, he was holding it either right there . . . either the outside or in between."

"Okay," the investigators replied.

"And he had his—he either had his hand or the handle or he had it in—on the cup—and I can't remember."

"That's okay," Kilgore said. "So he's laying there and you've made sure he's asleep. Okay. Tell me what happened then? Where did you get the bat from?"

"Down the hall. A little ways down the hall."

"Okay. And we were talking about that earlier, and is that what you hit your father with?"

"Yes."

"Okay," Kilgore said.

"Mainly the left side of his face and his head," Derek explained.

"Okay. Tell me about that now. And I know that's painful and we talked about it before, so tell me about it."

"I went in there," Derek continued. "I hit once and then I heard him moan and then I was afraid that he might wake up and see us so I just kept on hitting him."

"Okay," Kilgore said.

"Hit him somewhere around ten times."

"All the blows?" Sanderson asked. "What area?"

"The face—the face, the left side of the face and forehead."

"Okay," Kilgore said. "Well, you're saying the left but you're patting the right side of your face."

"Well, it was right to me 'cause he was laying down. Wait. No, it wasn't 'cause I was—I was hitting him. It was my right, his left."

"Okay, because you keep patting your right and I just want to make sure because the tape can't see what you're doing."

"Yeah," Derek said.

"That's why we have to explain everything so we make sure we get it all correct."

"Okay," Derek replied.

"Okay?" Kilgore asked. "All right, so what happens after that? Where's Alex at when this is going on?"

"He was right there beside me."

"Okay," Kilgore said.

"Watching me," Derek answered.

"Did he know you were going to do it?"

"Mm-hm. Well, he knew what was up when I grabbed the bat."

"How do you know he knew what was up?" Kilgore asked. "Did you say something to Alex when you grabbed the bat?"

"Not really," Derek said. "It was too late to go play baseball."

"What was y'all's conversation between the time he shoved Alex and the time that your father fell asleep, because we know y'all had some kind of conversation," Sanderson said.

"Well, Alex was just pretty—was really mad at him . . . and so, he was like you'd better go ahead and do it if you're going to do it. Kill him," Derek told them.

"Is that what Alex said?" Kilgore asked.

"Mm-hm. Somewhere, that's what he meant."

"Okay."

"I can't remember the exact words."

"He knew what you were going to do?" Sanderson asked the boy.

"Mm-hm," Derek answered.

"It was something y'all talked about. Is that correct or not?" Sanderson pressed.

"Yeah, but we didn't do specifics."

"Okay," Sanderson said. "Not exactly how or anything."

"Yeah, he just knew that something was going to happen."

"Okay," Kilgore said. "So what happens after that?"

"I—I . . . I killed him," Derek stammered. "I run . . . I immediately . . . I can't—I can't stand to see his face 'cause I was scared."

"What was your . . . I'm sorry," Sanderson said. "I don't mean to break in, but what was your initial feeling when you first did this?"

"Defense for Alex," Derek replied.

"No, I mean . . ." Sanderson tried to explain.

"What do you mean?" Derek asked.

"I mean how did you feel yourself when you first did this?"

"I was mad that he did anything like that."

"Okay," Sanderson pressed. "All I'm saying is, earlier you were asked if you knew the difference between right and wrong, okay. You do?"

"Mm-hm," Derek nodded.

"Okay," Sanderson said.

"But my anger just was so overwhelming that I just did what I thought was right."

Sanderson continued, "So after all this went down, then . . ."

"I threw the bat on the bed, lit the bed on fire, because I was scared of the evidence and everything. Scared of getting caught."

"Okay," Kilgore continued. "You lit the bed on fire. Did you light anything else on fire?"

"I tried to light the rug at the front door, but I don't think I did because I picked the rug up and I lit it. I lit the little frayed thing. . . ."

"You wet it?" Kilgore asked.

"I lit it," Derek repeated.

"Oh, I'm sorry," Kilgore said.

"Set it on fire," Derek said.

"I'm sorry," Kilgore said. "I thought you said you wet it. Okay, did you wet any of the house down?" The investigators knew accelerant had been used to ignite the blaze.

"No," Derek answered. He explained that he had used an aluminum bat on his father and had burned it along with Terry's bed. He said Alex was right behind him the entire time and together they ran out the back door.

"Okay, and where did y'all run to?" Kilgore asked.

"We just ran to—well, I don't know. I was just leading the way. We ran to a highway. We got somebody, a man, to pick us up and take us to Pace."

"Okay," Kilgore said. "Do you remember what he looked like?"

"No, I was too shook up about what happened to notice anything."

"You didn't know his name?" Sanderson asked.

"Mm-mm." Derek shook his head. He told the officers the man dropped them off in Pace. They ran to a subdivision, not far from his previous home with the Lays, where they hid in the woods for two nights.

"How did you get back to Pensacola today?"

"One of Rick's friends called him on his cell phone at the convenience store that we just walked up to."

"And did Rick come over and get you?"

"Mm-hm." Derek nodded.

"Okay, so y'all get in Rick's car. What's the conversation in Rick's car? What are y'all talking about?"

"He said he knew that something like this was going to happen and he was going to call Reggie so he could take us over here."

"You're talking about over here at the Sheriff's Office?"

"Yes."

Kilgore began wrapping up the interview. "Okay, is there anything else that you'd like to add or take away from this statement?"

"What statement?" Derek asked.

"The statement you just gave," Kilgore replied. He hadn't realized that Derek didn't understand law enforcement terminology and had no idea what a police statement was.

"He just—he told us that he called some friends and told them to be on the lookout."

"Who's that, now?" Sanderson asked. "I'm sorry. What are you talking about as far as that?" Everyone was confused.

"You talking about Rick?" Kilgore pressed.

"Rick's friends," Derek answered.

"Oh, okay," Sanderson said, seeming to brush the comment aside. The officers wrapped up the interview and asked the boy if they had been fair to him or threatened him in any way. Derek agreed he felt comfortable with them as well as with Deputy Reggie Jernigan, who had attended a portion of his interview.

"Is everything you told us the truth?" Kilgore asked.

"Yes, sir."

Sanderson thought the confession was chilling. As he listened, he was convinced the boys simply did not want to live with their father. Derek obviously preferred his life with the Lay family and resented his father's strict attitude. The two-hour-long interview was over, but the case against Derek King was just getting started. The investigators then turned their attention to his baby brother.

Chapter 7

"PRESENT IS ALEX DAVID KING. HIS ADDRESS IS 1104 MUSCOGEE ROAD IN PENSACOLA, FLORIDA. His date of birth is July 12, 1989, and Alex, you don't know your social security number, do you?"

The blond-headed boy shook his head.

Kilgore suggested that Alex pull his chair up a little closer to the desk so they could clearly get his voice on tape. The deputies then identified themselves as homicide investigators and advised Alex of his Miranda rights. He listened and signed a document confirming that he knew his rights. He answered the same simple questions they had asked of his brother. The twelve-year-old agreed that he too was smart enough to understand the situation.

"What I want you to do is kind of start about what happened," Kilgore said. "I understand that you had run away from home. Why don't you tell me about what happened Sunday right before you got picked up? You turned yourself in from running away."

"Yes, sir."

Alex was once again talking too softly, and Kilgore reminded him to speak up. "Tell us what happened."

"Yeah, all right," Alex replied, and the words poured out. "What happened Sunday. Okay. Derek, um . . . I went to ex-

plore the woods while Derek, he wanted to go to a friend's
house to make a phone call, so I went to explore the woods
to wait for him to come back and, uh, so whenever I came
out of the woods, I looked. . . . He hadn't shown up yet, and
I looked for him, and I couldn't find him. So I figured that he
had got caught, and so—but I didn't want to turn myself in
without that being the reason he didn't come back. And so I
just I spent the night in the woods waiting for him, and he
didn't show up. And so, I went to the Tom Thumb and I
called Rick 'cause I didn't know any other number I could
call, really. And so I decided I would just call Rick, and he
came and picked me up and, uh, while we were waiting, I
was talking to my grandmother, Joyce Tracy, um, so we
went—went across the street, McDonald's, to get something
to eat 'cause I was hungry. And after a while, went back
across the street . . . after a while, Terry and Derek showed
up. I was talking to Derek about what happened. He told me,
he filled me in on what had happened whenever he got
caught. Then, he had called someone and, uh, the ladies had
picked him up. Um, then they had called the police and
come pick him up and then he was taken to Terry."

Kilgore interrupted to clarify. "Okay. Now when you talk
about Terry, Terry's your dad. Is that correct?"

"Yes, sir."

"Okay, go ahead."

"But biologically he is not my dad. He's not my father. Biologically." This statement was new information to the investigators, but they moved on.

"Okay. Okay," Kilgore replied.

Alex repeated the same details Derek had given them. He
described their excursion to the flea market where they removed the missing persons posters, and their visit to Lewis
Tyson's home.

"And so while we were there, I was—we were talking about what would happen when we got home. And, uh, we were talking . . . we were sort of talking about him dying a little bit."

"Wait a minute, now," Kilgore interrupted. "Dying a little bit?"

"Well, him dying. We was talking about it a little bit but it was about him dying."

Investigator Sanderson spoke up. "What was the conversation about?"

"Pretty much it was like, I was saying I was scared about what would happen whenever we got home and I couldn't really handle it that much longer. So, we brought up the subject about his death, about, well about us killing him. . . ." Alex trailed off.

Sanderson asked, "Did you talk about how you were gonna do it?"

"No. Not then," Alex replied.

Kilgore asked, "Not then? Go ahead. So how long did you talk about that?"

"Not too long. We just went back to talking about Corvettes because that's my favorite car, so . . . we started on that. And so we went . . . while we were there we horse-played for a while. It was pretty late whenever we went home. It was in the night. And whenever we got home, he took a picture of Derek and of me before we went inside. We went inside, I went to use the rest room, and Derek went in the—in his room to play. He played. That was, um, that was before we took our . . . it was after we took our shoes off. . . . I think we took our shoes off. . . . So, then I—I noticed that Terry was in the green room. I went in there and then, well, he called me in there and then he asked—he started asking why I ran away, and I was saying because of what happened."

"And what had happened?" Kilgore asked.

"Well, the day that we ran away, before we went to the . . . to the school, he—he threw us around, and before we went to school that day, we couldn't take it anymore because we had, um, we had—well, he had done that before to us, um, so . . ."

Kilgore said, "Okay. Now you talk about he's done it before, I mean, what do you talk about him doing?"

Alex replied, "Abuse."

"Well, what type?"

"Mental and physical. Mental, he was staring us down every time we got in trouble. He was using, um, extreme eye contact."

"Okay. Extreme eye contact? Staring you down. Okay."

"And, um, and well, I had grown to where I could easily defend myself against that, which was rather simple because it's something dealing with the mind. Pretty strong in the aspect."

"Hear you're pretty strong in that aspect of the mind, aren't you?" Kilgore asked.

"Yeah," Alex said.

"So you could, you didn't have any problems with . . . the mental. . . ."

"Yeah, but Derek did because, well, and uh, I guess . . ." His voice lowered to a mumble. "And so."

"Okay, what about the physical abuse?" Kilgore asked. "You talked about that. What was he doing to you?"

"Well, he threw us around and whenever we were in the car he, um, we said something that we weren't supposed to or something like that, then sometimes he'd hit us and he'd tell us to shut up."

"Let me ask you, when he hit you, how, what would he hit you with? I mean how did he hit you?"

"Well, he hit me a couple of times. It wasn't very often

that he did but he hit me a couple of times with the back of his hand, well, basically slapped me across the face."

"Let me ask you this: the times that he'd slap you across the face and you say that he didn't do it much, was it because you were in trouble, or something had happened, or what?"

"Were you being disciplined?" Sanderson asked.

"No," Alex responded, "he was, um, he must have had a bad day and I just—I was talking and he hit me and told me to shut up." His voice became inaudible briefly, and then became audible again. ". . . a couple of the times. I think that was all the times he hit me. Wasn't very often."

"Wasn't very often? Okay."

"Not at all."

"Let me ask you this: we were talking about . . . earlier about being spanked for being disciplined. . . ."

"One time," Alex responded.

"Let me ask you this: did the times that you were spanked, was it because you got in trouble for something you weren't supposed to do?"

"Yes, sir." Alex said.

"Okay. All right. Tell me about that one time."

"The one time that he did use a stick, it was a long time ago, I got in trouble and he used the stick."

"Okay," Kilgore said. "How big was the stick?"

"I can't recollect that. It was too long ago. I was pretty young back then."

Sanderson asked, "You don't know if it was a little stick or if it was a big stick?"

Alex answered, "It wasn't—wasn't a little switch. I know that."

"All right, okay, so that time and then the other times you talk about it's because you had done something wrong. Is that correct?" Kilgore asked.

"Yeah. It was. He used his hand a few times, most of the time he just used the belt."

"Okay. How many times did he whip you with the belt?"

Alex said, "Well, I don't remember. I got in trouble so many times. I don't really remember."

Kilgore responded, "Okay. Did—Was it because you were doing something wrong?"

"Yeah," Alex said.

"Is that why you got in trouble?"

"Yeah. That's why. He'd spank me with the belt, but that's a long time ago. It didn't happen—hadn't happened except it just started not too long ago."

"Okay. Do you remember how many times you've been whipped with a belt?"

"No. It was quite a few times," Alex said.

Kilgore said, "Quite a few?"

"Yeah," Alex replied.

"How many's quite a few?"

Alex said, "I don't know. Well, more than just like, I think it was like ten or twenty times."

Kilgore asked, "Ten or twenty times and that's just been recently?"

"No," Alex replied. "Well, once recent, pretty recently. It wasn't till, well, it was a couple of months ago that he hit, that he spanked me with a belt. Last time he did it."

"Okay. So that's the last time he spanked you?"

"Yeah."

"Okay," Kilgore said, "so you're over at Lewis's house and you're talking about . . ."

"About, um . . ." Alex thought a minute. "Talking about, well, I was saying that I was afraid of what would happen when we got home and, um, it came up that we—we, um, that about killing him came up next."

"Okay," Kilgore said, "how did, I mean, how did it come up?"

Alex replied, "Well I was, we was talking about what might happen when we got home, and . . ."

"Okay. What did you think was gonna happen?"

"Well, we thought that he was gonna spank us then."

"But it turned out . . ." Kilgore began. "Well, go ahead. You thought he was gonna spank you. . . ."

Alex mumbled something unintelligible, ending with, "And use the mental abuse and physical."

"Okay." Kilgore said.

"We thought he was."

"Now you weren't too worried about the mental abuse, were you?" Kilgore asked.

"I wasn't worried at all about the mental abuse," Alex replied.

"Because . . ." Kilgore began.

"It got to where it had no effect on me," Alex replied.

"Okay," Kilgore said.

Alex began again, "So when we got home, um, took our shoes off, we went in our room to play, played around for a while. I went into the bathroom, and when I came out, Terry called me into the green room. He was talking about it and then, um, we were talking about it and he grabbed me by the wrist and he threw me onto the ground, but my arm hit something. I can't recollect what it was 'cause I was, you know, in motion. I was looking at the ground."

"Okay."

"But, uh, I hit something with this arm," Alex mumbled.

"Okay. And you're pointing to your left arm."

"Yes."

"Okay," Kilgore said. "You have to describe everything because the tape can't see. Okay, Let me ask you this. Let's go back real quick to the workbench. What you had talked about earlier . . . there was some lighter fluids and stuff. Tell us about that."

"All right. There's, uh, two cans of charcoal lighter, some—there's this off-brand type in a metal container and there wasn't much in it, and there was uh, there was another type, a better type that was in a plastic container. We didn't use any of it . . ." Alex mumbled something inaudible. ". . . we just lit the bed 'cause we knew the house was very vulnerable because it was so old, didn't know exactly how it was burnable but we just knew that it was and so we just lit the bed. The bed had several blankets, different blankets on it, so we knew that it would be a good igniter itself."

Alex told the investigators that after spending a couple of nights in the woods, they realized they could no longer live with the knowledge of what happened. He said Derek "got one of his lady friends to call Rick," and their father's friend soon picked them up at a convenience store.

". . . So on the way to Rick's house, we, um, talked about—me and Derek we both took turns telling Rick what happened. Um, so far as Terry's death and what led up to it, and whenever we got to Rick's house we each took a shower and, um, we cleaned off our clothes."

"Why'd you do that?" Kilgore asked.

"'Cause of, uh, it was a mess. We didn't really want to look so ragged, you know," replied Alex.

"Okay," Kilgore said.

"Look a little bit more presentable. So we cleaned off our clothes a little bit and so waited for Reggie to pick us up, take us to the Sheriff's Office."

"Okay. And that's how you ended up here."

"Yes," Alex replied.

"Okay," Sanderson said. "As far as Rick . . . You know Rick for a long time?

"Yeah," Alex answered.

"If anybody was to say okay, was Rick involved in this in any way . . . did Rick know . . . until you told him, did Rick know anything about what happened that night? Did he know beforehand it was gonna happen? Did he know right after?" Sanderson asked.

Alex answered, "He knew—I don't think he knew anything beforehand, uh, he said that he felt that it might come down to this, but we didn't tell him about it beforehand. After what's happened a couple of days, then he knew about it because we didn't contact him. After we ran away the first time, and I don't—I don't believe we made any contact. The reason I say that is because of Derek. Don't really know what happened, that is, a few times we did get separated or we were separated . . . and so Rick—we didn't contact Rick except to come pick us up. He picked me up the first time in the same . . ." His voiced dropped again, too low to hear.

"As far as the—I'm talking about as far as the death of your father—did Rick know before it was gonna happen that it was gonna happen?" Sanderson asked again.

"He didn't know for a fact but he had a feeling that it would," Alex replied.

"How do you know that?" Kilgore asked.

" 'Cause he told me about it. Out there they were talking about it."

"Out where?" Kilgore asked.

"Right out there in the waiting area," Alex replied.

"You talking about today?" Kilgore asked.

"Yeah," Alex said. "Today he said that."

"Well," Kilgore said, "we're talking . . . what was he saying?"

Alex mumbled something inaudible and then said, "Um, we were just saying . . ."

Kilgore said, "Go ahead and speak up a little bit 'cause you're—"

"All right. We were just . . . I was just talking stuff and he said that I—we weren't really talking about that, just talking about odd stuff, like a conversation instead of being bored."

"Okay," Kilgore replied.

"We were just making conversation, so I told Reggie, um, said I told Reggie that I had a feeling it might come down to this. And so he said, it was like Reggie said that he'd have to be listening to him more often," Alex explained.

"Did Rick come over there the other night?" Sanderson asked.

"No," Alex replied. "He had no involvement in it as far as anything . . ."

"If anybody was to ever say Rick was involved, Rick helped y'all or Rick was there, or Rick gave y'all a ride from there. If anybody was to say that, would that be true?" Sanderson asked.

"No," Alex repeated. "That would be false information."

"Let me ask you this," Kilgore said. "How do you feel about Terry's death now?"

"I have a mixture of feelings, really," replied Alex. "The same, uh, as I had. Well, after I calmed down it was just, I developed a mixture of feelings which I still have."

"Can you describe those for me?" asked Kilgore.

"Yes, um, I feel a little sad about it, a little sad, a little bit, um, a little relieved that we don't have to go through it, go through what he put us through again, the abuse, and a little bit. . . . Mainly I feel kind of down about. Because of the fact that you know, it was a death and I saw it and it's just kind of real disturbing."

"Okay, well, do you feel responsible?" Kilgore asked.

"Yeah."

"For his death?" Kilgore asked.

"Yes I do," Alex responded. "I feel mainly responsible.

Derek—Derek took the hits and—but I was the one that gave him the idea."

"You're the one that gave Derek the idea?" Kilgore asked.

"Yeah," Alex replied, "I feel I'm more responsible than Derek. Really. I mean, 'cause the fact that I gave him the idea and all."

"All right," said Sanderson, "let me ask you one other thing: as far as Terry, I know you were talking about the mental and the physical type abuse and all and it was sparse . . . I mean it was here and there, it sounds like. Was it or not?"

"The mental abuse was, uh . . . the mental abuse, it started a long time ago and had been going on for a real long time," Alex said.

"Okay."

"And, uh, I got informed—" Alex began.

Sanderson interrupted for clarification. "That was the staring and all that. Is that correct?"

"Yeah, the staring down."

"You got informed. What were you going to say?" Sanderson asked.

Alex continued. "I got informed by someone that he was doing this, and so—"

"Who informed you of that?" asked Kilgore.

"Um, I don't really want to say," Alex replied.

"Well, no," Kilgore said. "You need to tell us who informed you of it. It was Rick, wasn't it?"

"Mm, yeah," the boy answered reluctantly.

"Rick said that he was mentally abusing you?" Kilgore asked.

"Yeah, he told me that. . . . We had talked a lot and we were good friends and he said that he done mental abuse and he told me about it and then I started getting stronger toward him 'cause I knew what it was and I found a way to just sort of deflect . . ."

"Before Rick told you that," Sanderson said, "did it—"

"It affected me big-time," Alex replied.

"It did before that?" Sanderson asked.

"Mm-hm," Alex nodded.

"Okay. Okay," Sanderson said.

"But now, it didn't bother you?" Kilgore asked.

"It has no effect," Alex stated.

"Because you're mentally stronger," Kilgore said.

"Yes," said Alex. "Toward what he's doing." Under the investigators' probing, Alex also revealed that Terry did the best he could, providing clothes, toys, and gifts, although food was sometimes scarce when they fell on tough times. Alex also called his father reclusive and the only television he saw was at Rick's trailer.

"You haven't been enjoying it," Kilgore stated.

"Yeah," Alex replied. "We didn't have much entertainment at the house, just some books that I read about a thousand times and a couple of board games, but as far as the entertainment there, we didn't have much at all."

"You talk about Rick being a good friend. Did you use to write a lot in your diary? Do you have a diary?" Kilgore asked.

"I don't have one," Alex told him. "I did have one for a while but I really was never good at writing down my thoughts and my feelings. I can say them a lot better than writing them. I couldn't write them down."

"Has Rick been a good friend to you?" Kilgore asked.

"Yeah," said Alex. "He's a good friend. He's been good for me. He helped me out with Terry, you know, and he's—"

"Has he helped you out on some other things?" Kilgore asked.

"Well, learning," Alex replied. "He's helped, I watched him do a lot of his stuff and his work and he's explained it to me so he's helped me out on that and, uh, as far as what Terry was doing, so . . ."

The investigators ended the interview, having learned all they wanted to know. Sanderson was struck by how cool Alex remained, as if he were describing the slaughter of a complete stranger. The boy talked softly, but the details were chilling.

The brothers were arrested and charged with murder. While other children their age were getting ready to eat dinner or finish their homework for school the following morning, the King brothers were fingerprinted, photographed, and sent to juvenile jail.

As Sanderson and Kilgore watched them being led away, they were satisfied Terry King's killers were in custody. They were proud they had solved the high profile case in less than forty-eight hours, a rare treat lately for homicide investigators with the Escambia Sheriff's Office. More than half a dozen unsolved murders had piled up in the past year, bringing a barrage of questions from the media about the competency of the department. These arrests were much needed feathers in their caps, and the officers were pleased to share the news with the press.

Only instead of quieting the media's concerns, the clamor for answers grew louder.

Chapter 8

KEVIN BAILEY JUST WANTED TO GET IT OVER WITH. HE was standing in the yard with two other men, staring at the ruins of the house that Terry King had so happily rented from him. The cold December morning had nothing to do with the chill that settled over him as he looked at the lifeless house, the trampled flower beds, and the crime scene tape wound haphazardly around the home.

Kevin cut the flimsy plastic, realizing it probably had not stopped anyone from going through the house during the week since Terry's death. In fact, he was surprised the cops called the house "secure," since there was a gaping hole in the back wall and no one had made an effort to board it up. He had yet to see an officer consistently monitoring the place. Kevin suspected several people had gone through it, but he'd obediently waited until the Sheriff's Office released it to him. Once he got the green light, he quickly made an appointment to have his insurance adjustor and an out-of-town arson investigator examine the home before he had it demolished.

The men were about to go inside when the sheriff's crime scene van pulled into the yard. The deputies who emerged immediately resealed the house and banned Bailey and the others from entering. Kevin was irate with what he saw as

sloppy work and he demanded to know why they were re-
claiming the house they had just released to him. The officers told him they were looking for an aluminum bat and
then insisted that all three men leave the property. Kevin
walked away in frustration. Not only was the painstaking
process of demolishing the home put on hold, but more important, he wondered if the deputies investigating his
friend's death would get the job done right.

Deputy Ricky Barefield surveyed the damaged house for
the second time. It was eerily quiet, unlike the night he was
first called to the smoldering home, when dozens of firefighters were still hosing down hot spots and deputies were
busy shooing away onlookers. The crime scene officer had
shuffled around them in an attempt to collect evidence. The
task had been an important one for Barefield, who was still
in training. He called his supervisor before proceeding to let
her know how the scene looked, then went to work taking
pictures and videotaping it.

Today, he had plenty of help. Ten other investigators, including his supervisor—a forensics specialist—were converging on Terry King's tiny house, intent on finding a
murder weapon. Some of the officers snapped on gloves and
slipped into biohazard suits before they began sifting
through debris. They carefully searched the room by hand,
combing the entire floor and the remnants of Terry's bed, but
their efforts turned up only a melted glob of metal.

Escambia Investigator Glenn Gowitzke inspected it
closely. His primary job at the Sheriff's Office was computer crimes, but he also specialized in fire deaths. He was a
court-certified expert witness on fire investigations, based
on his training and experience as a longtime volunteer firefighter. The deputy was the size of a football linebacker, and
he easily tossed the glob in his hand.

The officers wondered if this unrecognizable object was

the melted remains of the murder weapon and the proof they needed to corroborate the brothers' confessions. Gowitzke thought not. He noted there was no aluminum underneath the burned bed and no aluminum sticking to the springs. He did not believe the fire had burned long enough or hot enough to completely consume the bat. He suspected the metal was all that remained of the window frame that once hung above the bed. The deputies bagged the glob for testing and intensified their search.

Armed with shovels and a chain saw, they tore through portions of the floor where the fire had burned through, and several officers crawled beneath the house. They sifted through more dirt, ash, and debris, patiently digging with their hands; but again, no bat. The search team tackled the rest of the house. They set up floodlights to illuminate every dark corner, peering behind cabinets, under the couch, and into boxes. The deputies covered the entire home, from the attic to the living room, and even tore apart the furniture. After several hours of fruitless labor, the panting crew stepped outside and walked the length of the entire yard, inch by inch. They were rewarded with a good stretch, but no murder weapon.

The deputies then loaded their equipment into the van and called it quits, leaving the ransacked house in their wake. As they departed, Ricky Barefield noted that people could come and go as they pleased.

Janet French had made the same observation the previous day when she pulled into town for Terry's funeral. She'd walked through the open door and collected some pictures and love notes she and Terry had written each other when they were still together. Janet only wanted personal keepsakes, but she realized the house was wide-open to any curious passerby.

Jimmy French and a family friend, Theresa Shumate, had

also gone through the King home hoping to find clues that would help them understand the gruesome crime. They happened upon a spiral notebook that turned out to be Alex's makeshift diary, where the boy poured out his thoughts and feelings. It read Biography, Do not read! Disregarding the stern warning, Jimmy and Theresa flipped through the pages and were stunned by what they read.

"My life used to be cloudy before I made friends with Rick," Alex wrote in a childish scrawl. "I had a whole lifetime ahead of me and I didn't know what to do with it. I had no goals. I was confused. What to be? Teacher? Governor? President? What?! I thought that was what life was about. But I was wrong. Rick let me see what I didn't understand. Life isn't about having a job. Life isn't about importance, fame. My ultimate goal in life now is what his is. It's about sharing your life with someone else's. Before I met Rick I was straight, but now I am gay."

Jimmy gripped the book tighter, his mind absorbing the implications. He hurriedly flipped through the remaining pages and found other shocking declarations: "Love is a powerful thing," "Alex King loves Ricky," and the initials AK/RC written together inside a carefully drawn heart.

Shocked, the pair immediately tried to get in touch with John Sanderson, but they were told he was unavailable. Hours passed with no word from the investigator, and they made several more unsuccessful attempts to contact Sanderson throughout the day. Jimmy's frustration grew. He wasn't sure what upset him the most: not having his calls returned or the cops neglecting to collect Alex's notebook and place it into evidence.

Later that evening, Lisa French arrived home to find her husband agitated. He told her that Sanderson had finally phoned at the end of the day. Jimmy felt the investigator seemed unconcerned with the diary or its contents, and his fury boiled over when Sanderson asked him to drop the book by his office.

"I told him, 'Get off your lazy ass and come get it yourself!'" He was convinced that Ricky Chavis was the key to solving Terry's murder, but he worried the investigators were too content with his grandsons' confessions to search for the truth.

Chapter 9

SUDDENLY, INFORMATION ABOUT THE KING FAMILY WAS invaluable. The brothers' arrests stunned the community as the local media raced to learn more. Who were these children? Where did they come from? Why would they do this? The questions were being debated in schools, at work, and in coffee shops. Reporter Mollye Barrows was on a mission to answer them.

The case was more than just an assignment for the journalist. She had a passion for her craft that included more than just regurgitating facts. Mollye wanted viewers to understand the people she wrote about and feel for their circumstances, whether their reaction was outrage or compassion. While Mollye enjoyed the local celebrity WEAR-TV gave her, she wanted to be respected for her work, not just for being "that girl on television." Complacency wouldn't accomplish that. There was a story behind this crime regardless of the boys' alleged guilt, and she was determined to hear it.

The investigators were saying little about the boys' history and their family. Mollye canvassed Terry King's neighborhood looking for clues about his life. She talked to one woman's eight-year-old grandson who had played with Alex during the months he lived along Muscogee Road.

"Did you like Alex?" Mollye asked the boy.

"Yeah, he was all right. He didn't really know how to do anything."

"What do you mean?" she asked.

"He didn't know how to ride a bike or play baseball. I thought everybody knew how to play baseball. He didn't really like his dad either."

"Did he say why?"

"Alex said he got mad and yelled at him when he did something wrong. I went over to ask Alex if he wanted to play and his dad told me no. He was sort of mean."

Mollye soon discovered that Derek had only recently moved in with his father and brother, having spent most of the past seven years living with a foster family. She learned that financial woes had forced Terry to place his children in Heritage Home. She shuffled through pictures of the children taken while they were there. Their shy, beseeching smiles provided no forewarning of the violence that was to come.

DAD A "CONTROL FREAK," FRIEND SAYS. The headline led the front page of the *Pensacola News Journal* the weekend following King's murder. The article featured a forty-year-old man who described himself as Terry King's only close friend. He approached the newspaper with his story on condition of anonymity.

The article read: "It just got to a point where they couldn't handle it." The self-professed "family friend" called King a "power freak" who isolated Alex and Derek. The friend said Terry's attempts at control included nailing the windows of his Cantonment home shut and installing double locks on the doors.

The mystery man maintained he never suspected the brothers had murder on their minds, but he added that Alex did tell him he wished his father were dead. He said that

Derek was also having trouble adjusting to his new life with Terry. The older brother had lived for years with the family of a local high school principal, enjoying an active social life. The "only close friend" said all of that came to a screeching halt when Derek moved in with his father.

He seemed eager to explain their actions, and his insights painted Terry King as an abusive father who pushed his children to commit murder. He claimed that concern for the boys drove him to share what he knew about Terry and his children, but his statements essentially indicted the entire family. The article revealed that Escambia sheriff's deputies had questioned him in connection with the brutal slaying. The family friend said he only wanted to help.

In fact, Investigators Sanderson and Kilgore were familiar with this anonymous Samaritan. They had interviewed him numerous times since Terry's murder. They found him to be unusually cooperative, but then, Ricky Chavis was always quick to do whatever he could to help anyone.

Ricky sat down with the deputies on December 2, 2001, for his first recorded statement. He was decidedly nervous. Ricky knew from previous arrests that he should appear cooperative but give little information. However, he was a talkative person by nature and he depended upon his friendly, chatty style of conversation to persuade others. He realized the most effective plan was to lie; he had to if he wanted to stay out of trouble. One false move and his good rapport with the investigators could deteriorate, resulting in his arrest. He decided to say that he had no involvement whatsoever. He was merely the person Alex and Derek called for help after they killed their father.

"All right, Rick. What we'd like to do is talk to you about Alex and Derek," Terry Kilgore began. "So in your own words, tell me about a phone call you received on the twenty-seventh of November."

"Okay." Rick took a deep breath and exhaled. "On Tuesday afternoon I received a phone call—oh God, I can't remember the time. I want to say about two-thirty. It was some girl on the phone. She said she had a message for me. She said, 'You need to look in the garbage can at the car wash behind the Tom Thumb store on East Spencerfield Road.' And I said, 'Okay. Thank you.' Then she hung up and I drove up there, found the note in the garbage can. I read it and I burned it." Ricky could have kept his answer simple, but instead he chose to create a bizarre cloak and dagger story he hoped would be convincing.

"What did the note say?" Kilgore asked.

"It said to drive up East Spencerfield Road slowly. So I did that. It wasn't too far and then I seen them pop out of the woods. Alex and Derek. So I pull over and they get in."

"Okay." Kilgore was anxious to hear what the boys had said to Rick. "Tell me what happens. What's said and what's going on."

"So as soon as they get in the car I says to them, 'Are y'all ready to turn y'all selves in, because if you're not, I'm taking y'all in anyway.' And they says, 'Yes, we're ready to go in. We're tired of running.'" Ricky sighed heavily, trying to convey the gentle countenance that said he was just a kind friend to these misguided boys.

"So on the way back they started talking about what happened. They started talking about what had happened and then Derek started to go into details." Ricky was eager to point the finger at Derek. "He said that Terry had slung Alex around. Then they just went to their rooms. After about fifteen minutes they came out and Derek was going after Terry. He grabbed a baseball bat and started swinging on Terry. I told him to shut up. I didn't want to hear no more. I broke down and was crying by then. Derek says, 'You doing okay?' and I just said, 'Yeah, I'm just real hurt and I'm real upset.' Alex and Derek didn't say hardly nothing on the trip back to Pensacola."

The entire story was a fabrication. There had been no secret note, no phone call to pick up the boys from the convenience store, no drive back to Pensacola, and no confession from Derek.

"They didn't say no more until we got to the house," Ricky continued. "We all walked in the house and I told Alex and Derek to sit on the couch. So that's when I picked up the phone and called Reggie. I advised him that I had both boys with me. I asked if he'd come on over and he said he'd be there in a minute."

Ricky paused to remember anything else he might want to have on the record. "Now I got both boys to take a shower. And I told 'em both, throw your clothes out, because you know, I figured they were probably dirty." The course of the investigation might have changed if the investigators had questioned Ricky's decision to do the laundry. Did Ricky wash the boys' clothing to destroy any physical evidence that could link them to the crime? Or did he launder the clothes because there was *no* evidence on the garments? Maybe the blood that splattered twelve feet around the victim, even sticking to the ceiling, simply never found its way onto Alex's and Derek's clothes. With this ingenious cover, Ricky could say that the washing had removed every trace of the dried blood. Unfortunately, the investigators neglected to hammer Ricky about his motive for washing the clothes, instead refocusing on the guilt of the children.

"Well, let me ask you this: you've known these kids for a long time and you've known Terry for a long time. Do you believe Derek when he tells you what he did?" Kilgore asked.

Ricky's response reads as if he had anticipated and prepared for this moment. He wanted to keep the investigators focused on Derek, and they had accommodated him by asking the right question. He paused as though considering his response, sighed, and answered, "I would almost have to," then added for effect, "because of his expression. I'm just like, 'Whoa!' I'm not used to nothing like this."

Kilgore nodded sympathetically. "I know it's just got to blow you away."

Ricky's eyes watered. "And I'm still having trouble accepting it. 'Cause look how young they are. Twelve and thirteen years old. They're only *children*."

"Well, sure," Kilgore soothed. "I know it. They're boys."

After a fifteen minute break, Kilgore began questioning Ricky about the events two weeks before the murder. Ricky described the day that Alex and Derek had run away.

"About five on November sixteenth I received a phone call from Alex. He asked if I'd come pick him and Derek up from the EZ Serve by their house. It took me about twenty minutes to get there," Ricky recalled. "As soon as they got in the car I says, 'Where's Terry?' They didn't tell me then that they had run away."

"Once we were moving, Alex said, 'We ran away from home.' He went into telling me that they couldn't handle being cooped up in the house with no entertainment. He said his dad was messing with their heads. Me and Alex talked about that before."

"Okay," Kilgore prompted. "And what was that about?"

"Once, we were sitting in my living room watching TV. Terry yelled 'Alex!' real loud and I jumped. I looked at Terry and I noticed Terry had this cold look on his face. I looked at Alex and then back at Terry. I noticed Alex had his head tilted down, and I got upset." Remnants of the anger were still evident on his face as he recounted the clash. The detectives moved right on by the conflict without inquiring further.

"Have you ever seen any physical abuse?" Sanderson asked.

"I have personally never seen any physical abuse," Ricky replied.

"Okay. You've got the boys and you're in the car. . . ." Kilgore brought him back to the story.

Ricky began to describe how he had taken the boys to his house, but he had to conceal the fact that they had stayed there for almost two weeks while he "helped" Terry King search frantically for his missing sons. Unfortunately, he hadn't given the specifics of this lie enough planning. He was creating details as he went and his delivery was shaky.

"I had to go, you know, went and bought a carton of cigarettes and filled the gas tank up. That's what it was. Oh, I wasn't sure on that one. . . . I got back to the house and they were gone. Then I went riding around." Ricky gave an elaborate, detailed description of each road he turned down. This fictional account was designed to convince detectives that after he had picked up the runaways and left them alone for a few minutes, they had run away from him also. In the hopes of convincing them that the boys had not been with him, Ricky referred the investigators back to the message from Alex they had copied from his answering machine.

"The evening of the seventeenth, I truly started helping Terry look for the boys. 'Cause I didn't feel right about them being off on their own. I did some driving around. Every day I was driving around. I went through three tanks of gas looking for 'em." Ricky seemed pleased with this touch. He was sure it portrayed him as a caring and devoted friend.

Throughout the interview, Ricky paced himself, stalling for time when necessary and claiming a bad short-term memory when he couldn't think of what to say. The investigators questioned him closely about his discovery of Alex in Pace. Ricky repeated that the boy had called him and he picked him up behind a convenience store in Pace before turning him over to Terry and Joyce.

"Okay. Now tell us about what you did that Sunday night," Kilgore said.

"Just piddled around the house doing odds and ends. I cooked up a little something to eat, which I hate cooking," he rambled. "So I was doing something to a PlayStation. I was working on a PlayStation. I was working on it, piddled with it, got tired of piddling with it." Ricky seemed to be growing more nervous. "I sat in the recliner, watched some TV." He quickly realized his mistake. If he was watching television during the time the murder was committed, he would be able to tell police what shows he had watched. He moved quickly to repair the mistake. "Um, I'm not sure what I was watching at that time. I started to doze off." That would fix things nicely. "About one-thirty I had the scanner locked on the fire department because I like listening to the fire department a lot."

"Mm-hm." Kilgore nodded.

"And, uh, I heard a call go out, you know, a fire call go out to a—you know, 1104 Muscogee Road. I jumped up, grabbed my keys, and I was gone." But this wasn't true. The fire report had gone out over the scanner without listing an address. Ricky told them he raced to Terry's house but officers at the scene had told him little. Kilgore and Sanderson were ready to conclude the statement.

"Can you think of anything else, Rick?" Kilgore asked.

Ricky wanted to end the statement by pointing the blame directly at Alex and Derek. "I just wish I knew why the boys done it," he finished, shaking his head.

Ricky left a free man. As he walked to his car, it was all he could do not to faint.

Ricky had cultivated a healthy grapevine with branches that snaked and weaved throughout the Sheriff's Office. Through this resource he learned that Lewis Tyson had told investigators that Alex and Derek had been with him while they were runaways. Ricky realized he was in trouble.

Three days later Ricky was once again talking with Sanderson, Kilgore, and the ominous tape recorder.

"All right, Rick," Kilgore began. "We appreciate you coming in. And I want to let you know that you are not under arrest and you're free to go. What I want to do is to get some things straight."

Rick began to tell his new, improved story. This time he admitted he had kept the boys when they ran away from Terry. He said the boys had hidden in the back bedroom each day when Terry had come to his house hoping for information on the runaways.

"Okay. Now let's go back and talk about the phone message that was left on your machine. That was a planned message, wasn't it?" Kilgore asked.

Ricky froze. He had forgotten about the message. In typical Ricky fashion, he skirted responsibility and pointed the blame at his two favorite scapegoats, Alex and Derek.

"It was planned between the two," Ricky said.

"Now wait a minute," Kilgore said, doubtful.

"I didn't help 'em on that," Ricky protested.

"You didn't help 'em on it, you didn't suggest it at all?" Kilgore prodded.

"No I didn't," Ricky argued. He hoped manufactured details would sound more convincing. "We stopped by there because I wanted to get something to drink and they wanted to use the phone. And I did inquire about that."

"You knew they were doing it?" Kilgore asked.

"I knew . . ." Ricky's voice trailed off. He did't want to get pinned down.

"Rick!" Kilgore demanded. He knew the boys would have no reason to make the phone call on their own. The only purpose it served was to protect Ricky.

"I knew," he admitted.

"You knew." Kilgore was making slow progress. "And it was planned before they called, wasn't it?"

"Yeah." Ricky felt like a trapped animal.

"Whose idea was it?"

"It was Alex's," Ricky insisted.

"Did you tell them you thought it was a good idea?"

"I told 'em, if that's what y'all want to do, go ahead and do it."

Shortly after the nerve-wracking interview, Ricky was the recipient of a special invitation. He was ordered to appear before the grand jury on December 11, 2001. The prospect of testifying filled him with horror. He was much more effective one-on-one, but to convince a room full of people was a daunting task.

The session started simply enough, with questions about his work and how he had met Terry King. He relaxed into the easy answers, but soon had to pay strict attention to keep track of his lies. He began by telling the grand jurors he lived alone. This served two purposes: to protect his brother Mike, who had been a witness to the events swirling around the King murder, and to protect himself from any information Mike might let slip.

He continued to perjure himself throughout the testimony, squirming miserably as the questions grew increasingly intense. He said he and Alex had never spent time alone together, denied telling the boy his father was mentally abusive, and had never given him marijuana.

Ricky was drained after testifying and ready to relax in the refuge of his well-protected trailer. However, home was a luxury Ricky would no longer be able to enjoy. He was about to take up residency at the Escambia County Jail.

On December 11, two weeks after the boys were arrested, Escambia sheriff's investigators charged forty-year-old Ricky Marvin Chavis with accessory after the fact to capital murder. Ricky's arrest made the already sensational case scandalous. His criminal history was public record and now a matter of public interest. His past transformed the murder into media mayhem.

Ricky Chavis was a convicted child molester. He had been arrested in 1984, charged with lewd and lascivious assault on a child and procuring minors for prostitution. The news of his arrest spread quickly, and the media descended on his trailer. Mollye Barrows arrived at 607½ Palm Court and eyed Ricky's neighborhood. He lived in an older, lower income area in West Pensacola. The street was lined with a mixture of trailers, rental houses, and middle-class homes. A run-down trailer with a rebel flag tacked up in the window sat to the east of Ricky's trailer; to the west, a brick home was surrounded by a well-tended yard and a chain-link fence.

Outside his trailer, Ricky's neighbors swarmed the street as soon as the news crews arrived. Some were huddled in groups, sharing "remember when" stories about Ricky. Others looked invitingly at the reporters and photographers, hoping to nab their fifteen minutes of fame. They were shocked that a child molester lived so close.

Mollye peered at the privacy fence surrounding Ricky's trailer with a mixture of awe and trepidation. She noted the electrified wire and a dozen or so cameras strategically placed around the property that enabled Ricky to survey his domain and keep track of who was at the gate.

"Why would anyone need a compound like this?" she asked her photographer.

Warning signs were securely nailed around the double doors that blocked unauthorized entrance. The postings sternly warned visitors against trespassing, to be wary of electrocution, and that they were being monitored. An intercom allowed for communication.

Mollye commented to her coworker, "Looks like this guy was all about *control*."

The gates were locked tightly and no one answered the intercom. The photographer was forced to climb on top of his news truck, a Chevy Blazer, and haul his equipment behind him. He gave a low whistle as he stared over the fence. "You should see this yard. It's right out of *Sanford and Son*."

Mollye laughed as he started shooting video. She was dying to get a look at the inner sanctum, but with her high heels and short skirt, she thought better of it. She settled for a peek between the planks of the privacy fence. She could make out scattered car parts and a number of vehicles. She turned her attention to the neighbors.

"We call it 'Fort Chavis,'" one woman told her.

Another man knew Ricky as a mechanic. "All I know from what I've been told is that he's a homosexual; other than that, he kept to himself. I brought my vehicle over to have it worked on."

Mollye learned that the gates guarding Ricky's home usually stayed locked until time for school to let out in the afternoon. Then they swung wide and teens, both boys and girls, converged on the popular hangout. One seventeen-year-old girl told Mollye off camera, "I used to go over there to get high. There were young boys going in and out of there all the time."

The reporter was not surprised neighborhood kids were attracted to Ricky's place. Those who had been inside said his trailer was geared toward entertainment. Visitors described an expensive entertainment center that offered television, video games, and a stereo. The teenage pot smoker went on to tell Mollye that it was well known kids could get cigarettes and drugs from the friendly mechanic.

Ricky also made it a point to endear himself to law enforcement. He listened to his police scanners fanatically. Two years earlier, he overheard deputies searching for a drug addict in his neighborhood. The suspect had just threatened a cab driver and slipped into the night, saying he intended to go out in a blaze of glory.

Ricky had climbed onto the roof of his trailer and scanned the streets, directing officers to the area where he heard the man running. The suspect had fatally shot a police dog and wounded a police officer before deputies killed him.

Mollye could just see the top of Ricky's trailer above the fence line. She pictured him standing there, frantically trying to point the cops in the right direction.

"He can be a pretty cool guy," one teen told her. "He'll give you stuff, like pot or food, but it's like he expects something in return."

Apparently, Ricky's friendship and generosity did not come without a price.

Chapter 10

RICKY CHAVIS HAD CALLED PENSACOLA HOME ALL OF his life. As a toddler, he demonstrated a phenomenal gift for mechanics, and no amount of chastising could prevent him from exploring anything that ran on electricity. At age three he could take apart and reassemble an AM radio with lightning speed. By five, when most parents were warning their children about electrical outlets, he was rewiring broken lamps.

Ricky's uncanny ability was a source of pride for his young mother, Brenda Chavis, who would laughingly scold him for dismantling her kitchen appliances. She didn't want to discourage her son's obvious gift, but when the proliferation of nuts and bolts on her kitchen floor wore on her patience, she'd hand Ricky the toolbox and shoo him outside to tackle his projects in the garage.

Jerry and Brenda Chavis divorced in 1966, hurling Ricky and his younger brother, Mike, into a churning sea of confusion. They had learned to accept their parents' angry arguments, but despite the years of animosity, the boys were devastated when the couple decisively severed their ties. According to Ricky and Mike, the brothers became ammunition in a brutal divorce war, and it seemed to them that they were used by the adults to assault one another and inflict as much pain as possible. The divorce hearing was a battle-ground, ending with Jerry in possession of the children and Brenda shouting obscenities at the judge. When the confused children asked when they would be going back to their mother's house, they were told they would never live with her again. With little explanation, the boys began their new lives in the home of their paternal grandparents.

In spite of being deprived of their mother, the years Ricky and Mike spent with their grandparents were happy and stable ones. Ricky was an easygoing child and always willing to help around the house, and Mike was sweet and compliant. The active children spent many carefree hours playing outdoors in the Florida sun, turning their hair white-blond and building strong, fit bodies. They spent their summers riding bicycles and having fierce watermelon seed spitting contests with neighborhood friends.

Jerry Chavis took little responsibility for his boys. Their grandmother, "Nanny," saw to their daily needs, preparing wonderful home-cooked meals complete with "scratch" biscuits. The grandparents also took the boys regularly to a Methodist church and provided them with a spiritual foundation rooted in strong Christian values.

Meanwhile, Jerry was busy falling in love again. His new bride was not eager to be a stepmother, but Jerry still moved his sons out of his parents' home and into his. Ricky was fourteen and Mike was twelve, and Jerry wanted to keep a close eye on the adolescent boys. But it was soon apparent that the newlyweds and the boys weren't destined to live happily ever after. Jerry informed his boys that they would be placed in foster care in a private home. He had arranged for them to temporarily live in a "nice house with other kids" and told his sons he would return for them in a few weeks. Unfortunately, the foster parents were motivated by money rather than compassion. Each child they took in represented more monthly income, and they greedily crammed ten children into their modest three-bedroom house.

When they arrived, Ricky and Mike told the other children that they wouldn't be there long. They refused to unpack for three weeks, believing that their dad would arrive at any moment. Weeks turned into months. Ricky and Mike took turns assuring each other that their dad was just behind schedule.

The brothers were grief stricken and confused when they finally realized their father wasn't coming back. They didn't know what they had done to cause their parents to abandon them. The lost boys saw only that they weren't worth the trouble to anyone.

But the cruelest blow was yet to come. The other kids were seasoned veterans of the foster system. Years of deprivation and cruelty had spawned children who elevated bullying to an art form. They took great pleasure in tormenting and intimidating the Chavis boys. Ricky was beaten up regularly.

On several occasions neighborhood children had the misfortune of riding bicycles too close to the foster kids, and were chased down and knocked off their bikes just for fun. Ricky deflected the abuse away from his younger brother by attracting the attention to himself. Smaller, weaker Mike was hardly noticed, but Ricky became a living target in a game of physical and emotional survival.

While there, the Chavises were witness to harrowing incidents of animal torture by the other foster children. On one occasion a puppy wandered onto the property and the ringleader of the group grabbed it, a brick, and a short piece of rope and took off running toward a small pond behind the house. Eliciting the help of another cruel boy, the two tied one end of the rope through a hole in the brick and the other so tightly around the puppy's throat that it squealed in pain.

On the count of three they tossed brick and puppy as far as they could, laughing as the horrified animal flew through the air and plunged into the pond. It splashed and struggled against the weight of the brick, finally losing the battle to keep its head above water and bobbing under for the last time. The Chavis boys were repulsed and sickened but knew better than to interfere. They were traumatized for weeks after the vicious incident.

But the brutality didn't stop there. One night while Ricky slept, the bullies crept into the room. They stood around his bed and watched him sleep, snickering in anticipation. Then they pounced, spraying shaving cream in his eyes and laughing at his anguish. Ricky knew his foster parents wouldn't help and any attempts to enlist their aid would result only in retaliation from the other children. Mike became a silent witness to his brother's suffering, comforting Ricky and trying to pick up the pieces after the vicious attacks.

Ricky's daily existence seemed hopeless. When his paternal grandmother attempted to visit and bring the brothers home with her, the foster home refused to allow it. The move would mean a loss of money and an opportunity for the boys to talk about their harrowing life.

The abuse left Ricky emotionally crippled, like a victim of polio. As an affected limb withers and becomes a handicap, Ricky's emotional growth was paralyzed and stunted. The years of mistreatment may have impaired his ability to become an adult capable of appropriate sentiments, leaving him doomed to remain that spiritually injured child. As usually happens with children who feel they have no control over their lives, Ricky became manipulative, and adept at ingratiating himself to others.

The foster home, clearly out of control, was finally closed down. Ricky Chavis was old enough to decide where he wanted to live, and chose to return to his grandparents. Mike was placed in a new foster home, which bore no resemblance to the old one. It was happy and healthy and the Chavis brothers finally found peace.

In 1978 seventeen-year-old Ricky attended Tate High School and also took classes at George Stone Vocational School, becoming adept at electronics, repairing cars, and wood crafts. These skills proved instrumental in shaping his life and personality. Ricky's mechanical ability was a source of pride for the young man who seldom received a pat on the back for achievement.

Jerry Chavis had already divorced his second wife and stayed busy with a string of failed relationships. At one point the boys' mother left her life in New Orleans to spend time with the children who were taken from her so young.

Ricky and Mike were thrilled to be reunited with their mom, and Mike decided to drop out of school after tenth grade and move in with her. Having been deprived of his mother since early childhood, Mike relished the renewed relationship. One of his sweetest memories was a scolding she gave him after he signed his truck over to a cousin who had fallen on tough times. The cousin defaulted on the loan, and Mike's mother sternly warned him about making better decisions. To Mike, the lecture was rare, and potent evidence of her maternal love.

By the time he was eighteen Ricky knew that he was gay, and he decided to tell his mother. He chose to break the news during an unusual occasion that found Ricky and his mother smoking pot together. He admitted that he was not attracted to women but felt a strong preference for men. He quietly waited for her reaction.

"I know," she said mellowly. "I was just wondering how long it was going to take for you to tell me." Then she smiled at him warmly, making his "coming out" experience much less painful than he had dared hope.

At the time, he had once again happily settled in his grandparents' home. He installed a construction trailer and a workshop behind their house and gathered his many friends to work on cars and party around the clock. It quickly became the neighborhood hangout.

Ricky was very popular and much admired by the gang. His genius for building something out of nothing was a source of amazement; even his bicycle inspired awe. It was equipped with a stereo, speakers, a CB radio, and a built-in charging system. A meter and little generators rolled against the wheels to produce power. The odd-looking bike attracted attention wherever he went, and he gladly answered questions until people walked away shaking their heads at the eccentric contraption.

One sunny summer day Ricky was digging through a Dumpster beside an auto repair garage when a thirteen-year-old boy rode by on a bicycle.

"Hey there," Ricky called, smiling. "Where are you going?"

"Home," the boy answered. He stopped his bike but seemed reluctant to talk to this man who was up to his elbows in trash.

"I'm Ricky. What's your name?" he asked.

"Herb," the boy said, then his eye caught the bizarre bike.

Ricky could see his interest. "I rigged that myself," he said, explaining how he built it from a collection of throwaway parts.

"My dad told me not to talk to strangers," Herb said, mounting his own bike. Herb's mother had left the home when he was a toddler, and his father was struggling to raise the five children she left behind.

"Well, your dad's right about that. There are some bad

people out there," Ricky acknowledged. "What church do you and your dad go to?"

"We go to a Pentecostal church, but I used to belong to the Seventh Day Adventist."

"Really? So does my uncle," Ricky replied.

"Well, I got to be going," Herb said.

"Wait a second," Ricky said. He pulled a pen and a scrap of paper from his shirt pocket and scribbled on it. "Here's my phone number. Call me sometime and I'll come pick you up and you can come out to the house."

"Okay, thanks," Herb said, and pedaled away. When he got home, he threw the paper away and promptly forgot about Ricky Chavis's invitation.

Ricky was happier than he had been in a long time. The party at his house was nonstop. He drank screwdrivers and beer, and soon the teenagers who hung out there began to embrace drugs. They took Quaaludes and smoked marijuana, then graduated to snorting a little coke on the rare occasions they could afford it.

The constant flow of traffic provided a perfect client list for selling pot. Ricky's outgoing personality helped him cultivate a thriving business, earning him a great deal of money and making a real job unnecessary. He bought huge quantities—trash bags full—from a man living in a nearby trailer park. Marijuana was plentiful in Northwest Florida, much of it homegrown. Between fixing cars and selling pot, Ricky was always "in the green."

He kept a pound of pot on hand for guests, stored in a filing cabinet in his workshop. The top drawer held his special reserve "good weed," and the bottom drawer held his home-grown. Many of the teenagers who partied there would pinch a little as they left. Ricky knew they were taking it but he didn't care. He wanted them to continue visiting.

* * *

One day when Ricky was driving his grandfather's Grand Torino, he spotted Herb Helton, who he had last seen while Dumpster-diving. He pulled over and smiled. "Remember me?" he asked Herb.

"Yeah," Herb answered. "You're the one with that crazy bike, aren't you?"

He laughed. "Right." After a few minutes of idle chat, Ricky asked, "When are you going to come out to the house?"

Herb shrugged. "I don't know. I don't want to get in trouble."

"That's okay," Ricky reassured him. "You won't get in any trouble. I can take you and bring you back any time you want. Really."

Thirteen-year-old Herb loaded his bike into the Grand Torino's trunk and headed for *Chez Chavis*. Once there, Ricky went out of his way to make his newest guest comfortable. Herb met several boys his age and he began to relax and enjoy the friendly comradery. Before dark, Ricky volunteered to drive Herb home. "You don't want to get your father mad," he counseled. But he stopped short of driving up to Herb's house, instead electing to unload the boy and his bike a block away. He knew that Herb's dad would be alarmed to see his son emerge from a stranger's car. Ricky said good-bye and waved as Herb pedaled off down the road.

Herb Helton became a regular fixture at Ricky's house. He sometimes rode his bike the twelve miles between their houses. But when he didn't feel like it, all he had to do was pick up the phone and Ricky would hustle right over to pick him up. He occasionally slept over on the weekends. One Friday afternoon they stopped at a Church's Chicken restaurant and Ricky bought lunch for Herb. Ricky got nothing for himself, but sat intently watching the boy eat.

Herb felt him staring and asked, "What?"

"I hope you like that meal," Ricky said.

Herb smiled and nodded. "I do," he replied.

"Good. Because it cost me three dollars," Ricky said, raising an eyebrow.

The comment made Herb uncomfortable. Did Ricky want something in return? The implication of the unspoken debt made him nervous. He declined to sleep over at Ricky's that night.

Herb felt good being one of the gang and he started bringing his friends, Randy and Ronnie, with him. They began sleeping over at Ricky's most every weekend, an arrangement Ricky loved.

Over the next year, Ricky and Randy grew close, spending a great deal of time together. Eleven-year-old Randy thought everything his nineteen-year-old friend did was cool.

One day Ricky was visiting Randy's house while his mother was away. He decided to teach Randy and his nine-year-old brother, Billy, about masturbation. Ricky lay on the floor and demonstrated the concept on himself, finishing his performance by ejaculating on the carpet. Little Billy thought it was "gross" and later told his mother about the man who "was playing with himself and went all over the floor!" The mother was furious and called all of the boys "little faggots." Unfortunately, she never called the police.

Ricky had a special fondness for Herb and would often say to him, "Answer me a question: when are we gettin' together?" The innuendo made Herb uneasy. The thirteen-year-old was unsure of what Ricky meant and usually just shrugged and changed the subject.

When Ricky's invitations to Herb were ignored, he decided to resort to another tactic: mutual masturbation. He began by hailing the virtues of self-gratification, talking about "jacking off" as if it was what all good friends did together. Then he lit up a joint, took a deep toke and passed it to Herb.

Next he gave Herb a girlie magazine to get him excited. Then taking off his own clothes, he treated the boy to a personal demonstration. He waited until the pot and pornography kicked in and Herb was in the highest state of arousal, then he slid next to him. It wasn't long before he had the boy, literally, in the palm of his hand.

Ricky's magnetic and manipulative personality had a strong impact on the teens who admired him. Ricky was a hedonist who exercised little restraint in his own life, and the results spilled over into his relationships, leaving permanent stains. He seemed to have little remorse, and was particularly adept at rationalizing bad behavior.

For example, he told himself that selling a little pot didn't hurt anyone. But the confidence that comes from succeeding in one criminal activity often leads to another. In fact, Ricky began burglarizing homes, and found that young, unsophisticated teens were particularly pliable and would follow him down any dark path he led them.

They drove around smoking pot during the day, planning the evening's activities. When Ricky spotted what he wanted, he often said, "I'd like to have that," and cruised slowly by checking out the best access. After dark he'd return with his adolescent accomplices.

He eased the boys into his criminal lifestyle by having them steal go-carts and bicycles they could keep. Driving through a neighborhood not far from his house, he found an expensive racing quality go-cart with roll bars, fancy tires, and a sleek black cobra painted on the hood. Ricky told Herb it was destined to be his.

In the early morning hours, Ricky killed the lights on his

1973 Chrysler Satellite Sebring and backed into the driveway. Herb was reluctant to steal, but ten-year-old Ronnie was Ricky's most promising protégé. He and Ricky silently crept out and loaded the go-cart into the trunk, slid back in the car, and gently pulled away. The crime came off like clockwork. Pleased with the smoothness of the operation, they immediately returned to Ricky's to unload and examine their prize.

Once cranked, the go-cart ran rough, knocking as though it had been damaged. The next day Ricky was out again, this time to steal a garden tiller. The tiller had a horizontal shaft compatible with the go-cart and its engine could be easily transplanted. Soon Herb had a thousand dollar go-cart that was the envy of his friends. His father was suspicious of the lavish gift and questioned Ricky about it on several different occasions. Ricky insisted he bought it for Herb, and promised to bring the receipt and owner's manual. The paperwork never materialized, and eventually Herb's dad stopped asking. All Herb had to do to keep it was lie effectively when someone questioned how it came to be his.

Ronnie was more fearless about stealing. He and Ricky would find a desirable residential spot and he'd simply knock on a door in the middle of the day. If someone answered, Ronnie would ask for directions, thank the homeowner and be on his way. If no one came to the door, he would jimmy the lock. Sometimes he resorted to simply kicking the door open. Then Herb, Ricky, and Ronnie would rush in, high on adrenaline, and grab stereos, televisions, everything they could quickly snatch. They'd stuff the goods into the Sebring's large trunk and speed away, never thinking about the devastated homeowners. But Ricky's luck eventually ran out, and he was caught and convicted of burglary, grand theft, and contributing to the delinquency of a minor. Still nineteen, he was sent to the county jail to await sentencing.

While in jail, Ricky was a model prisoner, well-liked by inmates and corrections officers alike. He knew more than anyone else about fast cars, a constant topic of conversation in jail. His vast knowledge earned him respect from the inmates, whose average education level ended at elementary school. He whiled away the hours by writing his thoughts in a journal. He also spent time chatting with a corrections officer named Reggie Jernigan, and he and the twenty-nine-year-old Reggie became fast friends. Their longtime relationship would later become the focus of great suspicion, considering that they were on opposite sides of the law.

As one of his release conditions, Ricky was required to get a job. He took a position at a convenience store a few blocks from his house. When the manager fired him a short time later, he told his friends, "I'm going to *get* that bitch."

The manager lived in a trailer park near Ricky's house, which made carrying out his scheme convenient. He crept into her yard after midnight and "serviced" her car with a cup of sugar in the gas tank and a full bottle of maple syrup in her engine. Smiling to himself, he headed home to await the gratifying results of his labors.

The next morning Ricky gathered his buddies for the show. He knew his boss's schedule. When she pulled onto the road a few blocks away, Ricky and his mates were sitting in his car betting on how far she would get. Ricky predicted that she'd only make it four blocks before her car would die, and he marked the spot by pointing out a particular pine tree on the side of the road. As the spectators watched her pass, Ricky said, "Three, two, one, *now!*" At that moment the car seized up and the stunned woman pulled onto the side of the road. She was directly beside the prophetic pine tree.

Cars were a constant throughout Ricky's life and the source of great pleasure. But their allure also kept him in constant trouble with the law; he just couldn't keep his sticky fingers off other people's vehicles.

One night he decided that a car awaiting repairs outside of a mechanic's garage should come home with him. Since the car's battery was dead, Ricky and his buddies slowly towed it behind his grandmother's car. Once safely installed at his home, Ricky began stripping the stolen vehicle. He just needed the parts.

The long arm of the law had no trouble reaching him. When they followed up on a tip and visited the Chavis home, he was caught red-handed with the stolen vehicle. Ricky earned a four-year stay at the Apalachicola Correctional Institution for the ridiculous crime. After serving only half his sentence, he was released on the condition that he would get a job and stay out of trouble. He moved back home with his grandparents, and was soon up to his old tricks.

When Ricky and his gang weren't stealing for profit, they did it for fun. Once, when he heard about a neighbor who had a car with a defective ignition, he and Ronnie made a special trip to determine if the car could be cranked without a key. They were delighted to find that it could, and took off with the vehicle on a reckless rampage, spinning doughnuts along a dirt road and driving at breakneck speed to Def Leppard's *"Foolin'"* blasting from the speakers. In a move inspired by the Dukes of Hazzard, Ricky attempted to sail over a hill into a clay pit. The hill turned out to be a cliff, and when the car became airborne, Ricky and Ronnie saw that the ground was much farther away than they expected. The screaming thieves came crashing down. The car hit nose first and folded like an accordion. The lucky outlaws emerged uninjured, laughing uncontrollably. They walked home that night, Ricky never realizing that he'd *left his wallet in the backseat*.

Early the next morning the police came knocking. A sleepy Ricky answered the door and was shocked to see two officers standing there. They asked him what he knew about a vehicle that had been run off into a clay pit. Ricky denied any knowledge but generously offered to ask around the neighborhood. When the deputies inquired about how his wallet had gotten into the backseat, Ricky realized it had fallen out of his pocket during the wild ride, but that he'd been too stoned to notice. Gifted in the art of deceit, he quickly crafted a lie, claiming that his wallet had been stolen several days earlier, probably by the same people who crashed the car! He peered inside the billfold and dejectedly shook his head, declaring that all of his cash was gone. But, he reasoned, he was lucky to have it back at all and had the officers to thank for that. Satisfied, the police left. Closing the door, Ricky turned and bowed as Ronnie broke into admiring applause for the award-worthy performance.

One afternoon Herb and Randy were in Ricky's garage passing the time. The three had been drinking liquor and smoking pot, and Ricky had passed out. Herb happened to glance under the bed and saw an amazing sight: a large shotgun.

"Check that out!" he exclaimed. He reached under the bed and gingerly slid the heavy weapon out, careful not to wake Ricky.

"It's so heavy," he said, grasping it with one hand.

"Wow," Randy said admiringly. "Let me hold it." Herb passed him the gun, and Randy placed it against his shoulder, closed one eye and peered down the barrel. He aimed it across the room and pretended to squeeze off a shot.

"Okay, my turn," Herb said, but Randy ignored him. "C'mon, Randy. I was the one who found it," he said, pulling at the gun.

"Wait." Randy pulled back and his index finger jerked against the trigger.

Ka-boom! The noise was deafening. Ricky awoke and leaped to his feet cursing and yelling. He quickly saw just how close he had come to death. Neither boy was hurt but the shot had whizzed past Ricky's head and blown a massive hole through the garage wall. Herb and Randy just stood there, mouths agape.

"Are you crazy?" Ricky screamed. "You could've killed us all! You're going home right now!" The boys were silent as he put them in the car.

Several weeks passed before Herb and Randy had the nerve to visit Ricky's house again. But when they did, they were relieved when Ricky welcomed them back with a smile. He had repaired the hole and added the event to his ever-growing repertory of wild stories with which to amuse his admirers.

At the age of twenty-two, Ricky was not shy about telling anyone, gay or straight, that he was a homosexual. However, he did *not* tell them that he desired young boys. He often found people surprised by his admission of a gay lifestyle. In fact, there was little outward evidence to point to his sexual preference. At six-foot-three and almost 200 pounds, he seemed as straight as the next guy. His voice was masculine and his penchant for working on cars helped him make acquaintances who might never have dreamed of befriending a gay man.

One chilly winter night in 1984 two young boys—Tommy Penton and his cousin, Mark Watkins—ran away from a juvenile treatment facility. They called Lonnie, a friend of

Ricky's, looking for a place to stay. The temperature was dropping quickly on the frigid January night, and the boys were grateful when Lonnie drove them to the Chavis house. Ricky welcomed them though he knew they were runaways.

Fourteen-year-old Tommy Penton was a beautiful child. He was a small boy with golden hair that he wore in a soft, feathered cut. Mark Watkins, a year younger, was a handsome, fun-loving boy who feared nothing. After feeding the ravenous boys, the foursome began to drink beer and smoke pot.

Later that evening the stoned, sleepy boys were shown to a bed. During the night, fourteen-year-old Tommy awoke to find Ricky sucking his penis. Mark experienced the same thing.

Almost two weeks later Tommy was still there, although Mark had left. Annie Penton, Tommy's mother, heard through the grapevine that her son was at Ricky Chavis's house. She and her cousin Jimmy headed over to reclaim him.

Annie discovered Tommy wasn't the only child at Ricky's place. There were boys everywhere. Jimmy knocked on the door, and when Tommy answered, he ordered him into his mother's van. Tommy did so without protesting.

Ricky was furious that Annie Penton had taken her son. He jumped in his car and peeled out after her. She looked in her rearview mirror and saw his car quickly advancing. She struggled not to panic. *She thought he was trying to run her off the road.*

The worried mother didn't know what to do. If she went home, she was afraid Ricky would follow her, but she also feared his dangerous driving would kill her, Jimmy, and Tommy. Terrified, Annie had one hope: she had to get to the Sheriff's Office.

The van swerved in and out of traffic trying to elude Ricky, but he continued to pursue her, screaming obscenities and riding only inches from Annie's bumper. By the time he realized where Annie was heading, there was little Ricky could do. She pulled right up to the front door of the Sheriff's Office, jumped out and ran inside. Seconds later when she emerged with an officer, Ricky was gone.

Upon questioning, Tommy admitted that Ricky had performed oral sex on him and then told him to "lay low" and not tell anyone. Ricky had confessed to Tommy that he was on probation and didn't want to go back to prison. Tommy told his mother that Lonnie had also molested him. Tommy's mother had no sympathy for the men who had sexually assaulted her son and pressed charges.

Exactly one month after Ricky took in the young runaways, he was arrested for lewd, lascivious, or indecent assault upon a child. Ricky testified against Lonnie, who received a fifteen-year sentence, and Ricky's betrayal of his friend paid off handsomely. In exchange for his testimony, he received only six months in jail and five years probation.

Ricky's short sentence and inadequate therapy was a license to reoffend, but that was okay with Florida; in 1985 child molesters were routinely released early to prey on additional victims. A National Institute of Health survey conducted in the early 1990s claimed an average of 148 victims per pedophile. After the time lost in jail, Ricky would have to work hard to catch up to his quota. By twenty-three, he was a free man. But he would have to exercise more caution; after all, he had made a promise to his mother that he would never return to jail.

But deviating from his criminal lifestyle was not an option. Two years after his release he was back to his old vices. The gang was reunited, and the parties at Ricky's place never seemed to end. Anyone too wasted to move could always crash at Ricky's trailer, sleeping off a hangover until the next party kicked in. These spontaneous slumber parties provided the convicted child molester with a pool of male, teenage sex partners. Even the straight guys were fair game. Ricky issued them invitations to "visit" him in the middle of the night. When one naive teen asked, "For what?" Ricky replied, "For *you,* man."

In addition to his home base, Ricky kept a room at Seville Inn in downtown Pensacola, where he worked as a maintenance man. He could stay on the property whenever he wished, a nice perk Ricky used for molesting many boys he knew who were scattered around town. Herb, Ronnie, and Randy were all visitors.

During this time, Herb was particularly troubled. Ricky had graduated Herb to oral sex. He felt immense shame about it, but Ricky pushed on. Herb blamed himself because of the sexual arousal he experienced. Ricky's timing was masterful—at the exact moment of no turning back, he gave the illusion that Herb was free to choose. This implied acquiescence kept Herb from blaming Ricky in a later moment of remorse. After all, according to Ricky's logic, he could have stopped if he wanted. Once this milestone was reached, the victim was in so deep that his conscience told him it was indeed his fault. To make matters worse, Ricky doted on Herb, exploiting the motherless boy's powerful need to be loved. Though Herb felt tremendous guilt, his devotion to the pedophile only deepened.

Many of the other boys were in the same boat. They found Ricky exciting, offering them "cool" but illegal enticements. Had he simply molested them and given them nothing in return, he could not have bought their silence. He ensured their loyalty by weaving his guilt with their own. If they betrayed him, they would inevitably open the Pandora's box of their own transgressions. Ricky's "we're all in this together" strategy ensured that he was insulated from liability.

Ricky was now engaging in oral sex with Herb and

Randy, but he had different ambitions for Ronnie, with whom he'd begun having anal sex. Ricky was obsessed with the boy. Ronnie's mother Velma suspected her son was being molested and repeatedly tried to separate him from the "parasite." But the boy was already tangled in Ricky's sticky web, and was too numb to break free.

While Velma was at work, Ricky would spend time at her trailer, molesting her son, eating her food, napping, and leaving just before she was due home. One afternoon, Ricky fell asleep and awoke to find the trailer engulfed in flames. He had forgotten to shut off a burner on the kitchen stove. Ricky was trapped in the back bedroom. In a blind panic, he literally beat his way outside, leaving a huge ragged hole in the trailer wall. Velma was devastated, her home utterly destroyed. Ricky later returned to the scene and photographed Ronnie posing in the ruins. He felt it would be a splendid addition to the scrapbook of his life.

Ricky believed he should never pay for anything that, with a little effort, he could steal. He was now not only stealing cars, but gasoline as well. Twice each week in the wee hours of the morning, he would load three teenage boys and four five-gallon gas cans into his Sebring. He drove alongside the railroad tracks and parked behind a local concrete company. With his electronic prowess, he disabled the alarm and crept inside. Then he and the boys located the gas pumps, which serviced a fleet of concrete mixers, and filled up the cans. The boys would trek back to the car with the stolen gas while Ricky stayed behind to reset the alarm and hide any sign of the intruders.

During one such outing, the boys, tired of hauling the heavy gas cans, stopped along the tracks to take a break and smoke a joint.

Herb was worried that the combination of fire and gasoline would toast them all. "Put that out," he ordered. "Ricky warned us about smoking." But the others ignored him. "You're going to blow yourselves up, assholes!" He then resorted to an age-old tactic: "I'm going to tell Ricky!"

None of the boys wanted Ricky to be upset. "You do and we'll all kick your ass!" one shouted. With that, Herb picked up a chunk of granite from the tracks and prepared to launch a preemptive strike. At that fortuitous moment Ricky returned to find his protégés smoking a joint, screaming obscenities, and squared off to do battle. He rushed them down the tracks and herded them into the car.

Once inside, he preached quite a sermon. Many parents had issued similar scoldings to their youngsters about the perils of smoking, cursing, and fighting, only Ricky's twisted lecture was designed to keep harmony among his juvenile outlaws and to keep his free gas operation running smoothly.

The stealing continued for a year and a half until the business owner noticed the missing gas and reported it to the police. The next time Ricky and his friends paid a visit for their illegal fill-up, they were arrested on the spot. Ricky was told that his friend, David Ward, had ratted him out, and the betrayal enraged him even more than his arrest.

In spite of his charming personality, the courts were growing tired of Ricky Chavis. With waning patience for repeat offenders, a judge revoked Ricky's probation and sentenced him to nine years in state prison.

Ricky continued to monitor the local news at home via the prison grapevine. Word had it that Tommy Penton, the child who had accused Ricky of molesting him, had died. The story buzzing through prison was that two kids on bicycles found Tommy hanging from a tree in a vacant lot, his death a revenge killing over a drug deal that turned sour. Tommy had allegedly been roughed up and threatened several days before he died. Although family and friends were convinced it was murder and told deputies of the previous attack, Tommy's death was ruled a "suicide." Investigators closed the case after only six hours.

Annie Penton was heartbroken and refused to accept the results of the meager investigation. But when she asked questions on her own, she started receiving threatening phone calls, telling her to back off or her other children would share Tommy's fate. Fearing for the safety of her family, she quietly buried her questions and her pain.

During his incarceration, another person from Ricky's nefarious past also met with a violent death. David Ward, who Ricky had been told was responsible for sending him to prison for the stolen gas, was brutally murdered. Three teenage boys followed Ward to a state park, where they shot him in the face just below his eye. Police questioned Ricky, wondering if he might have been responsible for arranging the murder, but they were never able to prove it.

Ricky served only three years of his nine-year sentence, then moved in with his paternal grandparents. But soon afterward his elderly "Papaw" suffered a fatal heart attack, and less than a year later Ricky's grandmother, "Nanny," died as well. Eager to sell the house and divide the estate, the family asked Ricky move out.

The Chavis brothers moved into a mobile home together. Ricky repaired cars, air conditioners, and just about anything mechanical to support himself and Mike. He continued to attract many friends, especially young teenaged boys, and taught them the skills that would likely lead down a tangled path to personal destruction.

Ricky now displayed the gay pride rainbow in the window of his home and boldly told everyone he met of his lifestyle. In fact, Ricky wasn't interested in other men—he was a pedophile, and his true sexual desire was for young boys.

As with many sex offenders, he was particularly skilled at locating troubled children and befriending ones from poor and dysfunctional families. He picked his victims with care, targeting weak, wounded, or needy children he could easily manipulate. Struggling families and their offspring provided a good hunting ground. These parents were often passive protectors, and their limited interference made his task of controlling them much easier. He preferred boys on the brink of puberty. Their sexual ignorance and curiosity made them particularly vulnerable. It was heartbreakingly easy.

Steve Bell, a young runaway, was one of those teens. Ricky knew the Bell family, having grown up with Steve's father and uncle. When Steve left home, Ricky saw his opportunity.

Ricky was an extremely fixated pedophile and a master of manipulation and control. He lavished the neglected teen with attention, providing the comfort and sympathy Steve never had. Soon, Steve moved in with the convicted child molester, and before long Ricky, who was thirty-two now, began having sex with the fourteen-year-old boy. He managed to convince Steve that it was his idea. Ricky was well aware that his pedophile's paradise would come quickly crashing down if school officials learned of the boy's home environment, and so Steve's education came to a screeching halt and he never returned to school after sixth grade.

Ricky was living the child molester's dream, and he was fiercely possessive of his victim. Steve was vulnerable and had suffered much in his young years. One evening, Steve told Ricky that he had been forcibly raped by a grown man when he was only eleven. Steve cried as he recounted the gruesome tale. Ricky was enraged. He knew the accused rapist and immediately called him on his CB radio, cursing and demanding to know why he had assaulted Steve. "Danny" laughingly told Ricky that he had enjoyed it and could have Steve again any time he wanted. Ricky was so incensed that he took a gun, jumped in his car, and sped over to Danny's house, intent on killing him. He parked his car a block from the house and crept into his yard. As he crouched in the bushes plotting the murder, he changed his mind. He realized that an hour earlier he had furiously threatened the man on a CB radio. When the police found Danny's body and came looking for the culprit, he would be the obvious suspect. Rethinking his vengeance, he settled on intimidation instead of violence. He climbed to the top of an antennae in Danny's yard and left a threatening note, then went home and called him again.

"I can kill you anytime I want," Ricky told him. "In fact, I almost killed you tonight." When Danny scoffed disbelievingly, Ricky told him to go look at the top of his antennae.

Danny walked outside, nervously looking over his shoulder, and saw a piece of paper flapping in the breeze from his antennae. Retrieving the note with shaking hands, he read: *I was here.*

Ricky continued to molest Steve, and his vicious temper would flare if the teenager showed attention to others. By 1998 the relationship had deteriorated so badly due to Ricky's blind rages that Steve feared for his life. He filed a restraining order, stating that the convicted felon had a gun and "follows me everywhere I go. There was a lot of violence in the past. I am afraid he might try to kill me." Steve fled to safety.

Ricky took the breakup badly. He sold his beloved black Monte Carlo, since it held so many memories of happier days with Steve. His first sexual assault on the boy had occurred in that car.

But always resilient, Ricky focused on the future instead of the past. And as he looked bravely ahead, his eyes beheld a glorious sight: a young angelic boy named Alex King.

Chapter 11

THE APPEAL OF HORRIFIC CRIME IS WELL KNOWN IN newsrooms across the country. Producers move the "*gory story*" to the top of the lineup, proclaiming, "If it bleeds, it leads!" Media coverage of heinous crimes is a win/win proposition: viewers want to know about the dangers lurking nearby, and the cesspool of iniquity never dries up.

Obviously, all stories are not created equal. Some events are but a passing blip on the screen of public interest, while others instantly grab headlines and transfix the masses for months on end. When the story of Terry King hit, production teams from all parts of the nation saluted smartly and boarded planes. Savvy network producers instantly knew this was a big one.

It's not unusual for an ordinary family to be living in peaceful obscurity one day, only to have some horrific event thrust it into the white-hot national spotlight the next. Such was the case with the King family. On the last Sunday of Terry King's life, his brother, Greg, was probably thinking of little more than the sermon he had heard at church that night or what to wear to work the next day. On Monday the police had broken the sad news of his brother's murder to Greg, and the local media had reported the story. One week later *Good Morning America* producers had flown Greg

King and his church pastor to New York and installed them in a lavish hotel. Greg was too numb from the horror of his brother's death to appreciate the heated toilet seats and caviar on the room service menu in the extravagant suite.

Early the next morning the two men were driven to the ABC network studio, where they sat in a small, cozy, three-chair set waiting for the cameras to dolly over and the lights to go up. Moments before the interview, anchor Charlie Gibson slid into his chair opposite Greg and focused on the man from Pensacola whose nephews were accused of murdering his only brother, just three days buried. In that instant, the King family departed obscurity and became the subject of conversation across the country.

Greg was quickly hunted down by the *Washington Post* and Court TV. Meanwhile, *Dateline NBC* was assigning a team to cover the story. With little but the basic details available, they flew into Pensacola and set about contacting the Kings' friends and relatives. Their list included grandmother Linda Walker, who was suffering from bronchitis. She was no match for the booking agents who made a living by persuading people in their most vulnerable times to confide the intimate details of their lives. They also interviewed "family friend" Ricky Chavis, who bemoaned the woeful tragedy, all the while implicating the young brothers. *Dateline* producers had no way of knowing that they were interviewing the man who would later stand trial for his role in the crime.

When attorney James Stokes heard Greg King's appeal on *Good Morning America*, he called and volunteered to take the case. Lawyers in Escambia County were required to accept one pro bono case annually. Stokes instantly decided he wanted this one. From what he already knew of the boys' situation, it would clearly be an uphill battle. But James Stokes was a warrior by nature.

Before embarking on a legal career, he had spent twenty

years in the Marine Corps, and possessed the pride that comes with that service. He flew a helicopter during the Gulf War, dropping off Navy SEALs for their clandestine missions. Stokes was a thrill seeker, and found skydiving a perfect outlet, completing more than 250 jumps as he trained to become a helicopter pilot. He thought helicopters were much more fun to fly than jets.

After his military service, he enrolled in law school at Florida State University in Tallahassee. While the school was respected for the education it offered students, it was best known for its national title-winning football team. The school attracted many of the best athletes in the country, as well as students who just wanted to be a part of the revelry surrounding the exciting team. Though James didn't care for the game, he quickly learned how seriously his peers felt about it when he arrived for his first semester and asked in all sincerity, "Does FSU have a football team?"

Upon graduation from law school, he took a job in the Public Defender's Office in Pensacola. He carried his *Semper Fidelis* attitude with him in his commitment to defending the accused, especially after he became convinced that prosecutors in Escambia County sometimes tried people they believed were innocent. Some defense attorneys felt that the county was an anomaly in that it was more likely to take people to trial based on probable *cause* rather than probable *conviction*. James believed that many more sexual battery and murder cases were won by defense lawyers in Pensacola than in any other part of the state, partly because they went to trial with less compelling evidence.

After two years of public defending, James decided to hang out his own shingle. He rented two rooms in the back of Pop's Attic, a small U-Haul storage business owned by his best friend. When his clients tried to locate his office for a first visit, they were often baffled. Pop's Attic looked like an old western general store, with its large porch and benches sitting alongside a pond full of geese. The concrete still bore impressions from their webbed feet when they'd waddled up to investigate the freshly poured sidewalk. More often than not, confused clients would drive away convinced that they had the wrong address, cruising up and down the country road before pulling back into the parking lot in dismay. The only clue to his presence was a humble signpost in the grass saying, JAMES STOKES, ESQUIRE.

James loved his job, although he constantly joked about how little money he made as a defense lawyer. He once agreed to represent a man who was down on his luck and short on money and set the fee for his services at a whopping one dollar. He fought hard and won the case but was never paid. He teased the client that he planned to take him to small claims court just as soon as his busy schedule permitted.

James far exceeded the minimum requirement for pro bono cases, taking a dozen each year for free or next to nothing. It caused an ongoing wrangle with his secretary, who tried in vain to convince him not to add more indigent clients to his already overburdened practice. Trying to slip in one more impoverished client, he told her, "Look what followed me home . . . can I keep it?" and ran out of the office laughing as she chased him into the parking lot scolding and waving the new client's file.

James's mistrust of law enforcement was evident on his business card. On the back he had imprinted: "Police can lie to you, your family and friends. Police will offer to make deals they cannot deliver on. Ask to speak to your attorney!" On one occasion he interfered with police whom he felt were harassing a homeless man simply in need of a place to rest. He explained the man's rights to him, then informed the police they were illegally badgering "his client." The police moved on to avoid spawning a court case over the trivial issue.

James's antics were also well known in court. He was not afraid to push the limits of a judge's tolerance. His emotional displays sometimes included screaming at witnesses, and had reduced several to tears.

One such example came to be known in the defense community as the "Yo Mama Case." It began when a Florida Highway Patrol officer was directing traffic around an accident early one evening. As a car with four young men drove by, they all yelled, "Yo mama!" at her. The officer was highly offended and immediately left her post to chase the youths down in her patrol car. They received a traffic citation, and decided to fight it in court. James Stokes was their lawyer.

The officer claimed she stopped them because she suspected they were drinking and driving. Stokes maintained they were only guilty of hurting her pride. On the stand, he asked her, "When they yelled at you, that made you mad, didn't it?"

"No," the officer responded.

"It didn't bother you at all?" James asked incredulously, his voice rising.

"No, it didn't," she said, trying to sound convincing. Her face was turning red.

"Then will you read all of the words that are *capitalized* in this report?" he asked.

"Yo . . . mama!" she answered reluctantly.

"If it didn't bother you at all, *then why did you capitalize all of the letters in* 'Yo mama!' *in your report?!*" James screamed. She broke into tears and asked to be excused. Years later the Yo Mama Case was still one of the favorite stories traded at criminal defense happy hours.

* * *

After James Stokes talked to Greg King and agreed to represent Alex and Derek, Greg immediately called Sharon Potter to represent them as well. While James was fiery and unpredictable, Sharon was calm and methodical. Their seemingly incongruent litigating styles complemented each other in the courtroom.

Sharon Potter wasn't born with a burning desire to practice law. Her interest evolved slowly over time as she saw her father return to law school in his forties. Early on, she preferred sewing, and she had her own seamstress business for years. Clients would bring her a picture from which she could design a pattern and make the garment. But her graceful side was balanced by an enormously competitive drive that manifested itself in a most unusual sport: Sharon Potter was a nationally ranked competitive trail equestrian.

Participants in the sport would ride fifty to a hundred miles cross-country, camping out at night. The horses and riders had to reach designated landmarks and were judged at obstacles along the way. The horses were watched closely for signs of health problems by veterinary doctors posted at checkpoints throughout the course. The sport could be grueling, but Sharon loved it. In 1988 she ranked third in the country.

Her sewing business had given her the freedom to travel and compete with her horses, but now she wanted a career with more of a future. She decided to return to school to pursue a law degree. Like James Stokes, she chose FSU, and three years later graduated with honors. After passing the bar, she accepted a position in the Public Defender's Office. The experience was valuable and she had a good track record, winning most of the cases she took to trial.

After several years in the Public Defender's Office she opened her own law office and embraced private practice with her usual level of determination. She was voted Criminal Defense Lawyer of the Year for 2000–2001. She rented a small but charming office in downtown Pensacola, within walking distance of the courthouse.

A few months later she agreed to cocounsel a death penalty case and was brought in to argue the penalty phase after the client had been convicted of murder. Her poignant appeal resulted in mercy from the jury, who gave the convicted man life in prison rather than death. It was a huge victory for her and won the respect of her peers.

Her law partner was equally dedicated. Dennis Corder often said, with a wry smile, that there were very few people who could put up with him, yet Sharon managed. His dry sense of humor and no-nonsense approach meshed well with her straightforward style, but more important, the litigators were ethical equals. They were willing to fight for a client, but not at the cost of compromising their personal standards.

Dennis and Sharon both attended law school at FSU in the early 1990s. Dennis was a phenomenal student and had a perfect score on the law school admissions test. He enrolled after his wife landed a job as an ophthalmologist in Tallahassee. The Florida climate was an adjustment for the man from Michigan, but he was soon immersed in his studies. Although Dennis and Sharon were moving along parallel paths, they remained strangers for several years. In fact, James Stokes was the one who caught Dennis's attention. He often saw the lanky Marine smoking outside the building and mistook the older man for a professor instead of a student.

Dennis Corder never doubted for a minute where his intellectual talents would be applied. Criminal defense suited him; he was an avid fan of the underdog. Crime was a part of life in his hometown of Detroit, where he'd once been mugged. In spite of that, he remained devoted to the rights of the defendant, and believed the methods law enforcement employed to solve crimes were often worse than the crimes themselves. He didn't watch cop shows much because he always found himself rooting for the accused to get off. Dennis wasn't out for blood, only a fair fight. He felt it was better to let one hundred guilty criminals go free than to send one innocent person to jail.

He and Sharon developed a mutual respect when they took on jobs at the Public Defender's Office in Pensacola. They spent several years there, juggling an average of fifty cases, sometimes as many as seventy. Often, the tremendous workload meant they never laid eyes on a client until the court date, even on plea day. When Sharon left for private practice, Dennis followed a year later and partnered with her.

Sharon had been in private practice for only a year and a half when Greg King called and asked her to help with the King case. He wanted a lawyer whose ethics were unimpeachable, and he'd heard that Sharon refused to step over the line of integrity. She played by the rules, not even permitting herself to engage in what some in the legal community jokingly referred to as "*strategic misrepresentations,*" also known as little white lies. James Stokes was less conventional in his handling of a case. He was creative and not afraid to shake things up when necessary.

The King case would prove to be challenging for a number of reasons, including the age of the clients. Sharon had been married for twenty-two years, James was a divorcee, and Dennis, also married, was admittedly not a "kid person." None of the attorneys had children, but during the upcoming year they would receive a crash course in extreme parenting.

The children's family decided that James would represent Alex and Sharon would take Derek. Since Alex had been raised without a mother, they felt he would relate better to James.

Derek certainly didn't seem like a child capable of brutal murder. He was friendly, energetic, and so very young. Sharon found him to be eager to please and very sensitive.

James and Alex had instant rapport. Alex had a marvelous wit, and the two teased each other relentlessly. Alex quicky figured out that James's Achilles' heel was his Marine pride, and he never missed an opportunity to bait his attorney with it. At one point he told James, "You seem more like a Navy man than a Marine," to which the lawyer replied, "Say that again and I'll tell the jury that you're guilty."

But there was little bantering between the boys and their attorneys the first day they all appeared in court together. Stokes and Potter were intent on having the boys released on bond. Although isolated from the general population, the children had been locked up at the Escambia County Jail, an adult facility, since their first degree murder indictment. Nearly a month later their attorneys were petitioning the court to let the brothers stay with family. The prosecutor had no intention of letting that happen. First degree murder suspects were usually held without bond until their trial, and these children were no exception in the eyes of the state.

In court that morning, the spectators were seated in a semicircle. The rows of chairs gradually elevated toward the back of the room, giving the audience an unobstructed view of the floor. The effect was a small-scale Roman arena, and the seats filled up fast.

Network and local television cameras lined the back wall, ready to give America its first glimpse of the boys who stood accused of beating their father to death with a baseball bat. Attorneys shuffled papers and chatted with staff from the County Clerk's Office while they waited for the hearing to begin. The brothers were not yet in the courtroom.

Sharon Potter was with Alex and Derek, discussing proper behavior in the courtroom until court security told her it was time to go. A door in the back of the courtroom swung open and all eyes turned to see who would walk through it. Sharon walked into the room seeming cool and reserved in a plain black suit. She was tall, and her straight brown hair hung in a long baby-fine pageboy. She was followed by Derek and then Alex. James Stokes lumbered in on a crutch, sporting a cast from a recent accident. His gray slacks and jacket hung loosely on his tall, angular frame.

"They're so *small*," someone whispered.

Shackles and chains around their ankles forced Alex and Derek to shuffle along slowly, while handcuffs swallowed their wrists. The brothers, wearing dark green jumpsuits, followed Sharon to the seating area and sank into chairs beside their attorneys. Their baby faces were angelic, and they hardly looked like teenagers. Derek was handsome in a roguish way. His dark hair was shaggy and in need of a cut. His wide blue eyes boldly scanned the crowd of spectators watching his every move. He appeared to be searching for a familiar face and found several. Derek raised his handcuffed hands for a small wave toward his family and former youth group leader, giving them a smile.

Alex was more subdued. While Derek returned the stares of onlookers, Alex's blue eyes were riveted to the floor or his attorney, anywhere but the crowd. When he reluctantly dragged his gaze upward, the small face could barely be seen over the banister. He appeared years younger than the birth date on his arrest report. His thick blond hair was wavy and unkempt.

Alex slowly rocked back and forth. When he wasn't biting the tip of his thumb, his small, delicate fingers clutched his chin and mouth. The boy was fragile; not just physically, but emotionally too.

Although noticeably nervous and sober, Derek had an interest in the proceedings that resembled fascination at a scary movie. He looked around with the wide-eyed wonder only children possess. His unmedicated ADHD would not allow him to sit still. His younger brother seemed utterly devoid of joy. He did not crack a smile and appeared as if he rarely did.

The boys' attorneys leaned in protectively as they whispered to their young clients. Sharon bent an attentive ear to Derek, while James gently put his hand to Alex's back as he talked to him.

David Rimmer stood calm and confident behind a table set aside for the prosecutor. He was a twenty-year veteran with the State Attorney's Office. He was tall, had thick gray hair, the same color as his mustache, and was thin, a testament to the time he dedicated to his job. As the top homicide prosecutor in the office, he had already taken forty-eight first degree murder cases to trial. He rarely lost one.

Rimmer had devoted most of his life to law enforcement. He started working for the Pensacola Police Department in 1971. He stayed only one year before joining the Escambia Sheriff's Office. There, he enjoyed serving the citizens of Escambia County for seven and a half years. In fact, he thought being a deputy was so much fun, he could hardly believe they paid him to do it, especially just running the streets on the midnight shift. However, he soon had bigger aspirations, and he signed up for law school in 1979 at the age of thirty-three. Three years later he walked away with a diploma and a job. Immediately following graduation, he signed on with the State Attorney's Office and began to work for State Attorney Curtis Golden, District One.

Twenty years later he was still devoted to his career. While some attorneys may have been daunted or distracted by the tremendous amount of media attention the case was drawing, David Rimmer was not. He could forget the cameras, as well as the packed courtroom, and focus only on the task at hand. An avid country music fan, he took one particular song to heart, "The Dance" by Lee Ann Womack. He believed the lyrics spoke of a prosecutor pushing forward and never taking the easy way out.

"All rise! The Honorable Kim Skievaski presiding." The deputy's announcement jolted the packed courtroom out of their seats. The Escambia Circuit Court judge strode into the room, black robes rustling as he took his place behind the bench. He quickly discussed some minor procedural issues before turning his attention to the question of bond. The boys' attorneys first set about to prove the brothers were indigent.

With Sharon by his side, Derek shuffled from his seat to a podium that stood before the judge. Sharon pulled the microphone down so he could speak into it clearly. He politely stated his name and answered Skievaski's questions about money, holdings, and his ability to access money. Derek's strong Southern accent rang thick and engaging through the courtroom. Two minutes later he was back in his seat.

Alex took tiny steps as he walked across the floor, his chains jangling. James towered above the child, a stark contrast to the boy's tiny frame. The crowd strained to listen as Alex answered the court's questions with the tremulous tenor of a boy younger than his twelve years. The judge quickly declared they were indigent.

Their attorneys argued that the brothers were not a flight risk since they would stay with family in protective custody. They pointed out the uniqueness of the situation, emphasizing their youth and inability to care for themselves. Derek and Alex watched somberly as their lawyers attempted to free them from jail.

David Rimmer rose quickly when the judge asked the State's position. "The State feels bond is inappropriate in the case, Your Honor," Rimmer began. "The State intends to show these children did willfully commit murder." He called Investigator John Sanderson to the witness stand. "Please state your name for the record," Rimmer said.

"John Sanderson, Escambia County investigator."

"And how long have you worked for the Sheriff's Office?"

"About twenty years."

"Did you interview Alex and Derek King on the evening of November 27, 2001?"

"I did."

"And what did they tell you about the death of their father, Terry King?"

"They confessed to killing him."

Rimmer pulled a handful of documents from his files and brought them before the judge. "The State moves to present these confessions before the court, Your Honor."

Skievaski peered over his glasses and tried to pin the prosecutor down. "Are you entering the confessions into evidence?"

Rimmer paused, "The State wishes to present them before the court to support the investigator's statements."

Skievaski waved them through and Rimmer quickly handed the papers to Sanderson.

"What did the boys tell you and Investigator Kilgore about the death of their father?"

"Derek told us he used a bat to beat his father to death. He said, 'I made sure he was asleep. I got the bat and I hit him over the head.' " In contrast to the brutal description, his tone was calm, professional.

Rimmer continued to probe. "Did he say how many times he swung the bat?"

Sanderson nodded and flipped through the confession. "Somewhere around ten times."

Reporters furiously took notes, while the cameras rolled.

The investigators went on to detail portions of Alex's

statements, noting that the boy clearly described seeing his
father's blood and brains. Many of the spectators looked
shocked as they attempted to make sense of what they heard.
How could a child beat his father to death with a baseball
bat, callously striking him over and over until the brains
were exposed?

Rimmer also showed the judge a poster board covered
with pictures of the crime scene. He quickly turned the
boards toward the boys' attorneys before handing them to
Skievaski. The crowd craned to get a better look at the photos, but Rimmer made it impossible for spectators to get a
glimpse of the gore.

Skievaski wasted no time in making his ruling. He denied
bond and ordered the boys be held in custody until the trial.

If the children were disappointed, it was hard to tell. Their
attitudes appeared to remain the same as court security led
the small, shackled figures back through the swinging door.
Derek smiled shyly at the deputies, while Alex kept his head
down and looked at the floor.

As people trickled out of the courtroom, reporters shifted
their attention to the confessions. Mollye Barrows was one
of many who wanted to see them. WEAR-TV and the *Pensacola News Journal* filed a motion to allow the press access
to the boys' statements.

A few days later at a separate hearing, the judge ruled that
the boys' statements were part of the public record, since
they were essentially entered as evidence during the bond
hearing. As soon as Skievaski issued his decision, Mollye
hurried to the clerk's office to make copies of the thick file
on the King case. The ruling basically opened up Pandora's
box, giving the press access to some of the evidence the
State had accumulated so far against the brothers.

The reporter pored over the statements. Some graphic details in the boys' accounts made her shudder, but some inconsistencies caught her attention. The reporter noted that Derek had confessed to hitting his father over the head ten times with the bat. Mollye thought the damage would be greater from ten hits.

She also noticed the boys used phrases like "extreme eye contact," "staring me down," and "mental abuse" when describing their father's allegedly abusive behavior. Aside from being flimsy complaints, Mollye thought it strange both boys used exactly the same words. She thought perhaps the brothers had lied to protect Ricky Chavis. She wondered if their lies stopped with regard to his role in the crime.

The reporter was also shocked to learn that Ricky Chavis was a good friend of an Escambia sheriff's deputy. As she read the transcripts, Mollye soon realized Reggie Jernigan not only brought the boys to the Sheriff's Office at Ricky's request, but that he was also there during portions of Derek's interview. Her concern intensified when she realized Derek had asked for the officer to be there for the interview, a request that was granted only after his initial request for Ricky Chavis was denied.

Mollye thought Derek's desire to have either man there was questionable, and she wondered how much of an influence Ricky had over the boys. She grew even more suspicious after reading that Ricky promised the brothers he had friends in the Sheriff's Office who would look out for them.

During Derek's questioning, Reggie had volunteered to "run and get the clothes" that the children had worn on the night of the murder. Sanderson said, "If you don't mind, would you go get them?" So Reggie and Ricky went together to retrieve the evidence. When they got to Ricky's trailer, the deputy allowed Ricky to decide which clothes to collect. "I had to go with what he said was their clothes," he would later state.

The journalist also learned from Alex's statements that Ricky had waited at the Sheriff's Office after delivering the boys to investigators. Mollye suspected Reggie kept Ricky abreast of all that was being said within the deputy's hearing.

Ricky explained to the investigators why he called his longtime friend after he picked up the boys. "When I got on the phone with Reg," he said, "I told him that I had both boys in my possession. I asked him if he would come over and let's take them down. He said he'd be there in just a few minutes."

Reggie told the same story to investigators: "He called me on Tuesday, the day after the homicide. It was about, I guess around two o'clock, two-fifteen. And he told me he found the boys in Santa Rosa County and he had just brought them to his house. I got off the phone with him and I called Investigator Terry Kilgore within thirty seconds."

When he arrived to take the brothers to the Sheriff's Office, Reggie insisted he told Ricky and the boys not to say a word to him about the case. He stayed with his friend throughout most of the afternoon's interrogations.

"He was upset about the boys." Reggie said. "I assumed that he knew something more that the boys had told him. I didn't ask him any questions and I didn't ask the boys any questions."

Reggie made frequent visits to "Fort Chavis," even in the middle of the night. There he had met Terry King and his sons, and sometimes saw the boys there without their father.

Mollye mulled over what she had read. As young, cherubic children with a heartbreaking family life, the boys were sympathetic suspects, but Mollye was not swayed by their appearance. She knew from past cases that children were capable of brutal acts. She was concerned because she suspected the brothers were pawns. Guilty or innocent, these children were being portrayed as demons, young killers who acted with the guile and ruthless intent of adults. Mollye suspected that Ricky's lascivious desire for young Alex King and his fear of being caught were strong motivation to spur him into action. Whether or not he swung the bat, Ricky Chavis appeared to be a manipulator who got what he wanted from the people around him. Devious motives were involved, but they might well have belonged to the puppet master who pulled the strings, Mollye thought, and not the children who danced.

Chapter 12

"**THERE WAS A COP CAR THERE ALL THE TIME,**" **THE** woman told Mollye. "That's why we were never really too worried about what went on there. We figured if a cop's there, it must be all right."

Mollye's questions about Ricky Chavis and his friendship with Reggie Jernigan had led her back to Ricky's neighborhood. Many people came forward shortly after Ricky's arrest, eager to share what they knew about their neighbor with reporters. According to them, Jernigan was a fixture at Ricky's place.

"He was there all hours of the day and night," the woman continued.

"Did you ever suspect their relationship extended beyond friendship?" Mollye asked.

She shook her head. "No, I think they were just friends, best friends." People who knew both of them agreed. Neighbors often spotted the two chatting in Ricky's yard. In fact, a friend of Ricky's was relieved to see the officer there one afternoon when she brought her van for repairs.

"My son had a problem with some kids wanting to jump him," the woman told Mollye. "Reggie's in uniform. He's in a police car. I went over there to talk to him about it. He said he worked in warrants arresting people who were wanted by the law. He said he couldn't do anything to help me." She was very upset with the deputy. "When you see a police car sitting in the driveway, it hurts your feelings when they won't help."

As with any big news event, some said they always knew "something was wrong" at Ricky's trailer. Others merely thought he was a regular guy who sometimes played his music too loud. Most agreed he easily attracted a crowd, especially teenagers.

One woman said Ricky had attempted to molest her son a couple of years earlier when the boy was fifteen. She said Ricky's place was once a regular hangout for both her son and older daughter.

"My daughter went there to smoke pot and my son played video games," she said. However, her son's visits soon came to an abrupt end. After a family argument one evening, the boy went to Ricky's trailer and was invited to spend the night. Ricky called the worried mother to let her know all was well, soothing her concerns. A couple of hours later she was alarmed when her distraught son called, anxious to come home. Later that evening, the teen refused to talk about what happened but indicated Ricky had "come on" to him. Until then, the mother had thought her children were in safe hands, especially since they told her that a cop was always hanging out at Ricky's home.

Mollye found the closeness between Reggie and the convicted felon suspicious. Numerous witnesses described them as more than just casual acquaintances, and she wondered just how deep their friendship ran. She took her questions to Jernigan's boss, Escambia Sheriff Ron McNesby.

McNesby, or "Ronnie Mac," as he was known, was just getting comfortable in his role as sheriff. He had been elected a year earlier after a hard fought campaign and marginal victory. The position was a lifelong dream for the middle-age man. He had spent most of his law enforcement career working his way up through the ranks of the Sheriff's Office, until he left the department several years prior to the election. He used the time to court campaign dollars and support.

The significance of the high profile King case was not lost on the media savvy politician. McNesby told Mollye he thought this would probably be the most important case of his career. She was chatting with him in his office as the photographer set up his equipment. The interview had been tough to schedule. As a crime reporter, Mollye often worked with local law enforcement. She sensed the sheriff was wary of the possibility of bad publicity, especially since the questioning revolved around one of the department's own.

McNesby sat across from her in a high-backed leather chair, a large desk separating the two. He was friendly, but Mollye knew this was not an interview he relished.

He defended the man he had known for more than two decades, saying Reggie was open about his friendship with Ricky Chavis. The sheriff pointed out that many deputies spend time with convicted criminals, but the relationships are often work related, like that of Reggie and Ricky. The officer worked in warrants, McNesby explained to Mollye, and his relationship with Ricky helped him gather information on suspects he wanted to apprehend.

Mollye was not entirely convinced. The reporter understood that the demands of police work could mean compromise to get the job done, but regularly fraternizing, if not *socializing,* with a convicted child molester seemed questionable.

"Considering what we now know—that Ricky Chavis is a convicted child molester, and that neighbors say he made no secret about smoking pot—doesn't it concern you that a deputy would spend so much time over there?" she asked.

McNesby admitted he was concerned, but insisted it was too soon to say if Reggie was aware of any illegal behavior.

Mollye pressed on. "Why was Reggie allowed to sit in on the boys' statements to investigators?"

The sheriff said he was told there was no family immediately available, and the boys knew Reggie from spending time at Ricky's, *with their father*, he emphasized. The sheriff wrapped up the interview by stating he was pursuing an internal investigation into Reggie's relationship with Ricky Chavis. Until it was completed, Reggie would continue to work in warrants.

Mollye headed back to the television station for the six o'clock newscast. She had less than two minutes of air time to boil the story down to its basic facts, easily digestible for mass consumption. The resulting story could seem ridiculously simple to the untrained observer. Many details of a story wind up on the proverbial editing room floor simply because there is not enough time to include them. In broadcast news, shorter is better. Good writers are known for their ability to say a lot in a little time, making the most of their words and still enabling the viewing public to grasp their meaning.

As she typed furiously, Mollye described Reggie's presence during the boys' police interviews. She also revealed his longstanding friendship with the convicted felon, the amount of time neighbors said Jernigan spent at his home, and the items police found during a search of Ricky's trailer, including marijuana, boys' clothing, and a picture of Alex tacked up on Ricky's bed.

She delivered the story from the studio, standing in front of a huge television. The graphic on the screen screamed

KING MURDER INVESTIGATION in bold red letters. She read her own words from the teleprompter, then watched the faces of those in the studio as they listened to the sound bite she chose from her interview with McNesby.

"Reggie doesn't deny that he has gone over there on numerous occasions," the sheriff explained, "and that they have become friends, but like I said, nothing that has been brought forward to us indicates any prior knowledge to what was going on in this case."

Mollye wrapped up her story by saying there was no word on when the internal investigation would be finished. She nodded as the anchor thanked her for her report, then stepped away after the camera operator gave her the cue that she was clear. As the anchor moved on to another story, Mollye quietly walked through the studio. She was careful her heels did not click on the polished cement floor. Viewers could hear extraneous noise during a live newscast. In fact, the entire newsroom could be seen behind the anchor desk.

Occasionally, the news director would send out a mass memo through station e-mail, warning those in the newsroom to keep it down during a newscast. Newsroom employees could be heard if they were laughing or arguing too loudly, and viewers could sometimes make out a police scanner screaming a high-pitched electronic warning that someone's house was on fire or there was a nasty car accident. Often, viewers could see a figure darting behind the anchors. It usually turned out to be a photographer, racing through the newsroom, risking bodily harm in an attempt to get a tape to the control room in time to make it to air.

The control room was where it all happened during a newscast. The producer, who wrote much of the show and organized the contents, acted as the liaison between the anchors on set, the reporters in the field or in the newsroom, and those working behind the scenes. The director ran the show, giving orders to those who ran the cameras, audio, and tapes. The tape editor kept tabs on stacks of tapes, the all-important visual element of the newscast, snatching tapes from hurried photographers and jamming them into the right machine, hoping to make deadline. He or she juggled dozens of tapes as stories were changed or dropped.

Occasionally there are mistakes. Mollye remembered one newscast in which the wrong tape was played over a tease. While the anchor read a few words detailing a story about animal cruelty coming after the commercial break, a tape for a medical segment played. The result was a bloody shot of a woman's breast implant being removed while the words HOG SLAUGHTER were boldly printed on the screen. The entire studio erupted in laughter. Behind-the-scenes action was often more compelling than what viewers were intended to see, and the same proved true with Reggie Jernigan.

Sheriff McNesby was squirming in the unwanted media glare. Mollye's report called the deputy's relationship with Ricky Chavis into question, an issue the Sheriff's Office apparently had not intended to address prior to the broadcast. McNesby, barely in office for a year, eagerly wanted to remain in the good graces of public opinion. The implication that one of his own officers was cavorting with a convicted child molester was an issue he could not afford to ignore, especially now that the county's voters would also be questioning Jernigan's actions and whether his boss endorsed his behavior.

The sheriff fired Jernigan two and a half months after the internal investigation began. Reggie's longtime friendship with Ricky Chavis had cost him his job. Mollye felt some of her suspicions about the deputy's behavior were justified when investigators found their relationship violated several policies, including those that prohibit officers from associating with criminals and engaging in conduct unbecoming to a member of the Sheriff's Office. Jernigan retaliated by saying the investigation and the charges were a result of media pressure.

The sheriff explained his decision, saying Reggie's friendship with Ricky was "unacceptable and caused extreme embarrassment to the community and his fellow officers." McNesby felt Jernigan's association with Ricky and to the high profile case reflected poorly on the Sheriff's Office, diminishing public respect and confidence in the administration.

Investigators made several discoveries that undermined Reggie's claim that his relationship with Ricky was based mostly on police work. Deputies discovered the two men exchanged more than just information. These facts were in their Report of Investigation.

They interviewed many of Ricky's acquaintances and neighbors who described Reggie's frequent visits with Ricky and said the two were well-known friends. During a search of Ricky's trailer, crime scene investigators found medication in a pill bottle that belonged to the officer. A discovery on the deputy's work computer also left no room for doubt that the officer knew of Ricky's sordid past. Jernigan had requested a copy of Ricky's criminal history in April 1998. The two men not only remained close in the years that followed, but their friendship had deepened. Mollye wondered to what extent.

Chapter 13

ALEX AND DEREK WERE TOLD THEY COULD EXPECT A special visitor soon. They were surprised to learn that their mother, Kelly Marino, would be coming to call. They had not seen her in more than three years, when her name had been Janet French. She remarried after she left Terry King, but later divorced, then changed her name—partly to hide from the ex-husband, and partly because she liked the name. "Kelly" was her favorite among Charlie's Angels.

Alex and Derek didn't know if they would recognize the woman who had given birth to them. After years of longing for her, Derek finally saw his mother walking toward him. He later told his grandmother Linda, "I didn't recognize her, but I knew it had to be the blonde." He remembered her as being thin, and now she carried extra pounds.

Kelly Marino's visit was short but sweet. For thirty minutes she sat with her sons, holding hands and telling them she loved them. After she left, she told a *Pensacola News Journal* reporter she just wasn't sure what she would do.

"Part of me wants to stay here and do whatever I can, but the other part of me tells me to just stay away." Kelly then returned to Lexington, Kentucky, where she lived with her new husband, two cats, and two guinea pigs.

Derek had recently been rejected by his foster family, and

seeing his mother walk away was another heart-wrenching blow. When his grandmother visited several days later, he poured out his hurt and sadness to her.

"I'm afraid everyone is going to forget about us," he said quietly to Linda. "No one will want to have anything to do with us by the time we get out of here."

"Paw Paw and I do, Derek," she quickly replied. Linda desperately wanted the court to grant her custody of both boys when they were released. Their mother had been out of their lives, and their father was dead. Where could they go? There was certainly no easy answer.

In the first few weeks after their arrest, it was obvious that Alex and Derek had totally bought into Ricky Chavis's lies. After visiting Derek, Frank and Nancy Lay were dumb-struck. They realized Ricky had planted the idea that jail was just a small bump in the road. "That sucker has told them that everything is going to work out and they're going to live together. It's going to be one big happy family," Frank Lay said.

Alex and Derek were convinced they would soon be free. Alex told his grandmother he wanted to live with Ricky Chavis. She gingerly reminded him he might not get out anytime soon, and sternly told him that he would *not* be going home with Ricky Chavis even if he did.

During part of their stay in the Escambia County Jail, the brothers were housed in the same cell. Tutors visited for one hour in the mornings, and the boys enjoyed their lessons and were cooperative students. Since Alex had only attended school sporadically during years of family instability, he was already a grade behind. He asked to be allowed to make it up during his time behind bars, but unfortunately, his placement in adult jail made that impossible. If they had been tried as juveniles, they would have enjoyed a full school schedule, but trying them as adults allowed them only the one-hour daily lesson. So, instead of using the long days to get ahead in school, both boys fell drastically behind. With little else to do, they spent hours gazing out of their window overlooking a grassy field.

Although their view revealed less activity than the one from the front of the building, the quality of the action they saw was novel. Since jail visitors were forbidden to bring gifts inside the facility, they frequently delivered tokens of their affection from the back field. At least once a week, women would face the building and brazenly lift their shirts, baring their breasts, to the enormous amusement and delight of inmates lucky enough to be staring out of their windows at that propitious moment. The inmates would shout the alert to others, and there would be a mad dash to the windows to see the show. On extra special occasions, such as wedding anniversaries and birthdays, some inspired women threw in a little dancing. The realization that this splendid diversion could happen at any moment was enough to compel some inmates to camp out at their windows.

Since Derek was the "talker" and Alex was adept at writing, the younger boy sometimes took dictation from his brother, acting as a social secretary and keeping up with Derek's correspondence. Alex wrote in tiny letters, squeezing as many words as possible onto the front and back of the page. When Derek did write, his letters were short and unfocused. He was not receiving medication for his attention deficit hyperactive disorder, and a task as simple as penning a brief letter took enormous concentration and was usually accomplished over a period of different sittings.

Once a week they were allowed an hour's worth of playtime on a basketball court in an outdoor recreation yard. Unfortunately, it came at the same time as Saturday morning cartoons, making them sacrifice one of the two rare pleasures in their lives. The playtime came and went in a blinding flash, then they tramped back upstairs and into their cell to wait another week.

They responded to the acute boredom as any child might. They roughhoused, had pillow fights, and played practical jokes on their guards. At one point they threw a sheet over a officer and wrestled with him. They were warned to settle down.

The brothers began to resign themselves to the jailhouse routine and adapt to their environment. They were growing in jail. Alex was still small, weighing just eighty pounds. His smile revealed a partially toothless grin; he was losing his *baby teeth*. They were so young that jailers feared they might fall out of bed, so neither boy was permitted to sleep on the top bunk in their adult prison cell. A special cot, which Derek referred to as a "canoe bed" because of its unusual shape, was brought in, and they took turns sleeping on it.

The boys' cell was located in a section of the jail called Special Housing, which was designed to provide more privacy than normal cells. The children were separated from the prison population, and away from dangerous adult inmates, by a black mesh screen, bars, and a glass enclosure. Shatterproof glass had recently replaced open bars in many cells, reducing the amount of spittle and urine flung at corrections officers. The door of the cell had a slot for meal trays, but outgoing Derek used it to shake hands with jail personnel whenever someone happened by. Inside the cell there was a desk and stool, a shelf, a toilet, a sink, and a small shower. The shower was separated from view by two block walls that jutted out into the room a few feet, allowing some privacy.

Ironically, some family members spent more time with Alex and Derek after they were incarcerated, than when they were free. They made sure there was always someone to see them at every visitation opportunity. Often, there were too many family members visiting, and the jail had to divide the hours up among them.

The boys' attorneys cautioned family members not to discuss the case with Alex and Derek since they felt it was in the boys' best interest to keep conversation light. Linda Walker was all too happy to comply; the last thing she wanted was to hear something she might later have to testify about in court. She and her husband Jimmy visited the boys twice every week. Alex and Derek were always happy to see their grandparents, and most of the time they seemed in good spirits. The Walkers often asked the boys what they wanted to be when they grew up. This simple question could help them measure their optimism about the future, and perhaps signal any depression they might be feeling.

But as the days dragged on, the boredom began to take its toll. The boys were restless and keyed up with no outlet for their adolescent energy. After months of idleness and isolation, Alex, feeling frustrated and helpless, attempted to run from corrections officers. He was quickly restrained and placed in the infirmary for observation. Another time he banged his head against his cell wall repeatedly. He was punished by being strapped into a restraint chair for five long hours with leather bands across his chest, lap, arms, and legs.

After two months in the same tiny cell, the boys needed a break from one another. Alex was moved to a separate cell next to Derek's. Since there was only one television, it remained in the original cell. Alex was quite content without it, passing the time reading and listening to music. Later, when jail overcrowding forced the two boys back into the same cell, they stayed up talking and drinking coffee until four in the morning.

* * *

Only two floors away, Ricky Chavis also sat isolated from the general population, plotting ways to get messages to Alex. Although he had no roommate, he was still able to communicate with other inmates. He quickly struck up a relationship with the man next door, Allen Kozelka. Both men were in protective custody, so officers took them to the exercise yard together. During their two hours outdoors, the men would stroll around the yard and chat, discussing their cases and building trust. Ricky was quick to tell Allen of his gay lifestyle.

Ricky was infatuated with Alex, and he talked about the boy nonstop. Allen was sickened by the obsession, but he let Ricky whine about his tormented love for the boy. Ricky also told Allen that he had a laptop computer, in addition to his home PC, where he stored all of his pictures of Alex. But, he said, it was long gone by the time police arrived with a search warrant.

Ricky's days were dreary, and he whiled away the hours pacing his cell, listening to the radio, and reading an occasional magazine from the book cart. With so much time and so little to do, he was consumed by his case. He desperately needed to contact the boys, but they were housed on the other side of the huge jail. Although difficult, the task was not impossible. Ricky's freakish form of genius was perfect for such challenges.

On a Saturday morning stroll in the recreation yard, Alex and Derek came across a message scratched into a cement sidewalk addressed to Alex. It told him to be bold and strong, that nothing had changed. Then, on March 14, Ricky was seen scratching another message to Alex with a small rock on the concrete. Officers transcribed it and entered the scrawl into evidence. "Alex don't trust . . ." is all he had time to write before he was caught.

Two weeks later Ricky had a hearing at the county courthouse. As he sat in the holding cell, he realized that the boys might later be placed in the same cell for their next hearing, and he decided to take a chance. When Ricky was removed from the cell, jailers discovered a message to Alex, this time written on the wall. It was transcribed, filed as a discovery exhibit, and released to the public:

I'm always thinking about ya. Hang in there. It will work out if nothing changes in the testimony. You know who not to trust. They are keeping us apart until this is over. Just say no. I think about you day and night. Please be careful. I'm with you and your thoughts. Our future depends on the outcome of us in court and what happens to us. Just be strong and please don't change anything and hang in there. You know what your lawyer did to me and that is not your fault but he is trying to break you down. Don't give in if a deal has been promised to get you to say yes about certain things that we know about. Just remember that. Be bold and be strong. Nothing has changed. I'm still here and watch who you trust. Everything's going alright so far. They want me bad. You all heard what they said and who said those things about me. And now be smart and sit back and listen. I'll still be waiting. Don't forget my address and phone number. What ever happens try to stay in touch with me or Mike, he is watching the house now. We will be kept apart. They are trying to make y'all talk and get me 50 years in prison. Remember what we talked about. They will try to make you believe that they already know and they really don't. It's a mind game. Don't be played and don't change nothing even under oath. Only you can make the difference. So please be strong minded and be bold. They will lie to you to get you to talk. So please . . . they will

*not keep their promises. They will lie to you to get you
to talk. Please don't give in. I'm still with you. ILU always and forever. You know who.*

The community was appalled by its brazenness, and convinced that Ricky Chavis had just signed and sealed his own
fate. The writing was removed before the boys could see it.

Fortunately, Ricky had devoted friends inside the jail
whom he could call upon in times of great need. On April 6
while cleaning out Derek's cell, an officer found a crumpled-
up piece of paper in the trash can. Straightening the page
out, the officer was amazed to find that it was a copy of the
letter found on the holding cell wall. Someone loyal to Ricky
had made sure that a page from the document penetrated the
high security around the boys and fell right into their small
hands.

Chapter 14

IN THE FIRST MONTHS OF 2002, THE NATIONAL MEDIA had moved on to other stories, but continued to monitor the progress of the King case. When attorney James Stokes accused Ricky Chavis of being Alex's so-called "adult lover," and questioned who really wielded the bat used to kill Terry King, the legal battle heated up.

The *Pensacola News Journal* ran a scathing article quoting Stokes and pointing the finger directly at Chavis. Stokes said that Chavis was at the King home the night of the crime, but before the murder. He also suggested that the boys' confessions to investigators could have been rehearsed, the result of Rick's efforts to coach the children during the time he hid them in his home after their father's murder. The public was riveted.

The reaction was just what James wanted. He was aware that an active child molester rarely stopped at one victim, and he called on others to come forward. "In cases where there is the possibility of sexual and emotional manipulation, the perpetrators and defendants often develop a bond of silence that can only be broken with the aid of information from local citizens," Stokes said. "The defense hopes that continued media coverage of facts already made public will promote the flow of information from concerned citizens to the defense."

Ricky was incensed by the publicity, and within days of the articles and news broadcasts his court-appointed attorney, Mike Rollo, filed a motion requesting the boys' attorneys be barred from communicating with the media. Rollo was a large man in his early fifties who bore a striking resemblance to Dick Cheney. In his gag order motion, Rollo stated that the *Pensacola News Journal* article was "exceedingly inflammatory," "unfair and prejudicial," and attempting to "assassinate Mr. Chavis's character." He argued that the article contained information that would not even be allowed to be presented in the trial. He later complained that it seemed as if the *News Journal* reporter was working as a part-time prosecutor.

At first James was outraged that one of his best weapons was being limited. He fought to keep communication lines with the press open, in order to give Alex a fair trial and allow the defense to conduct its own investigation to "uncover what really happened to Terry King." In his response to the court, he was quick to point out that the gag order was one-sided, only seeking to limit the defense from making statements to the press, not the State Attorney. "We must assume the concern for the judicial process does not include the statement by David Rimmer that 'there is no evidence Chavis, or anyone else, had a role in the crime,' " Stokes wrote. "Or the statement by Mr. Rimmer, 'Basically the boys were not happy and they killed him.' This conclusion could arguably influence the judicial process."

Stokes said that the State and Ricky were "tied at the hip," since he was the star witness against Alex. "The State Attorney's Office has concluded its investigation based totally upon the 'stories' the children told after Mr. Chavis spent two days with them 'getting the stories straight.' "

The judge from the King brothers' previous court appearances had rotated out, and the case now fell squarely into the lap of Escambia Circuit Court Judge Frank Bell. The sordid details of headlining crimes rarely captured more than a passing interest from the seasoned judge. He had presided over cases that drew huge national attention, like that of Paul Hill, who was convicted of killing an abortion doctor and a volunteer outside a Pensacola clinic in 1993.

Long since without hair, and possessing an accent that can only be found below the Mason-Dixon line, the sixty-two-year-old Bell had the Old South appeal of a hard-nosed magistrate who couldn't be easily swayed. He was said to have "a heart of granite" when dealing with criminals. When attorneys became long-winded, he often made no attempt to hide the fact that he was bored almost to the point of sleep, leaning far back in his chair and propping a knee on the bench.

Judge Bell realized the case was high profile, and he wasted no time granting Rollo's motion for a gag order. James and Sharon didn't fight it. It covered all public officials, court officers, and personnel who were connected to the case in any way. The gag order was a significant victory for Ricky, stopping potentially prejudicial information dead in its tracks. The attorneys were now prohibited from discussing the case with the media.

The public's appetite for information intensified. The tantalizing hints Stokes had dropped concerning Ricky's possible involvement with murder and molestation only fueled public suspicions that Chavis masterminded the killing, whether or not the boys actually committed the crime.

The brothers had testified before a grand jury, and the result was a fresh round of charges for Ricky Chavis. On April 10, 2002, he was indicted for first degree murder, arson, and sexual battery. The public feeding frenzy was renewed, but the boys' grand jury testimony was sealed, leaving outsiders to guess at who killed Terry King and why.

The *Pensacola News Journal* had no intention of patiently waiting for an answer. Nor did a new player in the drama, CBS News. A hearing was set to discuss relaxing the gag order, and network representatives from the CBS program *48 Hours* flew in from New York and Miami. They requested access to the defendants and their attorneys for interviews. As they reasoned, they didn't pose the same threat as the local media. They said that *48 Hours* was a documentary broadcast that cultivated stories over time. Since they didn't compete to be first to air a story, they had the luxury of spending as much time as needed to get the details right. This meant that they wouldn't air their coverage of the King case until well after the trials and sentencing, and therefore couldn't possibly prejudice the public's perception of the defendants.

Ricky's attorney countered that if the judge allowed only *48 Hours* access to the lawyers and the defendants, the local media would go ballistic. In the end, Judge Bell agreed that anyone who wished to talk would be allowed, but the media couldn't release the information until after the trials.

The judge used the same hearing to discuss whether to allow cameras in the courtroom. He acknowledged that other parts of the country had experienced unruliness as the result of cameras. But he reasoned that Florida approves of cameras in the courtroom, and said he had personally never had any problems with it, that after a while, you don't even realize the cameras are there, and you just try the case. He clearly supported the idea, and none of the attorneys raised objections.

The judge concluded the proceedings in typical Southern style: "Okay, folks. Appreciate y'all coming in."

The decision set the stage for a media frenzy that would not only stun the public, but put the Escambia legal system in the crosshairs.

Chapter 15

MOLLYE FELT THAT HER BEST CHANCE TO FIND THE truth was to go directly to the source. She called Mike Chavis, who arranged for her to visit his brother at the Escambia County Jail.

Visitation at the jail was scheduled for Sunday mornings at eight-thirty. Anxious to meet Ricky Chavis, she arrived a full hour early and was the first visitor to log in. The waiting room was somber. The shiny terrazzo floor was spotless. Thirty-six plastic chairs faced an imposing metal detector and two enormous automatic sliding gates that led to the prisoners. A sign hanging on the wall warned: "Keep noise level down. Control your children. Please keep them seated and do not let them roam or play in the lobby."

Mollye wore faded bell-bottom jeans and a blousy peasant shirt, fitting in well with the group gathering to share an hour with their loved ones behind bars. Several people recognized the reporter and smiled, but didn't try to engage her in conversation. Many visitors knew each other from their faithful Sunday visits, and chatted quietly among themselves. Here, they could discuss their most heartbreaking stories, knowing they were members of the same exclusive club. The result was a strange comradery rooted in sadness. Mollye felt like an intruder.

After waiting an hour for visitation to begin, she was calm

and ready when a deputy addressed the crowd: "Good morning, ladies and gentleman. In just a moment we'll begin visitation. First, a few details. There will be no books, papers, pencils, pens allowed in the visitation area. No food or gum is permitted. Purses must be left outside, and we have lockers available if you wish to use them. You may only bring your keys and your identification into the area. Visitors of prisoners in protective custody will be escorted back first and will communicate by phone. All others may visit behind screens. We'll begin now."

The deputy began calling numbers, and the visitors were herded through the metal detector and into a tiny, tightly packed holding room much like an elevator. Behind the crowd, the bars of the huge electric gate slid closed with an enormous echoing metallic *clang*.

The sound of vanishing freedom, Mollye thought. She couldn't help but believe the noise alone sent a powerful message to prisoners plotting escape.

As the first gate closed completely, Mollye noticed a list tacked to the wall outlining still more rules. She stifled a smile when she read rule number four: "No bra, no entrance!" She wondered if the compliance officer in charge of that item held a coveted position. The gate slid open and the guests of the Escambia County Jail rushed forth to meet their anxious hosts.

Ricky Chavis was already seated behind the thick glass partition when Mollye arrived. Distinct palm prints were smudged onto the glass that prevented desperate visitors and inmates from touching each other's hands. She slid into the metal folding chair where countless visitors had worn away the paint on the seat bottom. She picked up the phone. Ricky did the same, but before speaking into it, he took the receiver and cleaned it off with his baggy jumpsuit. Mollye followed his lead and did the same. She was dismayed to see that someone's greasy beige makeup was now wiped onto the bottom of her white shirt.

"Hi, Mollye," Ricky said in a strong Southern twang.

Mollye smiled but was shocked by Ricky's appearance. He looked nothing like she had imagined. At six-three and 150 pounds, he appeared thin and gaunt in his baggy green jumpsuit. He seemed self-conscious about his appearance and hurried to explain.

"I got my hair all cut off," he said, running his hand over his head. The little stubble of hair that remained outlined a receding hairline. "I'm only allowed two showers per week so I like to keep my hair short." He told her that the jail dentist had pulled three of his teeth, and that he planned to have all the remaining ones pulled and get dentures. But that was an investment he couldn't afford at this point. Each pulled tooth set him back ten dollars.

Mollye began asking about his childhood, and he answered all of her questions without flinching. Like his brother Mike, he had few good memories of his youth. Then she moved the conversation to his more recent past, specifically his relationship with Deputy Reggie Jernigan.

Ricky told her that he met Reggie, then a corrections officer, in 1980 while serving time in the county jail for burglary and grand theft. At twenty-nine, the deputy was ten years his senior. The men often chatted during Ricky's long hours of incarceration, but the two lost touch after his release. They became reacquainted about a year later.

"I was driving my black 1980 Monte Carlo down Brent Lane," Ricky recalled with a smile. "I didn't have a driver's license or the right tags. I see blue lights behind me and I pull over. I'm cursing, afraid I'm going to go back to jail. Then I see Reg walking up to my car. He told me, 'You got to be careful now,' and let me go. We've been friends ever since."

Although Ricky spent most of the 1980s behind bars, he and Reggie picked up where they'd left off shortly after he was released. They often talked while Reggie earned extra cash at an off-duty side job. The deputy was working security at the Sack and Save Food Store on Brent Lane where Ricky did his grocery shopping. Soon, Ricky was giving the deputy information he could use in his police work.

Reggie began spending more time at Ricky's place while he worked on the deputy's old van. The repairs enabled Reggie to keep it going until he could afford to trade it in.

Mollye remembered how Reggie had explained his friendship with the convicted felon. The account was in court files relating to King's murder.

"First it was mainly mechanic work and he was giving me information," Reggie said about Ricky Chavis. "He would get on hard times and need food. I even gave him food, gave him money to buy food. Once I tried to get some money fronted for information he was giving me, and there was so much bureaucratic paperwork we said the heck with it."

Ricky valued his friendship with the deputy and went out of his way to help Reggie in his professional and personal life. He told Mollye he had not had any contact with his longtime friend since his arrest, but he was hoping that Reggie would win the fight to get his job back.

Mollye asked Ricky why he was in protective custody, separated from the other inmates.

"I requested it," he answered quickly. "I don't want the *jail mentality* to rub off on me." Mollye thought it ironic that the convicted child molester wanted to preserve his lofty standards. She suspected that jailers feared harm might come to Ricky if he mixed with the broad prison population. Inmates are incredibly intolerant of certain crimes, particularly those involving children. While their moral fiber was a bit tattered by outsiders' standards, prisoners clung tenaciously to their own code of ethics. With so much time on their hands, they often reflected longingly on the families they left behind. They grew closer through letters and visits, and inmates talked with pride to others who had loving families waiting outside. Many were enraged at the thought that a child molester could be harming their children while they sat helplessly confined. Incarcerated child molesters were frequent victims of fatal beatings while in jail.

One such case occurred in Los Angeles, where an accused child molester was brutally bludgeoned to death by three inmates while in a holding cell. Sheriff's deputies at the jail were being investigated to determine if they either encouraged the beating or failed to stop it. Such brawls were termed "blood sport," and many bloodthirsty spectators saw little wrong with it. Child molesters made poor gladiators in the game. They were more accomplished at preying upon the younger and weaker, and stood little chance of surviving when released into the den of lions in prison. Pedophiles could expect a fatal beating to be waiting around any corner.

Isolating Ricky in a private cell, then allowing him visitors, reaped a bizarre harvest. The extroverted man was desperately talkative and didn't seem to mind any of Mollye's probing questions. He openly discussed Alex and Derek, his relationship with Terry, and the murder.

He told her that prosecutor David Rimmer and his attorney, Mike Rollo, had recently visited him. "They told me what Alex and Derek said in their grand jury testimony," Ricky said.

"And what was that?" she asked, trying to hide her eagerness. The records were sealed.

"They said that Alex and Derek testified that I committed the murder while they slept. Then I supposedly put them in the trunk of my car and drove them to my house." He rolled his eyes dismissively. "David Rimmer told me that he doesn't think I killed Terry. When the man prosecuting your case says that, it makes you feel a little bit better," he said reflectively.

Ricky had recently been to the jail barber. He said the barber had told him that he used the same number blade on the shaver that Alex did. Like an infatuated teenager, this tidbit of information seemed intimate and incredibly important to him.

Mollye asked Ricky about his life behind bars. He described his five-by-eight "private suite" complete with stainless steel toilet and sink combo, upper and lower bunk, single shelf, table and bench, and a much coveted window overlooking the jail parking lot. From this vantage point, he could monitor the comings and goings of visitors. This was a much different view than the back of the jail offered; it overlooked a grassy field through which occasional strollers walked on their way to a nearby fast food restaurant.

A cart with books and reading material rolled around every two weeks or so, and eager inmates awaited its arrival to provide temporary relief from endless hours of boredom. Ricky had been fortunate enough to find a 1958 edition of *National Geographic* magazine on the book cart, and rather than returning it when he should have, he hid it in his cell, hoping to keep the rare find for himself.

The tools he used to charm those on the outside were surprisingly effective on the inside as well. A number of times during the visit, deputies walked by and acknowledged Ricky with a nod and a smile. He seemed to know them all; even a nurse who strolled through waved to him. Ricky was a first-class networker even while in jail. He had recently been firing off notes to friends imploring them to write letters to the *Pensacola News Journal* and say positive things about him. He worried a great deal about the negative press he received, and spent much of his time trying to manipulate his image in the public eye. His efforts produced one faithful friend willing to stand alone in his defense. Her letter was printed in the newspaper and described the times Ricky had worked on her car free of charge. Ricky had cried when he read it. He pulled a well-worn clipping from inside his jumpsuit and pressed it against the window for Mollye to read.

Before long the visitation hour was over and she rose to leave. Ricky asked her to pause long enough in the parking lot to give him time to hurry back to his cell. From there he could wave through his small window. He knew his status in the jail was sure to soar now that the popular newswoman was his visitor.

Mollye took her time getting to her car, then looked up the side of the imposing building. She shaded her eyes against the blazing summer sun and strained to see inside the tiny window she knew was Ricky's. Suddenly there he was, waving enthusiastically, like a child leaving for summer camp. Only Ricky wasn't going anywhere.

On Monday morning Mollye received a letter at the station that erased any feelings of sympathy she might have felt for Ricky Chavis.

"Hello Mollye," the handwritten letter began. "My name is Herb and the reason I'm writing you is I have some information about Rick Chavis."

Mollye was fascinated. As she read, she learned that Herb Helton had met Rick in 1980, when he was thirteen and Ricky was eighteen. Herb described Ricky as friendly and seemingly sincere, the kind of guy a young teenage boy would admire. Ricky entertained him with his mechanical toys and abilities and offered him a "cool" place to hang out with other teenage boys, marijuana and alcohol. But according to Herb, Ricky's candy store wasn't free.

"Rick started having sex with boys from the neighborhood. I woke up after a night of partying and he would be embracing some kid." The three-page letter detailed more of Ricky's alleged suspicious behavior and the devastating toll it took on the people around him. Many of the details confirmed information Mollye already knew was true, lending credibility to Herb's claims.

Now in his early thirties, Herb was writing to her from the Escambia County Jail, where he was serving time for violating his probation. He had been arrested a year earlier for driving under the influence, and while on probation, a deputy stopped him for driving with a suspended license. In jail, he followed the King case closely, feeling a painful connection with the brothers. Herb felt compelled to come forward with what he knew.

"My concern about this terrible ordeal is those boys' future. Rick is a pedophile and a monster. It took a lot of nerve for me to write to you, Mollye. I just pray for all of this to end with the truth and justice. And most importantly a healing process for all involved."

Mollye immediately sent a letter to Herb. They began a three-month-long correspondence lasting the remainder of his jail sentence. During that time, Herb slowly revealed the horrific extent of Ricky Chavis's abuse and his methods for seducing children.

"I woke up countless times to him performing oral sex on me in the middle of the night. There were a lot of other young boys. I am sorry for not telling you before. I was too embarrassed. People look at you differently if they know something like this happened."

Mollye learned that Herb had received counseling at a Pensacola mental health center, but his wounds were deep. She wondered how many others bore scars from Ricky Chavis.

* * *

Sunday morning rolled around again and Mollye was due at the jail. Each visit with Ricky was enlightening, but this time she had theories to discuss. She had spent much of the week interviewing a number of people, including attorneys, family members, and investigators. Everyone had a hypothesis. The police believed Derek had killed his father while Alex watched. Family members were convinced Ricky Chavis wielded the bat while the children waited in his car.

The *theory du jour* was that someone had repositioned Terry's body after the murder. After all, said believers, how could a human head sustain ten violent blows, brutal enough to splash blood on the walls, yet still remain in a relaxed posture with arms and legs folded and a full coffee cup in the lap? It just didn't add up. They speculated that the killer delivered the first blow somewhere else, then carried the stunned Terry to the chair, where he then completed his morbid chore, folded the corpse, and departed. Having no access to the sealed crime scene photos, Mollye was at a huge disadvantage. All she could do was listen with fascination to those who had seen the body, and weigh their opinions objectively.

When Mollye was escorted back to the visitation area, Ricky greeted her warmly. With the trials just a month away, things were really heating up for him. They chatted about how preparations were coming along and how producers for television shows like *48 Hours*, *Dateline,* and Court TV were gathering information for their coverage.

"I'd like to talk with them," Ricky said without hesitation. "My attorney says he thinks it will be okay since the interviews won't air until after the trials."

Although Mollye said nothing, her instincts told her that Ricky couldn't possibly benefit from such an interview. She had already heard him referred to as "a cross between Gomer Pyle and Charles Manson."

Mollye moved the conversation toward the topic that she really wanted to discuss. "Ricky, there's a theory going around that Terry King's body was *repositioned*," she said, carefully watching his face. He raised his eyebrows but said nothing. Mollye continued, "You see, some folks think that if you take an aluminum bat and whack a person repeatedly on the head, that guy is likely to bounce around a bit."

"Hmm," Ricky said, pondering the idea. Then, warming to the game, he physically acted out the murder. Mollye watched, dumbfounded, as he first posed as the killer, delivering blows with an imaginary bat. *"Whack! Whack! Whack!"* he said. Then he sat in his chair and assumed the position of the beaten body, flopping and bouncing in response to the imaginary strikes. Mollye could hardly believe she was watching the man indicted for Terry King's murder cast himself as *victim* in the hideous, morbid drama. How could he claim to be Terry King's best friend and be so amused about the crushing of his skull? She fought to maintain her focus.

"Don't you think it's odd that the body was so composed after such a brutal assault?" she asked. "The arms were still folded, the feet were crossed. I think the body may have been repositioned after the beating. What do you think?"

"You're right," Ricky said thoughtfully. "The body would have moved."

"Well, if that's true," Mollye went on, "then what does that say to you?"

"That would say to me that it was premeditated," Ricky said without hesitation. Mollye could see the wheels turning in his head, but she had no idea where they were taking him. Since he consistently blamed Derek for the murder, she suspected he was twisting the "repositioning theory" to make the child look even more blameworthy.

The conversation came to a halt when the guard arrived to

escort Ricky back to his cell. Mollye thanked him for his time and told him she'd see him again next week. She believed each visit brought her a step closer to uncovering the enormity of Ricky Chavis's manipulation of the boys. As she watched him shuffle away from the visitation booth, she couldn't decide who had won this bizarre round of mental chess, but it was clear who the pawns were.

PART THREE
THE TANGLED WEB

*"The heart is deceitful above all things,
and desperately wicked:
who can know it?"*
Jeremiah. 17:9

Chapter 16

FOR YEARS TERRY KING'S LIFE HAD BEEN A QUIET struggle, devoid of much pleasure. He had no money for luxuries and sometimes not even enough for necessities. No one could remember a recent girlfriend, and his friendships were few. But now one of Terry's simple dreams was coming true: he was being reunited with his sons.

Derek's homecoming infused Terry's life with an element of energy and excitement that had been missing. Terry and Alex were low-key by nature, while Derek was bursting with high spirits. Though different, the brothers got along. For the first time in seven years, Alex had a live-in playmate, and Derek's deep desire to be with his family was finally realized. Through one another, each found a different kind of happiness.

Alex had always been a loner. His father's lifestyle limited his opportunities to socialize, so he had learned to fill his hours with books. His fondness for reading helped him develop an ability to focus and entertain himself for hours. Words substituted for friends. He developed a quick wit and an impressive vocabulary. He had no trouble holding a compelling conversation with adults.

During the early weeks of Derek's return, he and his father had many heart-to-heart talks. Terry tried to explain that although Alex lived with him, he had always wanted Derek to return, but his foster family didn't believe Terry could handle Derek and had discouraged the move. At first Derek missed his foster family and was reluctant to trust his newfound relationship with his father. But he slowly opened up to him, and each day settled more comfortably into his new life.

The first weeks of October 2001 brought the crisp, cool weather that Floridians wait for all year; air conditioners were shut off in favor of open windows, and light sweaters replaced the shorts and T-shirts of the previous month. Terry was still plagued by financial woes. He found himself short on cash and unable to pay his electric bill. After several notices, the company shut off his power.

When Ricky learned of Terry's plight, he didn't offer a loan, but instead suggested that Terry and the boys stay with him until he could afford to pay the outstanding bill. As a result, in the first week of October the Kings moved in with the two Chavis brothers, just in time to celebrate Ricky's fortieth birthday. Although the trailer was small, initially everyone got along. Terry enrolled Derek and Alex in Ransom Middle School, and with Ricky's encouragement, he signed a document granting Ricky permission to pick up the boys from school.

The living arrangements allowed Ricky the opportunity to learn all about Terry King, including his weaknesses. He soon honed in on Terry's troubled relationship with Linda and Jimmy Walker. The Walkers made it clear to Terry that they loved their grandsons and wanted to renew their relationship with them, especially Derek. They had developed a bond with the boy during the year he lived with them as a child. But Terry didn't trust them. He felt the Walkers not only wanted a relationship with Derek, but custody of him as well. Terry had no intention of letting anyone—especially the Walkers—interfere with his family.

He decided the best way to nip potential problems in the bud was to have Derek call them. Ricky was eagerly eavesdropping when Terry told Derek to tell his grandparents that he no longer wanted to see them. They were crushed, but knew Derek wasn't the one who wanted the separation.

Ricky was delighted. He was sure he could manipulate their unstable relationship with Terry and convince them he was an abusive father whose children should be seized. Ultimately he intended to keep Alex for himself. He went to work with determination, employing his savvy ability as a con artist. He began calling the Walkers frequently, capitalizing on their love for the boys. He portrayed himself as a concerned adult, unable to bear the abuse their grandchildren were suffering at Terry's hands.

The Walkers were horrified by Ricky's contrived stories. In desperation, they reluctantly considered reporting Terry to the Florida Department of Children and Families, knowing the move could remove the boys from their father. Ricky had offered to keep Alex, and Derek could live with them. While the Walkers agonized over the problem, Ricky added that Terry hated them and had threatened to kill Jimmy. To Ricky's disappointment, Jimmy didn't rise to the bait. He was not a man accustomed to solving problems with his fists. The Walkers needed more time and discussion before making a decision.

After planting the seeds of discord, Ricky focused on the iniquitous garden he was sowing in his own backyard. He loved keeping the children; he played games and talked with them for hours. He studied their every move and evaluated their feelings. Ricky used the opportunity to dig deep into their psyches, patiently searching for a soft, narrow space between the children and their father where he could drive a wedge.

Ricky slowly maneuvered the delicate balancing act of pulling the children closer to him while pushing their father away. The brothers listened with wide-eyed trust as he insinuated that Terry didn't understand them, that his occasional scolding proved his disrespect. Since Terry didn't spank his children, Ricky was unable to exploit physical abuse. Instead, he told Alex and Derek that their father's stares were cruelly abusive, pointing out that Terry was playing "mind games." Ricky smoothly positioned himself as their protector. Terry didn't allow them the freedom that young men deserve, but he, *Ricky*, understood. In fact, he proved it by furtively supplying the twelve- and thirteen-year-old children with marijuana and cigarettes. The constant drilling paid off; Alex and Derek began to distrust their father and instead turn to Ricky.

Two weeks before Halloween, Ricky delighted the boys with decorations. He hung black lights around his yard and rigged an elaborate ghost to fly from a cable on a tree. When the spook came floating down, sheet flapping, and jerked to a halt directly in front of an unprepared victim, the group rocked with laughter. Alex got into the Halloween spirit and asked his dad if he could use temporary spray-on hair coloring. Terry laughingly agreed. They all thought Alex looked hysterical with shiny black hair.

But the festivities didn't last. In the final days of October, the pressure of too many bodies in such a small space began to take its toll, and nerves grew raw. One evening, everyone was sitting in the trailer's tiny living room. Alex was playing video games and Terry grew impatient with the incessant noise. "Alex!" Terry yelled, and shot him the glare children understand without words. Alex immediately lowered the volume.

Terry had no way of knowing that the one word exclamation may have sealed his fate. Hearing Alex reprimanded, something dark and powerful rose up in Ricky. Fighting to suppress his rage, he snatched the keys to his Nissan Maxima and stormed outside before he found himself avenging his young lover.

He screeched onto Palm Court, slamming his fist onto the dashboard and cursing Terry King. His eyes burned with fury as he remembered the look on Alex's face. To him, the scolding was a travesty. He was adamant in believing children should not be scolded, but spoken to as equals.

Ricky sped down Brent Lane to blow off steam, gunning his car to twice the speed limit. After twenty minutes of aimless driving he stopped at a convenience store. Pumping gas with shaking hands, he breathed deeply and tried to relax. Returning home composed but still furious, Ricky walked into the trailer, speaking to no one, and retrieved the keys to his other car.

By the time he returned from his second trip, he was ready to confront Terry. Ricky stepped into the trailer, pointed his finger at Terry and commanded: "You! Outside!"

Terry was completely taken aback. "What's wrong?" he asked. He could see the intensity etched on Ricky's face. Ricky scolded the father for ten minutes. He accused him of being insensitive to Alex's feelings and warned that if he kept it up, he'd destroy Alex's self-esteem. As Ricky ranted, Terry tried to make sense of the fury. Why should Ricky care if he told his own child to behave? All he'd done was call the boy's name. Parents did that all the time. It was *normal*. He suddenly understood that Ricky was monstrously possessive of Alex, and that realization filled him with dread.

Terry said nothing, but knew he and his boys needed to get out. He quietly nodded his head in acknowledgment of Ricky's lecture then returned to his children.

Early the next morning, Terry went to see Lewis Tyson, who immediately agreed to loan him the money he needed to pay his electric bill. On November 1, Terry bid farewell to the trailer and the friendship offered by Ricky Chavis.

The following day, Terry drove his sons to school and informed the front office secretary, Debbie Alltop, that the boys would ride the school bus home from now on. She pulled the boys' checkout card and noted the change. He was relieved Ricky Chavis would never pick up his boys again. But in fact, he had neglected to specifically mention that Ricky was no longer authorized to pick up the boys.

Meanwhile, Ricky was in a blind panic. He worried his clash with Terry had done irreparable damage. The angry father had left with his children, perhaps permanently separating him from Alex. He had to fix things quickly.

Ricky summoned all of his ingratiating charm and phoned Ransom Middle School. He asked Debbie to let Alex and Derek know that he would give them a ride home. In spite of the numerous parents she had dealt with that day, the secretary clearly remembered Terry King's orders. Ricky was stunned to learn that Terry had already arranged for his children to take the bus home.

"Terry doesn't want these boys home alone while he's at work. You know what kids this age can get into," Ricky wheedled, flaunting his knowledge of middle-schoolers. "Terry wants me to keep 'em just until he can get home." Since Terry had neglected to formally take Ricky off of the sign-out list, Debbie relented. She sent a note to Alex and Derek letting them know they would be picked up and should come to the front office after their last class.

The boys were surprised, but said nothing when Ricky strolled into the front office that afternoon. "Your dad decided to have you come to my house until he gets off," he lied.

"Mr. Chavis, we need to speak to Mr. King," Ms. Alltop informed Ricky. "Would you please give him this note?"

"Sure." Ricky smiled, pocketing the slip of paper. It was a request for Terry to attend a conference. "I'll see that he gets it. Let's go, boys," he said, beckoning to Alex and Derek. They hoisted their book bags and followed him outside.

Ricky had no intention of delivering the note. He hoped the school secretary would assume Terry had blown off the conference. With any luck, she would forget about it.

"Whatever you do, don't let your dad know I picked you up today," he instructed the boys as soon as they were out of earshot. "You know how controlling he can be. He's upset and wants to hurt me by keeping us apart. Your father isn't thinking of what's best for you right now." Ricky sighed. "But there's a good reason for that, I suppose."

"What do you mean?" Alex asked, getting into the car.

Ricky cranked up the Maxima and pulled out of the parking lot. "Well, I wasn't going to tell you this, but now I guess I have to," he said, as if what he had to say pained him. "Terry hasn't been honest with you boys."

"He hasn't?" Derek said. The boys looked at each other questioningly.

Ricky shook his head like a reluctant messenger. "He didn't want you to know that he's Derek's real dad, but I'm afraid he's not your biological father, Alex." He paused a moment for the boy to comprehend the words. "Your mother was unfaithful to Terry, and you were fathered by another man."

"That can't be true," Alex said, shaking his head in denial. "Who told you that?"

"Linda Walker told me that. She said your father has

blond hair, not black like Terry's." Ricky added, "If you think about it, Derek looks just like Terry, but you don't." He watched as Alex leaned forward and searched his reflection in the rearview mirror.

"Why wouldn't anyone tell me?" Alex cried in distress. "Why would they keep it from me? Are you sure it's true?" He sincerely wanted to believe the only father he knew hadn't lied to him.

"Why would your grandmother say that about her own daughter if it wasn't true? It's not exactly flattering," Ricky concluded. Aware of the pain he was causing by convincing the boy that he had been deceived his whole life, he pushed on. "Linda told me herself. She said she had seen the guy sneaking out of your mom's house."

He watched as the blood drained from Alex's face. Ricky drove in silence, studying Alex as he quietly looked out the window. He had used the information to wound the boy, and now looked forward to the time when they could be alone together and he could administer his own brand of pain reliever. It was a perfect opportunity to draw the anguished child closer while destroying any remaining loyalty for his father. Ricky assured both boys they could count on him and could stay with him if things got too bad at home.

By the time Terry arrived home, Alex and Derek were there and Ricky was long gone. Terry quickly made dinner for the boys and all three headed for Pace Printing so he could complete his shift. When Terry finally returned home and fell into bed that night, he had no way of knowing that Ricky had slipped in under the radar and dropped a bomb that would devastate his family.

The next morning, a Friday, the King household was running behind schedule. Alex wasn't himself; he seemed absorbed in his own thoughts. By the time everyone was out the door, classes had already started. Terry accompanied Alex and Derek inside to sign the tardy log, then the boys scurried off to class.

"Good morning, Mr. King," Debbie Alltop greeted him. "Did Mr. Chavis give you the note about the conference?"

"What note?" Terry asked, alarmed.

"When he picked the boys up yesterday, I gave him a note and asked him to see that you got it. He assured me that he would."

Terry was furious. "You're telling me that Ricky Chavis picked Alex and Derek up *yesterday?*"

"Yes, he did." She explained that Chavis's name was still on the sign-out card and he had the authority to take them. "Would you like to take his name off?" she asked, pulling the card from her file box.

"Yes, I would," Terry replied. "May I see that?" Scanning the card, he was stunned to see Linda Walker's name listed as "Mother" on Derek's card but not Alex's. Terry had never given permission for the grandmother to pick up the boys. He insisted on seeing the school resource officer and giving him strict instructions that Ricky Chavis and Linda Walker were barred from checking out his children. The deputy assured him that would not be a problem.

Later in the day, Alex's class visited the school library. As soon as the students were set free to browse, Alex moved to the science section, found what he wanted, and took his selection to the checkout desk.

Alex often tried to solve his problems with books, and this one was no exception. He hoped that *Understanding DNA* would help him find out just who he belonged to.

Ricky was desperate to repair his friendship with Terry and continue seeing Alex. He made several efforts to make amends. He dropped by the King home unannounced, offering to repair a broken light pole in the front yard. Before Terry could object, Ricky grabbed a ladder and scurried up to examine the bulb. Terry turned and went back in the house.

Disheartened, Ricky returned home, but he soon had another ploy. Terry had no washing machine. Ricky quickly went to work repairing his grandmother's old one, hoping the peace offering would wash away his problems with Terry. But the determined father showed no interest in rebuilding the friendship. He realized Ricky had gone behind his back to get to his sons, and he no longer trusted him.

Ricky grew more frustrated and again dropped in on the Kings. Terry heard his car and met him outside, blocking Ricky's entrance to the house. Ricky tried to make conversation, but it soon became obvious that Terry had no intention of being cordial. As Ricky was about to give up, Alex appeared on the porch, smiling broadly.

"Hey, Rick," he said grinning.

"Hi, Alex," Ricky replied, trying to hide his pleasure at seeing the boy.

"Come on in for a few minutes," Alex offered. Ricky glanced at Terry and saw his jaw tighten, but he quickly slid past him into the house.

Inside, Ricky and the Kings sat in the green room, awkwardly looking at one another in silence. Terry made no effort to put Ricky at ease, hoping his message was clear: *stay away from my sons*. But Ricky couldn't stay away. He needed to know if Terry had discovered his dark secret. His access to Alex was blocked and he couldn't apply the pressure he needed to maintain the child's silence. Ricky knew if Terry learned the truth, he would be looking at another lengthy prison term. He had to get Alex alone, but getting around Terry wouldn't be easy.

Alex broke the tension. "Let me show you how I've been fixing up my room," he told Ricky.

Ricky hurried after Alex into the back bedroom, ignoring Terry's dark face. As soon as they were alone, he whispered, "I've got to talk to you. I'll pick you and Derek up after school on Friday. Don't take the bus. Meet me out front. Okay?"

Before Alex could reply, Terry was in the room. Ricky knew that his time was up, so he just said good-bye and left. After all, he had accomplished his goal.

That Friday, Ricky was plagued with doubts, wondering if the boys would defy their father. As he joined the long line of cars heading into Ransom Middle School, he frantically hoped Alex and Derek would be waiting for him out front. Inching forward, he scanned the mob of students. He didn't see the boys. Then he caught sight of Alex and felt a flood of relief. He had timed it well. No one would notice him in the mad rush of children eager to get home. As Alex got into the car, Ricky asked about Derek.

"He went back into the school," Alex said. "I'm not sure why. Maybe he had to go to the bathroom or just decided to ride the bus after all."

Ricky worried that Derek's disappearance might be a problem, but he couldn't pass up the opportunity to be alone with Alex. The impatient drivers behind him made it impossible to stall, and he pulled away from the curb.

When Derek appeared seconds later, Alex was gone. He decided he'd better call his dad at work. He told his father that he had missed the bus but Alex had probably taken it home. Terry hurried to the middle school and found Derek waiting alone.

"Sorry, Dad," he apologized.

"That's all right," Terry said, smiling. "I just took my dinner break a few minutes early. We'll stop by the house, pick up Alex, and then grab something to eat."

But the house was locked and empty when they arrived. Terry hurried next door to see Ed Harris, who told him that he'd seen the kids bounding off the school bus but Alex wasn't among them.

The worried father hoped that Alex had also just missed the bus. He slowly drove the four miles back to the middle school, searching along the way, but there was no sign of his son. The school's staff had not seen him since his last class, and Terry immediately suspected Ricky. He stopped at a pay phone, but got no answer at Ricky's trailer. Terry returned home and was just about to call the police when Alex walked in the door.

"Where have you been?" his father cried, overwhelmed with relief.

"I missed my bus and had to run home," Alex said.

Terry knew it was a lie. The boy had been missing for almost three hours and showed no signs of the hike. Terry was convinced Ricky had taken him, but Alex wouldn't budge from his story.

In fact, Ricky had driven him to a nearby field, just across the state line, where the two talked at length. Ricky knew he was on the verge of losing his young lover, but he had hatched a plan to keep that from happening.

He told Alex about Steve Bell, describing how the boy dropped out of school and lived with him for six years, and encouraged Alex to do the same. All he had to do was free himself of Terry, Ricky explained, and he would do his part by helping him hide. Ricky insisted that Derek should come along too. The convicted felon knew better than to leave the unpredictable boy behind to expose his secret. He revealed that he was already making arrangements for Derek to live with the Walkers. As Alex listened, Ricky insidiously reminded him that Terry wasn't even his biological father and was undeserving of the boy's loyalty.

On Saturday morning, November 10, Terry arranged to meet Ricky at McDonald's for breakfast. Ricky was delighted. He hoped the breakfast was an opportunity to heal the rift. His hopes were soon dashed when Terry pointedly asked him about his interest in the children. Eyes wide with feigned hurt, Ricky explained he was motivated by worry for him—Terry, a single father. He sympathized with Terry's back-breaking schedule and told him he could be a great source of help. When Terry didn't comment, Ricky assumed he was considering the prospect and mustered his ample arsenal of charm. He asked Terry to let him keep the boys, pointing out that his schedule was more flexible than Terry's and the free time would enable the financially strapped father to earn a better living. He emphasized that the boys would be happy with him and still have their needs met.

Now Terry knew exactly what Ricky wanted: *his children.* He had recently learned through the grapevine that Ricky had spent time in prison for molesting a child. In a rare moment of confrontation, Terry made it clear that he would never give up his boys.

Alex wasn't himself. He seemed more quiet and sullen than usual and began calling his father "Terry" instead of Dad. When Terry questioned him, Alex shrugged it off, but he was clearly heavyhearted. Terry pushed for answers, and Alex finally revealed that he wanted to be with Ricky. Terry was hurt and alarmed, realizing the problem was more severe than he had suspected.

He spent the remainder of the day in emotional turmoil. Ricky was after his sons and had somehow gained their confidence. He knew Ricky was waiting to pounce.

Terry told his sons they would be moving to Kentucky to stay with their mom. He hoped the lie would convince them that their relationship with Ricky was finished. Alex and Derek were shocked and fired a barrage of questions. How long would they be there? What was their mom like? They didn't know her, the boys cried. Terry was evasive. He also told them that Ricky had invited them over for dinner, an invitation he had accepted so they could say their good-byes. "This is the last time you'll see him," he said firmly.

On Sunday, Ricky was happily preparing for his guests. He hoped Terry was finally warming up to him, but when the Kings arrived, Alex and Terry were somber. Ricky soon understood why.

"We're leaving for Kentucky to stay with our mom," Alex announced.

Ricky was dumbstruck. Terry watched him closely as the news sunk in.

The horror Ricky felt at the prospect of losing Alex momentarily flashed across his face. He regained his composure, but inside the alarms were screaming. *He could not lose Alex. He had come too far to see it all disappear.* He knew he had to act quickly or risk never seeing the boy again. The thought clutched his heart like a cold fist. Terry didn't have a telephone, so Ricky couldn't even sneak a call to the boy. He would have to go behind Terry's back.

When the unsuspecting father disappeared to use the rest room, Ricky herded Alex into his back bedroom. He gave him twenty dollars and two keys to his house. He instructed him to run away from Terry and either call him or a cab. After a short visit, the Kings departed.

Terry was rattled. He knew the only way to keep Ricky Chavis away from his sons was to guard them constantly, but that was close to impossible. In spite of his efforts, Ricky had still found a way to pick them up from school. Monday morning, Terry accompanied the children to Ransom Middle School and informed the administrators that his children were moving to Kentucky. Friday would be their last day.

Later in the day he called Kelly—the name Janet had by now assumed. "I did something you probably won't like," he confessed. "I withdrew the boys from school and told the assistant principal they were moving to Kentucky to live with you."

"Why did you do that?" she asked. She wasn't angry, just curious.

"I'm afraid the boys will tell people I've been abusing them," he replied. "I fought too long to get them back to have them taken away again."

Kelly thought she understood. She knew Terry was afraid that her mother and Jimmy wanted to take the children away from him. In fact, he put a lock on his mailbox after someone started rifling through it. She didn't realize he was having trouble with Ricky Chavis. Always considerate of her feelings, Terry didn't want to upset her.

That week, Terry seldom let his sons out of his sight. He drove them to school every morning and scheduled his dinner break to pick them up minutes after they stepped off the school bus. When the weary father arrived home, the boys were nowhere to be found. They began playing hide and seek, forcing him to walk through the house and call their names until he heard laughter inside a closet or under a bed. After the daily ritual, Alex and Derek accompanied him to work until Terry went home around ten-thirty. Although the situation wasn't ideal, Terry felt it was safer than leaving them home alone.

By Friday morning he was ready to relax. He wearily

poured a cup of coffee while waiting for Alex and Derek to emerge from their bedroom. "Hurry up, boys," he called. We need to leave in five." Terry heard his sons talking quietly in the back bedroom.

Derek appeared in the kitchen and asked, "Dad, what time will you be home this afternoon?"

"Between four-forty and five," he answered. "You and Alex just come in the house and lock the door. I'll be right behind you."

"Okay," Derek said, and headed to the car. Alex followed him outside, and Terry stopped to lock the house. Ten minutes later they pulled up to the school and the boys tumbled out. Derek poked his head back in the window and asked Terry again, "What time did you say you'd be home?"

"A little before five," Terry reminded him. "Have a good 'last day.' "

That afternoon, when the bell signaled the beginning of the weekend, children poured out of school and made a mad dash to their buses. The uproar was always worse on Fridays. Alex and Derek found their seats and exchanged knowing glances. This was their last chance to change their minds. They trusted Ricky and thought he was only looking out for them. As they exited the bus, Derek told the kids he and Alex wouldn't be seeing them anymore. They were heading to Kentucky.

As soon as they arrived home, the boys sprang into action. The clock was ticking; they knew their father was due home in less than an hour and they would only have enough time to pack a few essential items. They took backpacks and knives and an item they felt was absolutely indispensable. It would turn out to be a monumental clue to their father of their whereabouts.

* * *

When Terry walked in the door a few minutes before five o'clock, he hollered, "I'm home, guys." Hearing no answer, he assumed they were hiding. He stepped into the kitchen and put on a pot of coffee. "You can come out now," he called over his shoulder. There was no answer.

He was lost in thought as the coffee machine sputtered. Pouring himself a cup, he pushed the door open and stepped out onto the porch. The yard work he and the boys had done was paying off. The shrubs looked healthy and the flowers in the recently planted bed were beautiful. He smiled to himself and took a sip of the steaming brew. After a few minutes, he went back inside the house to get his sons in gear.

"Let's go, boys," he called out, walking through the house. He was greeted with silence. He opened the bathroom door and pulled back the shower curtain. The stall stood empty.

Terry walked down the hall calling their names, feeling apprehensive. The game had never lasted this long. Quickening his pace, he strode down the hall, peering in each room and shouting his sons' names. "This isn't funny, boys. I want you to come out now," he called. Nothing. He ran through the house searching behind doors and under furniture. The moment he stepped into his own room he froze; someone had broken into his locked filing cabinet. The drawers stood open and papers were scattered around the room. He quickly flipped through the files, looking for his sons' records.

They were gone, and so were his children.

His heart jumped frantically in his chest and his hands began to shake. He fought to keep control as his mind spun through a series of possibilities. He knew his sons wouldn't care about their birth certificates. But he knew who would.

He began to search for other clues. What else was missing? He noticed his knives and the boys' backpacks were gone. That was strange. The boys' Sony PlayStation was also missing. He instantly knew his sons weren't hiding in the woods. They needed electricity for their video games.

Terry sprinted to his next door neighbor's yard, scanning the street for any sign of his children. He bypassed the front door, ran into the carport and frantically pounded on the screen door. Ed Harris appeared, but before he could speak, Terry blurted, "My kids are missing. Have you seen them?"

Ed shook his head. "No, I haven't seen them today at all." He was concerned about his distraught neighbor. The man looked as though he were falling apart. "Why don't you come inside and tell me what's going on?"

"Someone took my kids," Terry exclaimed, sitting down at the kitchen table. "And they also took some very important papers. My filing cabinet was broken into and some things are missing."

"What kind of papers?" Ed asked.

"My boys' birth certificates are gone. So is my diary."

Ed was puzzled. "Who would want those things?"

"The Walkers are the only ones who have a reason to want that stuff," Terry said firmly. "They're the grandparents who have been trying to get custody of Alex and Derek. I know they took the boys. It had to be them."

"Why don't you just go over there and get them?" Ed asked hotly. "Just put your foot down and tell them that they better butt out and let you raise your own kids." Ed didn't understand the soft-spoken father's demeanor. "If they had my kids, I'd kick the damn door down!"

Terry shook his head sadly. "If I go there, they'll kill me," he said quietly. He locked eyes with Ed. "They *will* kill me." Terry King wasn't given to drama, and Ed felt strangely convinced that his neighbor believed what he was saying.

"Well, what are you going to do?" Ed asked. "How can I help you?"

Terry King and Janet French were very happy early on in their relationship. He was 21 and she was 17 when they first met in 1986. *Courtesy of Linda Walker*

Derek and Alex with their parents. Terry and Janet's romantic relationship had ended by this time and she was pregnant with another man's twins.

Courtesy of Linda Walker

Two-year-old Alex and three-year-old Derek enjoy a day on the playground during the brief time they would live together. In just a few short years these same faces would become the focus of an international media frenzy.

Courtesy of Linda Walker

Ricky Chavis in his beloved Monte Carlo. He found that cars were a convenient way to cruise for potential victims.

Courtesy of Mike Chavis

Ricky Chavis, demonstrating the wanton attitude that made him popular with his teenage followers.

Courtesy of Mike Chavis

Ricky Chavis met Officer Reggie Jernigan in 1980 when Chavis was incarcerated in Escambia County Jail and struck up a friendship that would last more than two decades. The deputy is pictured here during one of his frequent visits to the convicted child molester's home.

Police Photo

Mollye Barrows reporting on the courthouse lawn in downtown Pensacola. Her assignment on the crime beat set her on the trail of the King story.

Courtesy of David McElfresh

Shy and hard-working, Terry King was happiest in the company of his children, family, and close friends. *Courtesy of Greg King*

Alex stands proudly with his father. The two enjoyed a close relationship until Ricky Chavis entered their lives. The pedophile drove a wedge between the father and son while plotting to keep Alex for himself.

Courtesy of Greg King

Fire ravaged Terry King's humble home in Cantonment, Florida, the night he was murdered. The heaviest damage was in his back bedroom, where the fire was started.   *Courtesy of Greg King*

Though Terry King was killed by violent blows to the head, fire-fighters discovered him in a relaxed position in his recliner, with his feet propped up and a full cup of coffee balanced on his hip.
Police Photo

A child's blanket and pillow were found on the couch next to the recliner.   *Police Photo*

Mike Chavis gives reporter Mollye Barrows a tour of Fort Chavis. His brother Ricky spent countless hours in this junkyard repairing vehicles for friends.   *Courtesy of Kathryn Medico*

Ricky Chavis's living room was a potent lure for young boys, with video games, a large screen TV, a stereo, and mirrored walls. Security cameras and monitors allowed the pedophile privacy to pursue his sordid lifestyle without the interference of prying eyes.

Courtesy of Mike Chavis

Mike Chavis peels back a rug, exposing the trap door leading to a concealed room beneath his trailer. This was one of many dark secrets Ricky Chavis hid from police.

Courtesy of Kathryn Medico

During the year that they awaited trial, Alex, 12, and Derek, 13, were held in the adult section of Escambia County Jail. Alex was so small he was still losing his baby teeth, and neither boy was allowed to sleep on a top bunk for fear he might fall off.

Courtesy of James Stokes

Jimmy and Linda Walker never missed a single visitation with Alex and Derek during their incarceration in Escambia County Jail.

Courtesy of Linda Walker

Derek King was a cooperative student but was permitted only one hour of school instruction per day during the year he spent in Escambia County Jail. If he and Alex had been tried as juveniles instead of adults, they would have received the standard school schedule.

Courtesy of James Stokes

Derek King's attorney, Sharon Potter, is a nationally ranked cross-country equestrian. Her demanding schedule finally forced her to trade trails for trials.

Courtesy of Kathryn Medico

James Stokes *(right)*, the attorney for Alex King, and his best friend, John Johnson, in their ultralight airplane. *Courtesy of Allison Johnson*

Dennis Corder was an avid skier. He and his wife frequently vacationed across the U.S. and Europe to hit the slopes. His suicide in 2003 was a shock for many.

Courtesy of Donna Corder

Prosecutor David Rimmer addresses a crowd on the courthouse lawn and defends his decision of trying the King brothers and Ricky Chavis for the same murder only one week apart.

Courtesy of Kathryn Medico

Herb Helton testifies about the devastation Ricky Chavis's criminal influence wrought in his life.

Courtesy of Kathryn Medico

Ricky Chavis looks on as his attorney Mike Rollo fights the lewd and lascivious and kidnapping charges. Chavis faced more than 170 years in prison if convicted.

Copyright 2003 Digital Film Dynamics

Alex King, the victim in Ricky Chavis's trial for child molesting, was brought into the courtroom in prison attire and dragging leg chains. Although he asked that the courtroom be cleared, he was made to testify to the humiliating details in front of a packed courtroom with cameras rolling.

Copyright 2003 Digital Film Dynamics

"Can I borrow your phone?" Terry asked. He still had no telephone service at his house.

"You sure can," Ed replied, happy to have some small way to help. "As a matter of fact I'll leave a phone out in the garage for you. Then you can get to it even if I'm not home."

"I appreciate that," Terry said.

"Use it as much as you like. Long distance or otherwise," Ed said.

Terry's first call was to the Escambia County Sheriff's Office. Within fifteen minutes a deputy was at his house filling out a missing persons report for Alex and Derek. Terry insisted the children weren't at a friend's house, but he suspected they might be with their maternal grandparents.

The deputy looked up. "And what are their names?" he asked.

"Linda and Jimmy Walker. They live close to here on Williams Ditch Road."

The deputy told Terry they'd check it out.

"I'm worried about their safety," Terry insisted.

The officer noted his concerns and left to log the report in his computer. Within minutes Alex and Derek were the subject of a BOLO—a "Be on the Lookout"—and their names joined many others on the national and state registries for missing children.

Chapter 17

RICKY KNEW HIS ACTIONS WITH ALEX AND DEREK WERE wrong. He realized that Terry King would be frantic with worry, but he didn't care. He wasn't thinking about what was right, he was focused solely on his obsession with Alex.

Ricky Chavis was a master of deception who had painstakingly set himself up in a double life. Outwardly, he displayed admirable traits: hard work, generosity, a willingness to help others. He invested much of his time doing favors for people, hoping to divert attention and suspicion away from his dark secrets.

He was amazingly skilled at adapting his mannerisms to fit the situation. While talking with rural folks, he would kick his accent up a notch. He became pious and stripped his vocabulary of curse words when dealing with the devout. He was particularly crafty with endearing himself to teenagers, peppering his speech with their modern expressions and mirroring their trends. In his living room he hung a sign that depicted the popular characters of South Park and read, CARTOONS KICK ASS! But that level of deception was child's play to Ricky; his cunning ran far deeper.

He moved into the realm of world-class when he became a registered police informant. He installed a police scanner inside his trailer and quickly set about doing auto repairs on police cruisers. This gave the convicted felon an incredible opportunity to endear himself to deputies and access information otherwise outside his reach. Finally, he had Reggie Jernigan park his patrol car in the front yard. Anyone even remotely concerned about Ricky Chavis would immediately relax when they saw that comforting sight.

Like many child molesters, Ricky was staging an elaborate production: setting the scene to look innocent, playing the role of benevolent neighbor, all the while secretly assaulting children.

Pedophilia has been around throughout history, but it took a giant leap forward with the introduction of the Internet. This horrendous world could be conveniently accessed with a keyboard and a search bar; the pedophile need only type in "Boy Love" to be instantly hooked into a society devoted to the predatory abuse and exploitation of male children. There, he could visit the site for NAMBLA—the North American Man/Boy Love Association—where a pedophile could feel right at home among friends. Formed in 1978, this organization sought to legitimize sex with children and strongly opposed age-of-consent laws. Theoretically a sixty-year-old man could have sex with a three-year-old boy, so long as it didn't turn violent.

The website included a publication called "Prisoners' Letters," where pen pals were encouraged to provide moral support to "incarcerated boy-lovers." This newsletter depicted prison as a harsh and hostile environment that could do damage to a molester's self-concept. Contributions and visits were encouraged, to help keep the poor fellow's spirits up.

But if large organizations didn't suit the Internet cruiser's tastes, there were 3,860,000 smaller sites, like the Underage Boy Love Site, which boasted naked preteens in a shocking picture gallery. Another website cultivated still younger victims and encouraged, "Sex before EIGHT or it's too late!"

In the long dark tunnels of cyberspace, the child molester

could finally express his most profound dreams and receive reinforcement from others who shared his perversion. This sense of comradery was a giant stamp of approval persuading the pedophile that the sexual exploitation of children was a good thing and that he was part of a broad-minded movement of enlightened people. Calling themselves "boy-lovers," they believed historians would look back and shake their heads at society's extreme oppression and narrow-minded views. But even the most delusional pedophile had to admit that those days were light-years away. Members of this clandestine club knew the dangers of exposure all too well; to continue to enjoy sex with children, they had to be fanatically secretive and constantly covering their tracks, for in spite of their passionate affirmations about their acts, it was still among the most serious of crimes.

However, Ricky Chavis had never been concerned about being a lawbreaker. After picking the boys up, Ricky drove them to Harold Smith's house. Smith was a friend he had known for many years who lived in the neighborhood. Ricky felt it was a safe place to stash the children in the event Terry King became suspicious and dropped by his trailer.

Ricky told Harold that Alex and Derek had run away from their abusive father and needed a place to stay for a few hours. Harold was reluctant to get involved in the family dispute. He had met Terry and Alex at Ricky's house on several occasions and couldn't recall anything worrisome about the father-and-son relationship.

Sensing his reluctance, Ricky quickly embellished the story, describing Terry as an unpredictable tyrant who beat his children with a belt for no reason and showed partiality to his older son, Derek. He lamented that Alex had even resorted to coloring his blond hair black in order to resemble his older brother and win his father's attention. In reality,

Alex had applied the spray-on color with his dad's approval for Halloween fun. But twisting the truth was Tricky Ricky's specialty.

Harold Smith finally relented when Ricky told him he and Reggie were trying to get help for the boys. Invoking Officer Jernigan's name convinced Harold the story was true, and he agreed to keep the children for a few hours.

With the boys safely deposited at Harold's, Ricky returned home and immediately called—Reggie Jernigan. Next, Ricky called the Sheriff's Office and learned Terry had filed a missing persons report. Four minutes later he called Reggie back with the news. Ricky knew Terry would suspect him, but his uniformed friend was the perfect cover. He asked Reggie to come right over, realizing that the deputy's presence would help defer suspicion.

Ricky was ready with a benign smile when Terry soon appeared at his door. Reggie was there, along with Mike. They said nothing as the frantic father fell apart before their eyes.

"Are the boys here?" he demanded, looking around for any sign of his sons.

"No, they aren't. Why?" Ricky asked, feigning innocence. "Didn't they come home from school?"

"Yes, but now they're missing. Do you know where they are?"

"I have no idea," Ricky lied smoothly. "I'll be glad to help you look for them," he offered. He chatted with Terry, although the worried man was still on edge. Unable to convince him with mere words, Ricky excused himself and went to use the rest room. This gave Terry a chance to furtively look around and satisfy himself that Alex and Derek weren't there. Ricky needed to send the troublesome father on his way so he could get down to business.

Terry was convinced either Ricky or the Walkers had

stashed his sons. "I'm going to go back up to the house in case they do show up," he said reluctantly.

"Well, don't worry too much," Ricky soothed. "I'm sure we'll find them." Terry turned and looked Ricky straight in the eye. Ricky's gaze never wavered as he added with a sympathetic nod, "It's going to be all right." His practiced concern melted into a self-satisfied smile as the heavyhearted father turned and walked away.

As soon as Terry left, Ricky ordered a pizza and went back to working the phones. Over the next few hours there was a flurry of calls between Ricky and the Smith house. *Sixteen*, to be exact. The boys wanted to go to Ricky's trailer, but he wasn't ready for them yet.

By ten-thirty that night Harold Smith was ready for bed. He asked his daughter to keep an eye on the children and said good night. At four in the morning Alex and Derek were tired of waiting and decided to leave. Harold's sixteen-year-old son "Bubba" walked the younger boys to Ricky's place. Although it was only four blocks away, the teenager knew drug dealers and criminals frequented the neighborhood, and he insisted on getting Alex and Derek there safely.

Early Saturday morning, on November 17, sheriff's deputies rolled to a stop in front of Linda and Jimmy Walker's small house. Rather than knocking on the front door, the two officers walked around to the backyard. Jimmy Walker, who had seen them pull up, met them outside and introduced himself.

"What can I do for you?" he asked, shaking their hands.

"We're looking for Alex and Derek King," they explained. "Are they here?"

"No, they are not," Jimmy said firmly. "Their mother called and told us that they had run away, but they're not here. I wish they were. You are welcome to come in the house and search. Look anywhere you want."

"That's okay," the officer said, declining the invitation. "Do you have any idea where they might have gone?"

"No," he said. "I have no idea."

Ricky smiled to himself; the boys were "home." While Terry King spent a sleepless night anguishing over his missing children, Ricky slept peacefully, knowing that Alex and Derek were tucked away in his high security compound. He awoke late Saturday morning and embraced the day with a smile. Now that he had successfully reached his first goal, it was time to work on the second: diverting attention away from himself. He piled the boys in his car, careful to hide them. He pulled down the backseat and they slipped into the trunk. With the backseat folded down, they could still see and talk to him, but when he wanted to hide his precious cargo, a flip of the seat would make them disappear from view.

He decided to make it look like the boys were staying in Pace, Derek's old stomping grounds. The plan supported the illusion that the boys were hiding in the woods, and made it appear that Derek had masterminded the runaway.

Ricky spotted an empty stand of pay phones near a Tom Thumb convenience store. He parked and glanced around the parking lot to make sure he wasn't noticed by a familiar face, then deposited some coins in one of the phones and dialed his home number. He motioned to Alex, who scrambled out of the car and took the receiver. Ricky scanned the store. In the event he was caught with the boys, he planned to say he had just found them.

"Hey, Rick. This is Alex," the boy began. "Me and Derek are doing fine. Don't worry about us." He looked at Ricky for further instructions.

"Say you're not coming home," Ricky whispered.

"Oh, and we're not coming home," he concluded. He looked up at Ricky for approval.

Ricky smiled and winked at the boy, then hung up the phone. "Perfect." he cooed.

Ricky was delighted with his craftiness. The message was sheer genius. As soon as he and the boys returned to his trailer, he pushed the play button on his answering machine and was greeted by Alex's familiar voice. Ricky was pleased with his convincing, manufactured alibi.

While he worked to hide his treasure, Terry was busy trying to find it. Joyce Tracy was a wonderful source of strength for her son. Though appearing tiny and delicate, she was tough and feisty. She devoted every waking moment to helping Terry locate Alex and Derek. Together they made and distributed posters of the missing boys.

Back at Fort Chavis, the children were trying to convince Mike Chavis to let them play video games. He had been watching television, but reluctantly allowed them to take over. Ricky settled into his worn recliner. His bliss was interrupted by a movement on one of his security monitors. The camera that aimed at his front gate was displaying a visitor. Terry King had come calling.

"Hurry, boys!" Ricky exclaimed. The boys dropped their game controllers and Ricky rushed them into the laundry room. He peeled back the carpet and quickly lifted the trapdoor. Alex and Derek dropped down into the hole Ricky had prepared for such occasions. Alex found the lamp and turned it on, flooding the tiny room with light. "Y'all be real quiet," Ricky directed as he closed the trapdoor and slid the carpet back into place. He then stashed the game controllers and opened the front gate for Terry.

"Any sign of the boys?" Terry asked, stepping through the front door. The worried father was standing only a few feet from his sons, huddled under the trailer.

"You better sit down, Terry. Alex called and left a mes-

sage on my answering machine," Ricky said, watching
Terry's face grow hopeful.

Alex's boyish voice filled the room.

"Check your caller ID. Where did they call from?" Terry
asked, enormously relieved to know that his sons were okay.

"Looks like they may be in Pace," Ricky said. "The phone
number starts with 983, and that's the exchange for that area."

"Well, Derek does know his way around there," conceded
Terry. "Play it again. It sounded like Alex was outside. I
could hear cars. I bet they were at a pay phone." Ricky re-
wound the message. "Did you catch someone else's voice in
the background?" Terry asked. "It sounded like someone
was telling him what to say."

"Must be Derek," Ricky said smoothly. "Let's write down
the number and see if we can find the pay phone. Then we
can narrow down the area they're in." Terry agreed with the
plan and the two men left to "locate" the phone.

Ricky didn't like it when Terry showed up at his house
unannounced, forcing him to scramble. He decided to lend
Terry a two-way radio. That way, Terry would think his
friend was helping him locate the missing boys, when in reality Ricky would be able to keep better tabs on him.

Terry was in torment. He was convinced that the phone
call from Alex had been planted, but he didn't know if it was
Ricky or the Walkers working to deceive him. If the Walkers
had driven the children to Pace to plant the call, why did
they have Alex call Rick Chavis? He wondered if they were
all collaborating.

Adding to his misery, Terry knew that whoever had his
children also had the keys to his home. He decided that it
would no longer be safe for him to sleep in his house. He put
a pillow and a blanket in his car. Fearing for his life, Terry
King drove to the T & W Flea Market and spent the cold
November night shivering in his car.

* * *

Terry regularly updated the boys' mother throughout the week. They were both convinced the Walkers had their children, and Kelly constantly called her mother, asking that she return them to Terry.

"We do *not* have the boys," Linda protested. "We wouldn't do that."

"But you must know where they are, Mom," her daughter pressed. "Otherwise you would be insane with worry. You don't even seem concerned," she insisted.

"Of course I am worried, but I just don't show my emotions like you do," Linda explained.

Terry King's life couldn't get much worse. His spent his days searching for his missing sons, but his evenings found him hard at work at Pace Printing. Although his income was meager, the job was his lifeline and he couldn't afford to lose it. He repeatedly called Ricky on his dinner break, desperately hoping for good news.

Ricky was not interested in restoring Terry's sanity; he only wanted the freedom to keep Alex without fear of discovery. He hoped to convince Terry to drop the missing persons report, but realized it wouldn't be easy. He told Terry that the report could lead to trouble if the children told police Terry abused them. The officers would have to file child endangerment reports and Terry would be investigated. These days, children could be removed from their parents for the slightest reason, Ricky explained. It would be better if they could find the children themselves, he urged. Terry agreed to think about it.

The next morning, Terry worried that Ricky was right. If the police found his boys and were convinced they were abused, it would open a can of worms. The Walkers could fight him for custody, and he didn't have the money for a

court battle. Each day, he drove slowly past the Walkers'
home to see if he could catch a glimpse of Alex or Derek.

On Thursday, Thanksgiving Day, Terry King had little to
be grateful for. Instead of enjoying a nice turkey dinner with
his loved ones, he spent the day scouring Pensacola in
search of his sons. He complained to the *Pensacola News
Journal* and Channel 3 News that his boys were missing and
the Sheriff's Office was doing little to find them.

His weary journey ended at the T & W Flea Market,
where he took part in a Thanksgiving cookout hosted by the
merchants. After dinner, Terry decided to sleep in his car at
the flea market. He was too fearful to return home.

Thanksgiving Day was much more enjoyable for Ricky
Chavis. He accepted an invitation to dine at the home of his
old partner in crime, Lonnie Early. Both men had served jail
terms for molesting Tommy Penton and Mark Watkins, and
they still remained friends. Ricky knew the young King boys
would be welcome at the convicted child molester's home
but said nothing about how they came to be with him.

Ricky had much to be thankful for. He was living his
dream; he had a prepubescent boy of his own and a perfect
place to hide him. Thanks to his ingenuity, everything was
going smoothly and he was relaxing in his new life with his
twelve-year-old lover. He no longer bothered to hide the
physical relationship. Derek saw him hold Alex on his lap,
fondle and French-kiss him, but Mike Chavis says he didn't
see anything inappropriate. Though Derek never said a word
to Ricky when he took Alex into his bed, he had become a
witness who would later pose the greatest threat to Ricky's
freedom.

Meanwhile, Terry was making the rounds, telling everyone
he knew about his missing boys. He felt that the more eyes

he had watching, the better his chances of finding them. On Friday he stopped by a friend's business. She already knew of the boys' disappearance and asked him about the search.

"I know who has my boys," he told her. "I'm going to go get him, because he's not a good person."

"What's his name?" she asked. "Is it anybody we know?"

"No," he replied. "And it's not anybody you want to know."

"Terry, you be careful," she cautioned. "Why don't you get the police to help?"

"I've tried everything I can think of to get them to help. They just don't seem to care about finding my boys."

His next stop was the T & W Flea Market. He bought a camouflage jacket from one business and told the owner, "I'm going hunting for my kids." He was also tired of his sleepless nights in the car, and the day after Thanksgiving he changed all the locks in his home. He then called Kelly and told her that the boys were still missing.

"You sound exhausted," she said. "Are you okay, Terry?"

"No, I'm not," he admitted. The phone grew silent. After a moment he quietly said, "I'm going to have some news for you Tuesday, maybe sooner."

Kelly was worried. "Tell me what you're talking about," she pleaded.

"I don't want to say anything yet, but I'm going to have some news for you." She didn't understand the intrigue and quizzed him further, but Terry refused to say more.

"I'll tell you when I call," he said. "Will you be at home?

"Yes. You call me any time day or night." She was anxious to help him, but realized he was stressed and not yet ready to talk. She was overwhelmed with sadness for Terry and felt compelled to apologize for causing him pain in the past. She wanted him to know that she knew he was a good man. The kind words were comforting to Terry. Kelly would later be glad that she had not let the opportunity pass.

After a week of confinement in the small trailer, Derek was growing restless. He had not brought his ADHD medication to the trailer and his high energy level was beginning to wear on his roommates. When he asked Ricky to drive him to Pace to visit a friend, it was the perfect opportunity for a breather.

Ricky dropped Derek at his friend's house, where the boy soon excused himself, saying he had things to do. With nowhere to go, Derek began walking toward his old neighborhood. Then he remembered a girl he knew from school who lived a few doors down from his former foster parents. Although he didn't know her very well, he did like her. Derek walked the mile to her house and rang the doorbell.

The teen was surprised to see her former schoolmate. Derek told her the Lays no longer wanted him and he was now a runaway from his real father, along with his brother Alex, who had planned the venture. He explained that their father was controlling and refused to let them watch television or play outside. In contrast, Derek told the girl, his father's friend Ricky was accommodating. He was allowing them to stay at his house, where they could smoke marijuana and skip school.

A half an hour later Derek called Ricky's house looking for a ride, but there was no answer. As he started to leave, Frank and Nancy Lay arrived, summoned by his friend's parents. Derek immediately realized he was in trouble and began to run. When Frank caught up with him, Derek was wild-eyed and agitated.

"What's going on? What are you doing, Derek?" asked Frank. "You can't keep running. We need to take you home."

"I don't want to go back home," Derek cried. "Please don't make me go back to my dad's." The Lays noticed that Derek seemed to be salivating excessively and kept spitting into the grass.

"What's wrong with you, Derek?" Nancy asked in alarm. She wondered if he was taking drugs. She and Frank exchanged worried looks.

"Let's just calm down and talk about this. We'll figure something out," Frank assured him. The couple's daughter was visiting with her three children, so they decided not to let Derek stay overnight with them. The boy was beside himself.

"We're not going to send you back home," Frank assured him. "But the law is looking for you, son. You're running from the law right now. The legal thing for me to do is to call the police. We'll let them know you're okay."

"But I'm supposed to meet my ride back up at the store," Derek protested.

"Well, your ride is helping you to avoid the law, and that's illegal," Frank said.

"But I've got to go," Derek begged.

"Derek," Nancy said. "The police will take you to a safe environment, a halfway house, so you won't have to worry about anything. And Monday we'll get involved and see what we can do."

The Lays called the Santa Rosa Sheriff's Office and a deputy was dispatched. En route, Deputy Leonard Thomas punched Derek's name into his computer and immediately found the boy listed as a runaway.

"Thank you for coming, officer," Frank said, shaking his hand. "This is my wife, Nancy, and this is Derek." The Lays briefly explained Derek's relationship as an ex-foster child, and told Deputy Thomas how the boy had been recently returned to his father because of disciplinary problems.

"Where have you been staying?" Frank asked the boy.

Derek shivered as the four stood in the Lays' front yard on the cold November night. "We've been staying at Rick's house. He helped us run away. He's trying to get us away from our dad," Derek explained.

Frank and Nancy were instantly alarmed. "How old is this guy, Derek?"

"He's my dad's age," Derek replied.

Frank immediately suspected foul play. "Now listen," he said, choosing his words carefully. "You're a pretty smart boy. What's the deal here? An older man wanting to do this for you guys? And he's doing it behind your dad's back?"

Derek hurried to explain that Ricky let them play games and it was fun. He said his dad wouldn't let him play outside.

The deputy was also growing suspicious. "Has this man ever abused you sexually or touched you inappropriately?"

"No," Derek replied.

The Lays insisted that the deputy write down Ricky Chavis's name and address. "There's something wrong with a man who's forty years old, not married, and he's befriending all these children," Frank told Deputy Thomas.

"I know what you mean," he responded.

"I don't want to go back home," Derek said. "My dad is playing mind games with me."

"It can't be that bad, Derek," Frank said. "Alex has lived there with him all these years."

"Alex hates him. He'd like to see him dead," he said offhandedly.

No one took the comment seriously; they thought it was just boy talk. And even though it aroused no concern to Derek's former foster parents and a sheriff's deputy, the innocuous statement would be later twisted into "a *plan* to kill Terry King" and used as a weapon to try to convict

Derek and Alex. In his deposition, Deputy Leonard Thomas stated that no one ever said there was a plan to kill Terry King.

Frank turned to Derek. "Son, you call me," he said. "Wherever you wind up, you call me and I will get back with you Monday."

In spite of Frank and Nancy's pledge that Derek would not return home, within the hour deputies ignored their advice and delivered Derek to his father.

Derek was relieved to find that his father was happy to have him back rather than angry. He didn't reveal where Alex was. Ricky had made it clear that if anything went wrong, he was not to be blamed.

Derek told his father that he and Alex had been camping out in the woods at Pace. Terry immediately drove there to search the woods on the cold November night. Unable to find Alex, Terry began knocking on doors in the nearby neighborhood hoping someone had seen him. He had no way of knowing his child was warm and cozy behind the walls of Fort Chavis.

While waiting in the car Joyce asked Derek about his reason for running away. His explanation made little sense.

"I don't know, really," Derek told her. "I guess I want to ride my bicycle more. Dad won't let me ride my bike in the highway."

Derek also revealed that he no longer wanted to attend school. As the new kid, he was constantly tormented. Joyce wasn't satisfied. She was convinced someone had taken them. She talked with Derek at length and found that despite those few complaints, he seemed quite happy with his father.

Meanwhile, Ricky was coming unglued. Earlier that evening he had driven to Pace to pick up Derek but the boy was nowhere to be found. He was terrified someone had spotted the runaway and picked him up or perhaps Derek decided to betray him and go back to his father. He hoped it was only a mistake and Derek would soon call.

With growing fear Ricky realized the boy's disappearance was a big problem. Derek knew a lot of secrets. Derek had seen him caress and kiss Alex. He had also seen his brother sleeping in the same bed with him. Ricky had smoked pot with the boys and had hidden them under the trapdoor. And technically, he was guilty of kidnapping. If Derek exposed those secrets to Terry, Ricky knew he would go back to prison for life.

It was just a matter of time. Terry would be enraged if he learned that his sons were hiding right under his feet each time he had come to the trailer. But worse still, when Terry discovered that he had been molesting Alex, he would go to the police. No doubt about it; he was on his way back to prison for a long time. Panic seized him.

Ricky took the same action he usually did when the stresses of life became too great to bear; he fired up a joint and called Deputy Reggie Jernigan. He wanted to know what the cops knew. He also called Linda Walker to step up the pressure, telling her how much he hated for Derek to go back to his abusive father.

"There ain't no tellin' what Terry's going to do to him," he said. He knew his final declaration would push her over the edge: "Terry told me that he's going to give Derek away again."

Linda Walker was shaken. Although she was usually in bed before ten o'clock, she couldn't possibly sleep now. Concerned that Terry was mistreating her grandson, she called the Department of Children and Families to file a child abuse report. She begged the report taker to find out why her grandchildren had run away and gave a grim account of the ordeal they had suffered throughout their lives. She added Ricky Chavis's name as a reliable source for more information.

After midnight Terry called Ricky on the two-way radio and told him that Derek was home. Ricky held his breath, wondering if Terry was on to him.

"The cops picked up Derek in Pace," Terry told him, "but I'm still looking for Alex. Can I come by?"

"No," Ricky said. "I'm going to bed." Maybe Terry didn't know the truth. Yet. Derek was a loose cannon; it was only a matter of time before the capricious boy said the wrong thing and sent the cavalry charging to Fort Chavis. They would storm his trailer, rip open the trapdoor, and find Alex's small face peering up at them. It could happen at any moment. He knew that in the morning he would have to send Alex home to deal with Derek. The boy's assignment would be damage control.

Sunday morning, November 25, was crisp and cool, and Terry King greeted it with optimism. He had the feeling that this would be the day he would find Alex and finally have both of his boys home and safe. But it wouldn't be easy.

At one o'clock that afternoon Joyce Tracy was scouring Pace in search of her grandson when Ricky called her cell phone and asked if she had found Alex. He was relieved to learn Joyce and Terry were still in the dark.

"Well, I'm on my way to help you look for him," he lied easily, arranging to meet her at a Tom Thumb convenience store.

Once in Pace, he phoned her again, this time with good news: he had found Alex! A few minutes later Alex was reunited with his grandmother. Since Terry wasn't there, Ricky suggested he and Alex run across the street to McDonald's to get Alex some lunch while Joyce waited for Terry and Derek to arrive.

Alex and Ricky were leaning casually against the car when Terry pulled into the parking lot. Terry jumped out and approached the pair, but Ricky met Terry before he could embrace his son and pulled him off to the side. Alex greeted his grandmother and then quickly slid into Terry's car with Derek.

Terry was cold, but Ricky was determined to maintain a relationship. "Why don't you and the boys come by for dinner tonight?" Ricky begged. He expected Terry would interrogate the children, and he wanted to know what, if anything, Terry had learned by dinnertime.

"All right," Terry said.

Ricky wasn't sure he would show, but he wasn't too worried. He already knew that he would see the boys again that night.

On Sunday afternoon Denise Aue, an investigator with the Florida Department of Children and Families, pulled into the driveway at 1104 Muscogee Road. She had been assigned the case when Linda Walker's complaint hit her desk. Denise had the responsibility of attempting to make contact within twenty-four hours of a complaint.

She parked in the grass driveway, assessing the condition of the small wooden home. There was a well-maintained flower bed neatly surrounded by a small fence. The child abuse investigator walked around to the front, noting the porch was adorned with a flag, a God Bless America sign, and Christmas greenery on the railings. She knocked on the front door and waited, but no one answered. Since there was no car in the driveway, Denise assumed no one was home and she wedged her business card in the door. She had twenty-four hours to make another attempt to talk with Terry King.

By then he would be dead.

Chapter 18

MOLLYE WALKED IN THE DOOR OF HER SMALL APART-
ment and was suddenly surrounded by her cats. She flipped
through her mail, mentally prioritizing the good stuff from
the junk. A plain white envelope caught her attention; it bore
the name *Ricky Chavis*, via the Escambia County Jail. This
letter quickly moved into "open first" status.

Ricky opened politely: "I hope this letter finds you in
good spirits." His handwriting was neat and legible on the
plain white paper. "I'm doing alright considering where I'm
at." He then went on to share his impatience over his im-
pending court date, wishing to get it over with.

Mollye was surprised to read that Ricky already knew the
murder and arson charges would disappear, but was uncertain about the accessory after the fact indictment. The reporter wondered just how he "knew" those things, and made
a mental note to review his prediction after the verdicts.

He invited her to ask any questions. Even from his jail
cell, Ricky was still hard at work trying to control the flow of
information. He had drawn a painstaking floor plan of Terry
King's house. Sitting down at her kitchen table, Mollye flat-
tened out the page to examine it.

Scanning the layout, she noted Ricky's meticulous attention to detail. He included closets, furniture, and even the

hot water heater. The hand-drawn layout showed his intimate knowledge of the home flawlessly burned into his brain.

While Ricky fought for freedom, his friend Reggie Jernigan was also struggling to get his job back. He did not take the dismissal quietly. He had no intention of giving up his hard-earned career and subsequently losing his retirement benefits. He filed a petition with the Escambia County Civil Service Board to have his position reinstated.

In his request, Reggie admitted his friendship with Chavis showed poor judgment, but he believed the discipline was excessive. He blamed the administration's change of heart on the press. The thrust of his defense was based not on his own actions, but rather, the fact that other officers were guilty of the same violations. "Should I have been fired for something so many do?" Reggie begged.

The deputy's "don't blame me when everybody else is doing it" argument did not fall on deaf ears. The sheriff reluctantly put Reggie back to work in court security. Although he did not receive back pay for the months he was fired, his retirement benefits remained intact.

The community was outraged. Letters to the editor of the *Pensacola News Journal* denounced the sheriff's decision. Many were suspicious of the officer's involvement with a convicted child molester and believed Jernigan did not belong on the force. But Mollye knew of one person who would be pleased with the administration's change of heart.

Stepping out of her apartment and into the brutal August heat, Mollye headed back to the Escambia jail for another Sunday visit with Ricky, intending to weed out some morsel of truth. Obviously Ricky was possessive of Alex, but would he have resorted to murder? She was determined to find out. In the visiting area, Ricky was in his usual state of self-pity.

"I let my hair grow out a little, and damn it, I have gray hair! Before I got locked up I had no gray at all." He was relieved that Reggie was back at work. The news gave him hope that his freedom might also be restored as easily as his friend's job.

Ricky told Mollye it would be best if he didn't discuss the case, then immediately began talking about it. Once again he was careful not to implicate himself, but his obsession with Alex gave him away. Ricky was very critical of Terry's abilities as a father.

His voice was tight with anger as he told Mollye about an incident when Terry yelled Alex's name while they were all living in his trailer. Infuriated that Terry would take such an attitude with the boy, he confronted him, but according to Ricky, the abusive father not only rejected his advice, but his friendship as well. Although the argument took place months ago, rage underscored Ricky's every word.

Mollye was spellbound by the fury she saw still burning in his unnaturally bright eyes. She could feel heat crawl up her neck, and resisted the urge to break eye contact. He spun the story to make himself look caring, but Mollye had a different take: he didn't want *anyone* messing with *his* baby. Her suspicions were confirmed. He was abnormally, perhaps murderously, protective of the boy.

As if realizing his mistake, Ricky's demeanor abruptly changed. The enraged convict instantly became the friendly, harmless bumpkin. His outrage disappeared behind a wide smile and he began talking animatedly about happier times he had enjoyed with his brother Mike. Mollye was stunned at the sudden transformation. Before long, visitation hour was over and she rose to leave. Ricky reminded her to wait in the parking lot until he could wave from his cell.

As she drove away, Mollye grabbed her miniature tape recorder and began dictating the details of her conversation with Ricky. Like a camera coming into focus, she saw a clearer picture of the events that led up to Terry's death. The key to his murder appeared to lie in one word: Alex. Terry shouted the boy's name in a moment of parental frustration, and Ricky's reaction had set a chain of events in motion.

Terry had also withdrawn from Ricky after the confrontation. That piqued the reporter's interest. If the angry father shut him out, she realized, Ricky had far more to lose than just a casual friendship. She remembered, then, that she'd heard something about Ricky's falling out with Terry. Had Ricky talked to the investigators about it?

As soon as she arrived home she pulled out the heavy file containing Ricky's police statements. Thumbing through them, she found not one, but *three* references to the argument. Each time Ricky mentioned it and began to describe how angry he was, the deputies moved on, missing the opportunity to learn more about the clash. They seemed fixated on the children's guilt and dismissed the possibility that Ricky may have been motivated to kill Terry King.

In one statement, Ricky said he never saw Terry physically abuse the children; however, he did tell them, "The only major thing I seen was that one incident in my living room where he yelled, and it—"

He had been interrupted by John Sanderson before he could elaborate. "Yeah okay," Sanderson said.

But Ricky pushed on. "I mean it was loud."

"Right," Sanderson acknowledged.

"And I . . . I couldn't understand why he got on to Alex that night," Ricky continued. "I couldn't understand it."

The investigator attempted to move Ricky beyond this topic, only to have him return to it immediately. "But then when I noticed, when that incident happened in my living room, that raised concern, and I got upset with that."

Yet again the deputies missed his cue. Mollye noted that Ricky clearly told them how upset he was. In fact, he couldn't let the subject go despite their disinterest. Why didn't they ask him about it? How did the fight affect his relationship with Terry? Why did he care so much about remaining close? Mollye realized that Ricky must have been desperate to repair the friendship and stay close to Alex. She pulled out all three of Ricky's recorded statements and found the incident mentioned in each one. She removed those pages, highlighted the lines, and taped them to the wall. The pages read:

> . . . *and I got upset* . . .
> . . . *and I got upset with that* . . .
> . . . *and that bothered me.*

Mollye wondered if this angry altercation had begun the countdown to Terry's death.

Chapter 19

BEFORE THE TRIALS WERE SCHEDULED TO BEGIN, Sharon Potter and Dennis Corder arranged for Derek to meet with a mental health expert. Clinical psychologist Dr. Ron Yarbrough had a thriving private practice in Pensacola and had testified in numerous cases throughout his career. He first met with Derek, then later listened to his taped confession to police. After two sessions he was ready to share his findings with David Rimmer, Mike Rollo, and Derek's attorneys.

Dr. Yarbrough informed the attorneys that Derek's IQ was 123, meaning that he was smarter than ninety-three out of a hundred children in a random sample. The psychologist also provided fascinating insight into Derek's inner world. "I asked him for five wishes. Number three was that his mother and father would get back together again. And that's just unbelievable to me that somebody with his IQ would not realize that his daddy and mama didn't love each other; but that's his fantasy. That he could have a good family."

David Rimmer asked about Derek's feelings for his mother.

"He didn't say much about his mother because he doesn't know her," Dr. Yarbrough responded. "He said that he's kind of mad that she hasn't spent any time with him, but it seemed to be an afterthought, not a consciously burning thing. He wanted a picture of where she lives in Kentucky and her husband."

Although Derek desperately longed for a family, he seemed to only hold out hope for a relationship with his brother. "What he believes is that Alex and he will be together forever," the doctor remarked. "He thinks like a little boy and not like a teenager. And the little boy says, 'Alex and I will be together,' and that's his family."

Dr. Yarbrough moved on to discuss the feelings Derek had about himself. "I think he's got a poor self-concept," he observed. "He doesn't have a lot of attention. He's a small boy, although he's a very good-looking young man." Dr. Yarbrough had asked Derek, "Do you ever bully others?" and Derek had responded, "I couldn't ever bully anybody. I'm the littlest guy around."

The psychologist laughed remembering something decidedly *big* about Derek: his appetite. "You know this kid, for a little bitty skinny guy, loves to eat," he recalled. "He ate like a machine when he was in here. He ate five cupcakes at our second meeting." Sharon Potter smiled. The Derek she knew was always hungry.

"Do you have an opinion as to whether or not his confession is truthful?" David Rimmer asked. With the lack of physical evidence, much of the case hung on Derek's statement to police.

"My opinion is, it is *not*," the doctor replied, then explained his conclusion. He described his first office visit with the boy. "Derek is playing with this, touching that, and chattering constantly. His reaction time between questions is zero. He answers quickly and usually interrupts before the question is asked," the doctor explained. "When I heard the taped confession, I said, 'This is not like Derek at all.' There was one section that was forty-eight seconds, where he was trying to respond and formulate an answer. That is not Derek King. The amount of words and type of words that he used were not typical of what I would consider anything that Derek would produce."

He pointed out the confusion in Derek's description of how his father was killed. "There are questions where he's saying that he hit his daddy on the right side of the head, and the officer then comes back and said, 'Oh, I thought you said you hit your daddy on the left side of the head, but you're patting your right side. Was it the right side or the left side?' which to me it appeared to be leading. I believe he botched even what he tried to go over, because the plan was too intricate."

Mike Rollo wanted to know more about the plan. "Let me ask you: did he ever specially tell you that Rick Chavis sat him down, grilled him with the details of what went on inside the house, and said this is how it's got to be, you've got to say this? Did he ever give you any statements saying I had a skull session with Rick Chavis and this is how it went?"

"Yes, sir," Dr. Yarbrough replied. "He specifically said, 'We practiced for two days.' "

"Did he ever tell you how he could be convinced to confess to a homicide that he did not commit?" the attorney continued.

"Yes, sir," the psychologist answered. "There were a couple of components to that. One was that Ricky said that if they used the abuse thing, that they would get out in three weeks and that it would be self-defense and that nothing would happen to them and they could live with him and could do whatever they wanted to, smoke dope or whatever."

"Did he have any reflection on that now, any hindsight ability to look at that now as a poor plan or not very well thought out?" Rollo asked.

"Yes, sir. He said, 'Not at the time but now six, eight months in jail, I think it's a real stupid plan.' And he is angry about participating in it, and angry about Rick."

The psychologist said he and Derek had discussed the night of his father's death. "He told me that he didn't commit a crime," he recounted. "He told me that Ricky came to pick he and Alex up, and that Alex had made arrangements for Ricky to do this and left a back door unlocked. And that Ricky came in after his dad was asleep and they snuck out. He looked at his dad, who was sitting in the chair. He said nothing there was unusual. His dad had a coffee cup in his hand, and then they left and went out in the trunk of the car and they stayed out there for a while, and then they left and went to Ricky's house and I believe he said they stopped several times on the way to Ricky's house."

"Did Derek tell you why he was with Chavis when they ran away?" Rimmer asked. "I mean, did he say that he wanted to be with Chavis?"

"Yes, sir," the doctor replied. "He wanted to be with his brother, and his brother wanted to be with Chavis. He clearly was very, very excited about being with Alex, and seems to still be excited, even in jail, about being with Alex," he explained. "He wanted to be with his brother, and there were other things that he got to do at Ricky's that he never got to do at his dad's. So he enjoyed those, as well."

Dr. Yarbrough stated that Derek was a very bright young man but one who had a severe and difficult case of attention deficit hyperactive disorder.

"Would his impulsiveness and his hyperactivity play a part in him making a sudden decision to kill his father with a baseball bat, if in fact he killed his father with a baseball bat?" David Rimmer wanted to know.

"If he were to have killed his father, it would have been more like a crime of passion, a reactive event instead of a planned thing, but he's never shown any history of kicking a dog or slapping a dog or of even pushing a dog away," he observed. "And the best predictor of future behavior is past behavior."

Between visits, Dr. Yarbrough had spoken at length with Frank and Nancy Lay, seeking background information about their experiences with Derek. He told the attorneys that the Lays felt Derek was very compassionate, that he was kind. Nancy told him her foster son would worry about her if she was sick, and she remembered that Derek would sit and stroke the family cat for hours. Frank also said that Derek was extremely good with their grandchildren, who were toddlers; he thought it was unusual that an adolescent Derek's age would be willing to play with little kids. "He really liked doing that," Frank had said. "And it was him being a little kid himself."

The psychologist explained Derek's thought processes: "His thinking is immature, scattered, it's just not cohesive and goal directed. Derek is in *the now*. He is not a leader. This intricate plan of where they were hidden and the runaway, there's no way this could have been concocted, in my opinion."

The deposition had not provided much help for Mike Rollo's defense of Ricky Chavis. The attorney invited the doctor to add anything he wished before he wrapped up. "Did you reach any other conclusions?"

The psychologist reflected on the time he spent with Derek, then chose his words carefully. "Basically, that he didn't have the capacity to plan and use forethought, as would be required to have carried out the complicated acts involving murder."

PART FOUR
ON WITH THE SHOW

*"A lie can travel halfway around the world
while the truth is putting on its shoes."*
Mark Twain

Chapter 20

THE SHACKLES AROUND RICKY CHAVIS'S ANKLES FORCED him to take baby steps as he made his way through the tiny courtroom. He was wearing a green prison jumper, his arms clasped together at the wrists with handcuffs. He smiled nervously at the guards who watched him, before taking a seat in the small jury box. Scanning the room for a familiar face, his eyes finally settled on Mollye Barrows, seated on the press bench behind him. Ricky's trial was scheduled to start in just three days. His attorney, Mike Rollo, had requested a hearing to have the murder charge dismissed, and Mollye was there to cover it along with several other local reporters and photographers.

He and Mollye exchanged the familiar smiles of acquaintances, and Mollye noticed the other journalists casting curious glances her way.

"How are you?" Ricky asked quietly.

"Fine," Mollye answered. "And you?"

"Okay," he said, shrugging his broad shoulders like a doubtful little boy. A local newspaper photographer was watching closely. Ricky then lifted his shackled arms chest high and crossed his fingers, a small, hopeful smile on his face. The photographer's camera was clicking wildly when the judge walked to the bench.

Mike Rollo argued that the first degree murder charge

against his client should be dropped because the prosecution was presenting competing theories of the same crime. At issue was the King brothers' statements to the grand jury. Mike said the boys' original confessions and later testimony to grand jurors were at odds and the State should not be allowed to present both versions. Rollo questioned the State's plan to argue that *both* Ricky and the boys murdered Terry King.

David Rimmer insisted he intended to argue that only Derek had actually swung the bat, but he agreed he did have some concerns. Jury selection for both murder trials was looming ahead, immediately following the weekend.

"I don't know what to do," Rimmer told the court. "This has bothered me for quite some time. I've got some things in my own mind I'm thinking about." He seemed bewildered. "I'll make a decision before the weekend. I want to do the right thing. I don't want to prosecute anyone that's not guilty."

The hearing also gave the media its first tantalizing glimpse at the boys' grand jury testimony. The court allowed Rollo to discuss it in order to argue his motion.

Reporters scribbled furiously, taking down the highly coveted details of the previously sealed statements. Alex and Derek had told grand jurors they waited outside while Ricky Chavis had beaten their father to death with a baseball bat. Alex also revealed that Ricky had been molesting him for months and that the fear of losing him spurred Ricky into his murderous actions. Despite Rollo's argument, the judge ruled that Ricky's case was headed to court.

The Chavis story led Channel 3's newscast that night and headlined the *Pensacola News Journal* the following morning. Mollye shook her head in amusement when she picked up the paper and saw Ricky's picture, front page center. The accused murderer and child molester looked out at the reader, crossing his fingers in a hopeful gesture above his handcuffed wrists. Mollye knew he had been smiling at her. She wondered if he would still feel like grinning after his trial.

Monday morning, 140 Escambia County citizens were packed into a large courtroom at the M.C. Blanchard Judicial Building. Attorneys hoped the potential jury pool would provide enough people who would impartially evaluate both trials, untainted by pretrial publicity. Whittling down the numbers would be an all-day process. David Rimmer, Sharon Potter, and James Stokes began by describing the cases. They explained to the crowded courtroom that the trials would follow back-to-back, and as a result of extensive media coverage, the attorneys had already agreed to keep both verdicts sealed until each trial was finished. They were concerned the outcome of one might affect the other.

Shortly into the polling process, the attorneys discovered they weren't the only ones asking questions. Once the potential jurors understood the premise of the cases, some had queries of their own.

One middle-age man stood up in the crowd and looked at Rimmer. "On this sealing the verdict on Chavis? Are they all three charged with the same crime, of killing this man?"

"Yes," Rimmer answered firmly.

"So if Chavis is convicted of doing it, how could the boys have done it?" All eyes turned to Rimmer. Even the masses, relatively uneducated in the intricacies of legal analysis, had already honed in on the phenomenon that would continue to plague the State's case.

"Remember when I was telling you about being a principal?" Rimmer said. "Remember the illustration I gave you? Two guys robbing a convenience store, one guy goes in with a gun, the other guy is driving the getaway car. If somebody is helping somebody else commit a crime—"

The inquisitive man interrupted. "Even though Chavis has done it, you're saying that they were principals to it, even if they didn't actually commit it?"

"Well, I can't comment on the evidence," Rimmer said, "but, I mean, that's a legal thing that would be up to you to decide. It would be up to you to decide whether or not you feel that Derek and Alex were the actual perpetrators, or Derek was the actual perpetrator and Alex was only there encouraging him, or vice versa. See, that's the legal concept of being a principal." Rimmer decided to wrap up the conversation, and turned quickly to another query.

The attorneys eventually moved into a much smaller room, where they individually polled potential jurors, three at a time, about their ability to judge the case fairly. Several members of the media attended, including Mollye. She paid particular attention to Derek and Alex.

When the boys walked into the room, they were immediately drawn to a large window overlooking a nearby parking lot. They gazed with wide-eyed awe at the cars below, riveted by a flashy Camaro and a shiny Corvette. The brothers faced the possibility of life in prison; no first date, no high school prom, an existence isolated from the outside world, and yet a set of wheels and buff coat of paint caught their attention better than the hearing at hand.

Alex, oblivious to the seating protocol, plopped down in a chair and wound up sitting next to Judge Bell, never realizing he was positioned next to the most powerful person in the legal process. Derek sat next to a hefty court security officer, who separated him from the press, but it didn't stop him from teasing the deputy or smiling at the reporters.

The questioning took several hours. Alex listened and even participated in the process, but occasionally he leaned back in his chair, swiveled and stared at the ceiling. He was neatly dressed in khakis and a gray button-down shirt with a sharply pressed collar. Derek also appeared like he was dressed for Sunday school, in a blue and white striped shirt, blue tie, and navy blue pants. He looked over at his brother, then turned to the officer beside him and spoke with a smile. "Alex looks good in a tie, he's been in that jumpsuit."

While Alex and James often consulted about particular jurors, Derek had a more difficult time concentrating, obviously battling with his attention deficit disorder. He couldn't stop fidgeting with his hands, his clothes, or his chair. In fact, he questioned Sharon Potter about the mysterious handle on his chair, unaware that it adjusted height. She promptly informed him that it was an ejection seat. Derek contained himself for an hour, then curiosity got the better of him. He tapped his fingers on the handle, then finally gave it a firm pull. When his chair dropped a notch instead of catapulting through the ceiling, Derek snapped his head to look at Sharon and grinned broadly.

The potential jurors filing in and out of the room also watched the boys with curiosity. Many said they had seen some media coverage of the case but had no opinion. Some admitted they had already made up their minds about the crime. Others felt they simply could not be impartial, fearing sympathy for the children would affect their decision.

"It would bother me," said a father of two sons. "I don't . . ." He looked at Derek and smiled, then finished in a faltering voice. "I just couldn't do it."

One woman doubted she could set sympathy aside. "I look at those boys and I have grandsons that age," she said, walking away with wet cheeks. She wasn't the only one.

Another woman was also too upset to answer questions. "They brought tears to my eyes when I first came in," she said in a choked voice.

The boys watched the proceedings with interest, but appeared relatively unaffected by the swell of emotion around them. Derek continued to playfully torment the deputy beside him. He tapped the officer's shoe with his own foot and continued to whisper, until the guard put his fingers to his lips and gave the boy a good-natured gesture to hush. The day was wearing long for them all.

They went well into the evening, the attorneys finally seating a jury of six to hear the brothers' trial and choosing twelve others to decide if Ricky Chavis murdered Terry King. They would begin hearing evidence in a matter of hours.

The man who had once thrived on being the center of attention with his young followers squirmed under the unblinking media eye. He was overwhelmed by publicity and self-pity as he was transported to the courthouse the morning his murder trial began.

The M.C. Blanchard Judicial Building was ground zero for the press. News trucks, cameras, and television reporters competed for space on the courtyard as the State prepared to try Ricky Chavis for the death of Terry King. Court TV crews were busy erecting a tent, in an attempt to keep their court reporter from sweltering during her live reports in the late August heat. Mollye was amazed at the transformation. Her local stomping grounds had become a temporary campsite for every major network, as well as print and magazine reporters. She joined the crowd of spectators filing into the courthouse.

Upstairs, people packed the hallway leading to the courtroom where the proceedings were to be held. Many were divided into camps. Terry King's mother, Joyce, and his brother Greg huddled close to one wall with a friend from church. Farther down, Terry's father, Wilbur King, sat with his wife. Across the hall the boys' mother, Kelly Marino, was surrounded by a much larger crowd, including her mother, father, stepparents, and their extended families. Mike Chavis and a number of witnesses who apparently knew each other stood quietly apart, looking subdued and wary. Derek's foster parents, Frank and Nancy Lay, sat talking to the investigators. Unconcerned with boundaries, television and newspaper reporters mixed and mingled within the groups, attempting to cultivate relationships they hoped would blossom into revealing interviews.

Mollye hurried upstairs, her black bag loaded with notepads and makeup swinging heavily against her leg. She squeezed into the crowded courtroom and took a seat on the packed media bench.

Ricky looked as persecuted as he felt. He slouched in his chair in an olive gray suit. He attempted to joke with the deputies in the courtroom and occasionally smiled nervously at the reporters who were quietly assessing him. His efforts to appear friendly backfired; his decaying dental condition had left his smile in shambles, similar to a jack-o'-lantern. Mollye knew Ricky had been encouraged since the summer jail visit he received from Mike Rollo and David Rimmer. According to Ricky, the prosecutor had told him that he, himself, did not believe Ricky to be guilty. However, that had been two months ago, and Ricky was once again terrified at the possibility of a murder conviction.

Stokes, Potter, and Corder sat in the back of the courtroom. They suspected this trial could possibly be a dress rehearsal for the prosecution's case against the King brothers, and they wanted to know what Rimmer had in mind for their clients.

Judge Bell and the jury soon entered the room, and the attorneys began their opening statements. Rimmer strode be-

fore the jury and introduced himself with his usual composure, but he was noticeably lacking in enthusiasm. He outlined the details of the heinous crime, the boys' confessions
to the police, as well as their relationship with Ricky
Chavis and their father. Although his delivery was typically
brief and to the point, his words were uninspired, as if he
were going through the motions. There were no passionate
pleas for justice, no earnest gestures made to emphasize
disgusted accusations that Ricky was a conniving murderer; in fact, he only pointed the finger at the children
whose trial had not yet begun, at least technically. He told
jurors there was no question Ricky was involved in the
murder, but they would hear testimony that it was Alex who
had a "plan" to kill Terry King, because they preferred
Ricky's company to their father's. The prosecutor made it
clear that the King boys had lied to the investigators, but he
failed to mention that Ricky Chavis had lied in every one
of his interviews, depositions, and recorded statements to
the police, even admitting to some acts of deception that
were designed solely to protect himself from trouble with
the law.

"You listen to all the evidence," Rimmer advised the jury.
"It's going to be up to you to decide whether or not Ricky
Chavis was involved in the murder of Terry King, or
whether or not he had no involvement in that murder whatsoever. It's going to be up to you. That's all I've got to say."

Mollye was not surprised at his curt remarks, subtly
damning the brothers. She remembered a conversation she
had with the prosecutor earlier that summer concerning the
case. He fervently believed the children were guilty of murder and jokingly told her he was convinced that if he snuck
into Derek's jail cell at night and gently pulled back his hair,
he would find 666 forged into his scalp.

Essentially, Rimmer and Mike Rollo were fighting toward

the same end—to assign blame to the King boys. Rollo's dramatic accusations in his lengthy opening arguments echoed the prosecutor's belief. The defense attorney promptly accused Alex and Derek of the brutal beating, saying Alex had plotted the murder and Derek helped execute the plan. He called their testimony to the grand jury, which accused Ricky of killing their father, the "new and improved story." Derek, he adamantly told jurors, was an unfeeling psychopath who constantly lied, stole, manipulated, and caused problems both at home and at school. He insisted that the evidence—specifically the boys' confessions—would show the children were the killers and his client was just a man with good intentions who was caught up in a bad situation.

"He had no motive to kill Terry King, who's been described as eccentric, strange, odd, reclusive," Rollo said. "Was he concerned about the way that Terry was treating his children, especially since Derek came back? Yes, he was. Did he want to see the boys prosper? Yes. Does it make any sense to think there would be any evidence to suggest that he would want to kill Terry King in order to rescue the boys?"

Ricky quietly listened, like a saint with his halo glowing brightly.

Reporters listened in rapt attention as the State called a string of witnesses who described the fiery scene in which Terry's brutalized body had been found.

State Fire Marshal Investigator Kevin Fiedor testified that the brothers' shoes had been sent to a state laboratory for comparison with cans of accelerant taken from the scene. Although the test results showed that the chemical found on the shoes was not the one used to start the fire, Rimmer did not tell the jury this. The crime scene analysts had carefully collected clothing and shoes from the boys, but Ricky's clothes and shoes were never taken for testing.

Leonard Thomas was called to the stand. The Santa Rosa County deputy had met Derek when he had been picked up in Pace by Frank and Nancy Lay. Thomas testified that the Lays told him Derek was very upset and had pleaded with the officer not to send him home. Rimmer had few questions for Thomas, except to ask the deputy about Derek's demeanor and if he found a lighter in Derek's pocket, a discovery Thomas had made.

Rollo moved in dramatically. "Were you present when Derek King admitted to the Lays that *he* and Alex had a plan to kill their father?"

"No, sir," Thomas answered. Thomas knew the words had not been spoken. Derek had said, "Alex hates him. He'd like to see him dead." But somehow the phrase had become a "plan to kill Terry," which was far more indicting. Rimmer also planned to use these words himself when he prosecuted the boys.

Technically, Ricky was the one on trial for her son's death, but Joyce Tracy realized her grandsons were the focal point, and she made a staunch effort to defend them when she was called to the witness stand. The sixty-six-year-old woman looked crisp and credible in her pink dress suit, flower lapel pin, and high-collared blouse. Her skirt dipped conservatively below her knees, and she wore perfectly shined patent leather shoes on her tiny feet as she daintily approached the stand. A courtroom deputy took her hand and gently assisted her up the two steps into the witness box. The petite woman was the epitome of "Grandmother," but she was candid and refused to be swayed by Rollo's attempts to paint her as biased.

"Okay. Now you recognize it's pretty significant whenever Alex told you that Derek killed his father? I mean, that's a significant statement, isn't it?" He was referring to her conversation with Alex at the juvenile detention center shortly after his arrest.

"I didn't take it that he meant Derek killed his father," Joyce replied.

"That's what he said," Rollo insisted.

"I didn't say he killed his father."

"That's what Alex said," Rollo replied.

"No."

"Is there some misunderstanding here? I thought you just told us that you visited Alex at the jail, and you asked him who killed Terry King, your son, and he said Derek."

She drew her diminutive frame up straighter and looked the defense attorney in the eyes. Her voice rose slightly. "He said, 'Derek *and*. . . . ' "

"Yeah," Rollo replied, "and he didn't say anything else. He said Derek, didn't he?"

"And," she said stubbornly.

"He said Derek, D-E-R-E-K, Derek, did he not?"

Her voice rose again, "Sir, he said, 'Derek *and* . . .''

"And we'll never know what that means?"

"But he did say the word."

Joyce had the last word on this issue. Rollo was unable to put words in her mouth, but he did make his point with the jury. Rimmer could have stopped Rollo from repeatedly asking the beleaguered grandmother the same question, but he remained silent. After all, she would be his witness again next week.

Mollye rushed out of the courtroom and headed for the live truck. Her deadline for the midday report was coming up fast and she still had to log sound bites. Downstairs, her photographer was already setting up his shot on the lawn of the Judicial Center. Mollye hopped into the truck and began the tedious process of tracking down the ten or fifteen seconds of sound that she would include in her story. She went through several tapes before transcribing the testimony she wanted. Mollye wrote a general recap of the morning's events on a legal pad while the photographer edited and fed video back to the station. The two enjoyed the cool air-conditioning of the truck before reluctantly getting out into the August heat. Then she stood before the camera, waiting for her on-air cue. She turned to the camera as the opening sounds of the newscast rang in her ear.

"Attorneys gave opening arguments this morning," Mollye recounted. "The defense says Alex and Derek King are cold-blooded killers. The State is asking jurors to decide if that's true. . . ." By the time Mollye finished her broadcast, the trial broke for lunch. The reporter was impatient for the hour break to end when she learned the State's next witness was Alex King.

Chapter 21

THE COURTROOM WAS SILENT WHEN THE SIDE DOOR opened and the small boy walked in. He looked like a child of nine or ten, rather than thirteen. Mollye watched Ricky's face intently as Alex approached the witness stand. His eyes were riveted to the boy. The jurors also watched Alex as he made his way to the witness stand in his green jumpsuit, handcuffs pinning his tiny wrists. Mollye was stunned to see him wearing the restraints. She had covered plenty of other trials where convicted adult criminals had been allowed to testify without shackles. She wondered if the State truly considered this eighty-five-pound boy a risk, or possibly hoped to imply that this child was a threat to society.

Alex took a seat in the witness box and dropped his eyes to the floor. Cameras clicked furiously when the boy raised his shackled hands in an attempt to swear his oath before the court, the handcuffs appearing larger than his arms. The boy was also forced to face the graphic pictures of his father's bloody, beaten body. The crime scene photos were propped up directly in front of him, and although Alex looked down most of time, periodically he would stare at the pictures for a few moments and shake his head almost imperceptibly, as if in denial or shock.

Rimmer was quick to let jurors know Alex was also

charged with first degree murder. He was abrupt with the young prisoner, handling Alex as if he were a liar, instead of his key witness against the man who was supposed to be on trial.

"Do you know Ricky Chavis?" Rimmer asked the boy. Alex locked his eyes to his hands folded on the bench before him, answering yes. The prosecutor then asked him to identify Chavis. The handcuffs forced the child to raise both hands. He looked up long enough to point to Ricky Chavis and immediately dropped his head.

Rimmer then began a brutal line of questioning that helped jurors understand Alex's relationship with Ricky Chavis. He was curt as he asked Alex if he had once believed he was in love with the forty-year-old man, and systematically produced one love letter after another that Alex had written to him. The boy answered each question politely, looking embarrassed.

"Did you write this?" Rimmer asked, displaying one of Alex's notes.

"Yes, sir."

"What does it say?"

" 'I love you, Rick,' " Alex read, his voice barely above a whisper.

"Is this your handwriting?" he asked again, and insisted the boy read it aloud.

Alex looked up long enough to take the paper. " 'Alex David King loves Ricky Marvin Chavis so much, always and forever.' " His head dropped again. The process continued for well over a dozen letters.

Rollo objected. He didn't want all the letters entered into evidence for fear the jury would see the extent of his client's relationship with the child and realize his possessiveness could be a motive for murder. Judge Bell overruled Rollo's objection.

The prosecutor continued with his barrage of questions on Alex's childish love letters. "In that note did you say at the end of it, 'Before I met Rick I was straight, but now I'm gay'?"

"Yes, sir."

"Why did you think you were gay?"

Alex hardly moved, refusing to look up. "Because Rick had told me that." The boy said he had a sexual relationship with Chavis that began before his father's death, but Ricky had hidden it from Terry. As he testified about the details, including how often and where they had been intimate, as well as his desire to live with Ricky, Alex's quiet voice became even softer.

"Why did you want to be with Rick?" Rimmer asked.

The boy's voice grew almost inaudible. "Because I was in love with Rick and—because of the different—like he let me play video games and stuff, like he had game machines. It was funner over at his house, I guess."

"Alex, when you were at Ricky Chavis's house, did he ever give you any marijuana?"

"Yes, sir."

"How did you feel about your dad at that time?"

"I don't know. I love my dad." But Alex admitted that he did call his dad by his first name when he was angry.

"Now, after you ran away on November sixteenth and you were reunited with your dad and your brother on Sunday, November the twenty-fifth, did you have a conversation with Rick Chavis over in Pace in Santa Rosa County that Sunday afternoon?"

"Yes, sir."

"What was that conversation about?" Rimmer asked.

"He took me over to McDonald's and told me to like make sure like we were home at twelve o'clock so that he would pick us up, told me to make sure the back door was unlocked."

Alex described what they did during the hours before his father was murdered. He said his dad went into the "green room" while he and Derek went into their room to play board games. Then, Alex said, he began to set Rick's plan into motion.

"I went to the bathroom—I unlocked the back door, used the bathroom, came back to our room. And me and Derek waited there for a while. Derek fell asleep and—Rick came in our room and he told—woke Derek up and told us to be quiet." Alex said Ricky then had them wait in his car. They folded down the backseats and crawled into the trunk, where they hid until he returned.

"Okay, so you and your brother get in the trunk. Where was Rick at that point?"

"In the house, I believe."

"Okay. Then what happened?" Many of the jurors leaned forward as the boy continued.

"We waited there for a while and he got—I heard him get in the car and asked us if we were all right and we said yes, and he started the car."

Alex said Ricky told them what happened after they returned to his trailer. "Well, he took us inside, said that there had been a fight, said there had been an accident, and said that my dad was dead. And then he said that he'd—he said that he had done it for us and like he—he said that our dad would have killed us before he would let us go live with him."

"Did Rick want you to come and live with him?"

"Yes, sir."

"When you got back to Rick's house that night, did he wash your clothes?"

"No, sir."

"Did Rick tell you how the fight happened?"

"Well, he said that he was—that he had done it to protect us, but not really."

"Did he give you any details at all?"

"Yes, sir. He said that a bat had been involved."

"Did he tell you where he hit your dad with the bat?"

"He said in the head." The Court TV camera zoomed in tight on the boy, while reporters scribbled on their notebooks. This was the first time the public had heard his own account of the crime. He revealed that Ricky had kept him and Derek at his home for nearly two days, convincing them to take the fall for their father's murder, before he turned the children over to investigators.

"What did Rick Chavis say?" Rimmer asked.

"Well, he wanted us to take the blame for it 'cause we could get off with like self-defense and he knew police officers that could back us up and he told me—us—a story and kept going over it."

"What story did he tell you that he kept going over?"

"I don't remember it too well but I had been—like I had been thrown, like my dad had thrown me across the room or something and like Derek had killed him to protect me."

"So Rick Chavis told you to tell the police that Derek had thrown you across the room?"

"Yes, sir."

"And that Derek had killed him to protect you?"

"Yes, sir."

"Now is that what Rick Chavis had told you to tell the police?"

"Yes, sir."

Mollye shook her head in amazement as she took notes. Ricky claimed that he "only wanted to help" the children, but he had wasted little time delivering the boys into the hands of the Sheriff's Office. If they had been guilty, a friend who was genuinely concerned would have taken the boys to an attorney, who could maneuver them through the legal system and work out a deal that was in their best interests. But Ricky, a convicted felon, didn't do that. He had made a career of criminal behavior as well as avoiding the consequences. Through Ricky's efforts, law enforcement had focused on the children, deflecting any suspicion from him.

Alex testified that Ricky called his friend Deputy Reggie Jernigan to pick them up and bring them to the Sheriff's Office. Once they arrived, they recited the tale Chavis had given them. Rimmer appeared to grow more annoyed with the boy as he stubbornly stuck to his story. At one point he asked the child if he had ever deliberately hurt himself while he was in jail.

"Yes, sir," Alex answered quietly.

"Why were you doing that, Alex?" Rimmer demanded.

"Because it was colorful."

"Colorful for whom?" Rimmer asked.

"Me."

"Why did you want to be colorful? Did you think it would help you when you testified?"

"No, sir."

There was a long pause. Long enough for people in the courtroom to wonder why the prosecutor had pursued that line of questioning and why the court allowed the prosecutor to proceed in his blatantly hostile examination of Alex. Ricky didn't need Mike Rollo. He had David Rimmer on his side.

"And it's your testimony that Rick Chavis killed your father?" the prosecutor finally asked.

"Yes, sir."

Finished with his questions, Rimmer returned to his seat. Alex was motionless on the stand while he waited for Mike Rollo to take over where Rimmer had left off.

Glasses and suit in place, Rollo interrogated Alex with disdain. "Before your testimony today, you met with your attorney all weekend, didn't you?"

Alex responded that he had.

At the back of the room, James Stokes realized where Rollo was going. The defense attorney intended to imply he had coached the boy on what to say on the stand.

"All day Saturday, all day Sunday until late in the evening; isn't that true?" Rollo pushed.

"Yes," Alex said.

"Your attorney is James Stokes?"

Strokes was practically hopping in his seat, itching to come to his client's defense. He glanced at Rimmer, who was taking notes as if he had no intention of interfering.

"He became your attorney shortly after you confessed to killing your father, did he not?" Rollo continued. "And when he first met with you, he told you not to make any other statements or talk to anyone about what you—"

Stokes's tall, lanky frame was suddenly towering above the seated crowd. *"Objection!"* he said loudly, his voice tempered with a hint of caution. He walked slowly toward the bench, fully expecting to be reprimanded.

Judge Bell turned to him in surprise. "Mr. Stokes, this is not your trial," he said, then looked at Rollo. "We've got a problem here. Mr. Rimmer is representing the State and you're representing Mr. Chavis. Mr. Stokes is representing the witness, but not in this trial. Obviously those types of questions are, I think, sort of lawyer/client privilege. I don't want to inject myself into a role here, but who's—" Judge Bell turned to James. "Mr. Stokes, I guess since he's your client—"

"I object," Stokes repeated. "This is attorney/client privilege."

"It seems pretty obvious to me," Bell agreed.

Rollo defended his question. "I think the question can be asked under the law, and if there is an assertion of privilege that's made at that time . . ." He looked at Rimmer, who remained silent. ". . . apparently Mr. Stokes is making it." Rollo was merely stating the obvious, but the remark spoke volumes. Stokes had to object because Rimmer certainly wasn't going to do it.

The judge sustained Stokes's objection, and the former Marine lumbered back to his seat, surprised and relieved he hadn't been tossed out of the courtroom.

Rollo turned back to Alex and rephrased his question, asking the boy if Stokes had been his attorney since shortly after his confession to the police, during the time he testified before the grand jury, and up until this trial. Alex agreed that was true.

"And that's when you changed your story and stated under oath that, in fact, all of your confessions to killing your father or standing by while Derek killed your father, the murder that you planned, that's when you said, no, that really didn't happen; isn't that true?"

Alex wasn't rattled. "Yes, sir," he replied.

Rollo fired one question after another, his doubt and disgust with Alex's answers ringing in every syllable. He continued the barrage for more than an hour, hoping to wear the thirteen-year-old boy down, tear into his weaknesses and expose any inconsistencies in his statements. Mollye kept a close eye on Ricky during the interrogation, wondering if he felt protective now, as his own defense attorney attacked the child he claimed to care so much about.

Ricky stared at Alex, a strange look on his face that Mollye recognized as yet another of his unsuccessful attempts to look pleasant, caring, and misunderstood. Alex sat on the witness stand, an offering on Ricky's altar of perverted self-gratification and self-preservation. This was the culmination of Ricky's insidious manipulations and betrayals.

Mollye turned her attention back to Alex. Instead of completely undermining the boy's credibility, Rollo's harsh interrogation had helped induce sympathy for the boy. Alex was relieved when he was finally allowed to leave the stand after nearly two hours.

Judge Bell watched him disappear into another room, his handcuffs jangling on his wrists, then called the attorneys to the bench. "When you brought that last witness out, the youngest, Alex, they had him in handcuffs. What's the reason for that?"

"I don't know," Rimmer said. "I didn't have anything to do with it."

Rollo shrugged. "I didn't either."

Bell ordered the security officers to remove Derek's handcuffs before bringing the boy into the courtroom. "These guys are kids," he chastised. "They're not going anywhere."

Derek's arms were swinging by his side when he walked into the courtroom, his outgoing demeanor the opposite of Alex's withdrawn composure. He looked as angelic as his brother, even in a green jumpsuit, his pale skin contrasting sharply with his dark hair. Derek took his seat in the witness chair and immediately began looking around the courtroom; at the gallery, at the jury, Ricky Chavis, and the judge, seemingly interested in everything that was going on. His voice was loud and clear as he was sworn in, and he looked directly at the attorneys as they spoke to him.

He had not received his ADHD medication during his months in jail, and the lack of medication was apparent as he sat in the witness box, fidgeting. Derek quickly moved through the same routine as his brother, identifying Ricky

Chavis and explaining the series of events that led up to the first occasion they ran away to be with him.

"Why did you want to be with Rick?" Rimmer asked the boy.

"I don't know, I guess because my brother did," Derek said, his Southern accent ringing clearly throughout the courtroom. Derek testified that Ricky had encouraged them to run away, even making the arrangements by giving Alex money and two keys to his home. He said they would hide from their father in a small room underneath Ricky's trailer, accessed through a trapdoor in the floor. After he was returned to Terry, Derek said he kept quiet about Alex's whereabouts because he didn't want to get his brother and Ricky "in trouble."

Rimmer directed Derek's attention to the night of the murder, and the boy described the same scene for the jury that his brother had detailed.

"What happened after you got back to Rick's house?" Rimmer said.

Derek reflected. "Let's see. We went to Rick's house, we sat down, and we were watching TV, we smoked some marijuana. Then after we smoked—well, yeah, smoked it, went—then I went to sleep. Then I was woken up—well, I woke up, then watched some more TV, and then me, Rick, and Alex went into his bedroom and we—well, we didn't go to sleep, we just sat up in there and talked." He couldn't remember what they had talked about but he said they stayed there until the news came on in the morning.

Listening appeared to be an effort for Derek. He answered the questions, but occasionally became confused. Each time Rimmer paused to review his notes, Derek gazed around the room, hoping to spot a familiar face. Rimmer, however, was keenly focused.

"Did he ask you and Alex to do anything for him?" Rimmer asked.

"Cover for him," Derek replied.

"What do you mean?"

"Well, take the blame."

"What did he say about you and Alex taking the blame?"

"He said that we had to take the blame for him because he promised his mom right before she died that he would never get locked up again."

There was an audible gasp from the crowd at Derek's answer, but he seemed bewildered, looking from the judge to the jury to the attorneys. Sitting in the back, Sharon Potter bit back a smile, realizing her client hadn't been instructed not to mention Ricky's prison time. The attorneys approached the bench and Rollo demanded a mistrial, stating the damage Derek's comment had done to Ricky Chavis's case was incurable. Judge Bell dismissed his claim, saying people go to jail for many crimes, both serious and minor. It was a déjà vu moment for Mollye. Ricky had told her about that same pledge he made to his mother before cancer took her life. The only way Derek could have known about the promise was if Ricky had also said it to him.

A short time later Mike Rollo was ready to take his shot at the eldest King brother. His first line of business was to remind Derek he could be prosecuted for perjury. The boy responded with his typical eager-to-please nod. Rollo was on a mission to destroy the boy's credibility.

"Now back at grand jury, you told them that you got in trouble a lot when you lived with the Lays, right; do you remember telling them that?"

"Yes," Derek answered.

"Because you brought a lighter to school and you stole

some money and you would lie to them; do you remember telling the grand jurors that?"

"Yes," he said matter-of-factly.

"And you said when asked by Mr. Rimmer would you lie to them a lot, you said not a lot, but you would lie to them if you did things wrong, right? Did you answer that sometimes you would lie to the Lays if you did something wrong?"

"I think so, yes."

"Okay. Because that's the truth. You would lie to the Lays if they caught you doing something wrong, right?"

"Yes."

"So when you're caught doing something wrong, that's what you do, you lie about it, right?"

"Not all the time," Derek said simply.

"Just sometimes?"

"I guess." If Mike Rollo expected some sign of discomfort, he was disappointed. Rollo then tried to home in on the inconsistencies in Derek's statements.

"Do you remember back when Mr. Rimmer asked you before the grand jury, 'How many times do you know of personally that Rick Chavis had sex with Alex?' And do you remember your answer was, 'None'?"

"Not *personally*," he said, as if shocked at the thought that he would see it firsthand.

Rollo looked smug, either missing or ignoring Derek's meaning. "So you don't know?"

"No, just from what Alex has told me."

"Well, let me ask you about Alex; does he ever lie?"

"I haven't known him to."

"Never once?"

"Not that I remember, no, sir."

"So as far as the brothers, you're the one who tells lies, but Alex tells the truth; right?"

"I guess," was Derek's uninhibited response.

Rollo became biting and sarcastic as the questioning continued. He grilled Derek about the night of the murder, hammering away at the differences between Derek's confession to the police and his statements to the grand jury. Derek said he agreed to take the fall for killing his father because Ricky convinced them they could live with him once they were out of prison, a plan that couldn't work if he were also convicted. Ricky told them claiming self-defense was the answer.

"We would all get off—like Rick said," Derek explained. "We would all get off and we could live with Rick."

"Happily ever after?" Rollo asked with his typical sarcasm.

"Yeah, but if we didn't say that, we would all three go to prison if we didn't take the blame for him. I don't know why, but I trusted him because he's been in trouble with the law before and I thought he knew what he was talking about. He's been in that situation."

Potter and Corder exchanged smiles. Once again Rollo turned to the judge and asked him to strike the comment. Judge Bell turned to the jury in his offhanded way. "Ladies and gentlemen, that response about the fact that Mr. Chavis had been in trouble before is really not a proper response. Sometimes during the course of the trial that type of information is proper, sometimes it's improper. In this particular case at this point, it's improper. So I realize he's just testifying and he doesn't understand what the rules are, but disregard that comment."

Rollo continued. "Let me ask you, Derek, about when you lived with the Lays. Isn't it a fact you were always in trouble when you lived with Nancy and Frank Lay?"

"Mostly because of my grades," he answered.

"Didn't have anything to do with the fact that you liked to start fires or anything?"

"No."

"You never tried to do that?"

"When I was younger, yes."

"Okay. Let me ask you, one time did you ever, just as kind of a joke, put gasoline in some tiki torches out by the pool there at the Lays' house?"

"No. They kept blaming me for that, but I did not do that," Derek insisted.

"So somebody else snuck up and did that, it wasn't you; is that right?"

Rollo's determined efforts to paint Derek as a liar, a thief, and a pyromaniac went uncontested by the prosecutor. Rollo seemed unconcerned with the truth. His game was perception, and with these insinuations, he was laying the groundwork for an encore performance later in the trial.

"So, Derek, it's fair to say you were in trouble at the Lays' all the time, right?"

"Yes."

Rollo implied that when the Lays returned Derek to his father, he must have resented leaving the luxuries of a well-to-do family. He listed the roster of so-called advantages the boy had with the Lays that he lacked with his father: new clothes, their large, lovely home, things they bought him, trips they took, their swimming pool.

"Because to be fair, Terry King didn't have nearly the surroundings they had and you wore kind of shabby clothes and you didn't have friends and people made fun of you at school. It wasn't any fun, isn't that true?" Rollo insisted.

Derek swallowed hard, clearly struggling not to cry; so

hard in fact that he began to have difficulty speaking. "What are you saying, that I didn't like my dad's house?"

Rollo pushed on. "Yes," he said.

The tears Derek could no longer control spilled down his cheeks. The boy's voice cracked and faltered as he tried to answer. "I didn't like it with him, when I was there with him or around with him," he choked, as if the admission wrenched him apart. His voice broke. "But he said that he would make it better and that he'd—he'd—he'd—he would help us and like make it better and give us stuff, like get a TV and stuff like that, but he didn't have a chance to . . ." Derek fell apart, openly sobbing as the tears came faster than he could wipe them away.

"You ran away from all that before he had a chance to do that, didn't you?" Rollo pressed.

"Yes," Derek said.

"And you ran away over to your foster parents' neighborhood, right? You wanted to go back over there, right?

"Well—Well, I saw Alex with people that he liked and I thought maybe I could be with some of my friends, so—and Rick didn't have any idea. He just—I meant, Rick didn't have any—he didn't have any objection."

A chorus of sniffles and quiet comments rippled through the courtroom. Some were dabbing at their eyes, while others wept into crumpled tissues. If Rollo hoped to make Derek appear heartless to the jury, he failed. Mollye had ceased to be surprised when Rimmer failed to object, but she, and many others in the courtroom, hoped someone would step in and give the boy a chance to compose himself.

"He was trying to help you do whatever you wanted to do, right?" Rollo said, clearly unaffected by the boy's tears. Derek could only nod. "Is that right?" Rollo repeated.

"Yes," Derek replied. His emotional dam had cracked and his small chest heaved with sobs, but Rollo plowed ahead.

"Okay. So when you're in runaway status, you went over to the Lays' neighborhood and in fact visited—"

He could go on no longer. Derek looked pleadingly at Judge Bell, who was watching him with concern. "I'm sorry," Derek said. "Can I please take a break, Judge?"

The courtroom broke into pandemonium. Derek's family was ready to spring to their feet and sweep him off the stand. Other spectators were outraged the questioning had been allowed to continue as long as it did. People were sobbing, touched by the child's anguish. Even some of the jurors were wiping their eyes.

Judge Bell called a fifteen-minute recess, and Sharon Potter quickly left her seat and hurried after Derek. In a side room, away from the prying eyes of the courtroom, she held the boy while he leaned over a table, sobbing into her arms. He told her his dad *was* going to make it better for them, only he never had a chance and Mr. Rollo shouldn't say such "bad things" about his father. He was frustrated that the defense attorney would imply his father wasn't providing a good life for them, as if Terry were somehow inferior to the Lays. Sharon listened patiently, offering comfort. Eventually he was calm enough to return to the witness box.

Back on the stand, Rollo took up where he left off. "Derek, before we took a break, I was asking about when you ran away, you went over to your foster parents' neighborhood, right?"

"Yes, sir."

"Isn't it true that before you were handed over to the deputy who took you back over to the county line, that you told Nancy that you and Alex, your brother, had a plan to kill your father?"

"No, sir."

"Never said that to Mrs. Nancy Lay?"

"No, sir."

Rollo wrapped up his interrogation a short time later, and Rimmer stepped in with a few more questions.

"Why did you decide to change your story and say that Rick actually killed your dad?" Rimmer asked.

"Because I didn't want to spend the rest of my life in prison taking the fall for somebody else's act." As if teammates in a relay race, Rimmer moved aside again and passed the torch to Rollo.

"And isn't the reason you changed your story from your first confession was because you really don't want to spend the rest of your life in jail?" Rollo asked.

"Covering for somebody else," Derek answered.

"You don't want to spend the rest of your life in jail, do you?"

"If I was truly guilty and that was the consequences for my actions, then, yes."

"So if you are truly guilty and a jury finds you guilty, you are prepared to spend the rest of your life in prison for something that a jury might think you did, right?"

"If they find me guilty."

"You don't have any problem with that, do you?"

Derek looked as if he couldn't believe his ears. "Yes, I have a problem with that!"

Mollye raced outside, her deadline fast approaching. She leaped into the live truck and began comparing her notes to the video, looking for the sound bites she wanted. Derek's tearful testimony would lead the evening newscast. Then she stepped outside ready for her first report. Other reporters stood ready for their evening broadcasts. They were all essentially writing the same story: the convicted child molester versus the children who looked like angels. Who would the jury believe?

Chapter 22

DAY TWO OF THE CHAVIS TRIAL PROGRESSED MUCH like the previous one, but it lacked the brothers' riveting testimony. Rimmer called witnesses who provided evidence of Ricky's infatuation with young Alex, including the testimony of a crime scene analyst who found Alex's picture taped to the mirrored headboard of Ricky's bed, and a corrections officer who caught Ricky scratching a message to the boy in the jail recreation area. He also called Investigator John Sanderson, who testified that although they found no evidence linking Ricky to the crime scene, his behavior was suspicious. Chavis admitted he had driven to the King home twice on the night of the murder. He also said that he hid the boys from their father as well as sheriff's deputies and also lied to the cops during all of his numerous interviews. Still, the confessions of the King brothers convinced Sanderson they were the killers.

During his cross examination of the investigator, Rollo played those taped confessions. The jury listened to the boys' young voices describe the murder of their father. In the courtroom, Ricky was solemn but appeared unconcerned, his feet spread apart, fidgeting under his chair. Soon after the tapes were played, Rimmer rested his case against Ricky Chavis.

The jury left the room while Bell heard Rollo's expected motions for acquittal. The defense attorney argued there was no proof that Ricky had swung the bat that killed Terry King. He also said the State's alternative case, based on the principal theory, was nonsense; his client couldn't have helped the boys murder a man they denied killing.

Bell agreed there simply wasn't enough evidence to support the State's principal theory, and threw it out. However, he ruled the trial could proceed on the basis that Ricky was the perpetrator. Rimmer argued that his perpetrator case was weak, since it was based on the testimony of two suspects who originally confessed to the murder. Bell decided there was just enough evidence to go forward.

Rimmer was in a quandary. He didn't believe Chavis was the killer, and yet that was essentially the case he now had to present to the jury. Although reluctant, he plowed ahead on the argument that he would let the jurors decide if Chavis was guilty.

Rollo was in the proverbial catbird's seat. The case was an unexpected pot of gold. He was in the national spotlight, defending a convicted pedophile, the world's worst sort of villain, against a murder charge. If he could snag an acquittal, it could help establish his career and possibly land him more lucrative cases. The fact that the prosecutor agreed that his client wasn't guilty made his task ridiculously easy.

Escambia Sheriff's Deputy Reggie Jernigan was his first witness. Many members of the press finally saw the deputy Ricky Chavis called friend. Although he had distanced himself from Chavis since his arrest, Jernigan was clearly loyal to him on the stand. Under Rollo's direction, he described Ricky as a peaceful person who had never even suggested hurting anyone. The defense attorney asked him to recount an occasion when he saw the King brothers beat a junk car in Ricky's yard with a short-handled sledgehammer. The officer said dramatically that Derek was "going at it like some-body possessed." Enthused at his choice of words, Rollo latched onto the description.

"Possessed of what?" he asked excitedly.

"I have no idea," Reggie said. His fountain of descriptive adjectives had apparently dried up.

Jurors went home with the testimony of the boys' mother, Kelly Marino, ringing in their ears. The woman who had been assigned much of the blame for her sons' present circumstances was reluctant to take her seat in the witness box. However, she testified truthfully that the boys confessed during her first visit with them. A friend who had been with her also revealed that, sadly, Derek didn't recognize his mother when she arrived. The woman said Derek began to cry and confessed, "I wish I hadn't done it." When they pressed him for details, he stuck to the story that he killed his father with a bat because he was "defending Alex." The investigators were waiting for Kelly when her visit ended, and she relayed what her children had said. She now resented the fact that the investigators had encouraged her to talk to her sons for that purpose, putting her in the position of testifying against her own children. However, Kelly's statements would not be as damning to her boys as the testimony Mike Rollo had planned the following day.

Dr. James Larson was a trial lawyer's dream. The middle-age psychologist was educated, friendly, and articulate. His specialty included studying children who killed their parents, and he used catchy layman's terms the jurors could easily understand. The courtroom was fascinated that morning as he began describing the characteristics of child killers. He talked extensively about one group in particular, the psychopath, or "Ted Bundy type," as he called it.

"He could be smart, well-educated, well-groomed, good

with words, convincing, but the motives are evil, the motives are cruel," Larson said. "The things that give them pleasure are not the same things that give us pleasure."

Under Rollo's direction, Larson told the jury that the major defining characteristic of a psychopath is lack of conscience. Other characteristics included the inability to conform and dangerous pleasure-seeking behavior such as taking drugs. These self-centered, impulsive children could also have attention deficit hyperactive disorder.

The psychologist revealed that these warped individuals began displaying certain behavior problems early on: lying, stealing, fascination with fire and weapons, or hurting animals.

Mollye was quickly jotting down his words point by point. As she wrote, one question kept turning over in her mind: had Dr. Larson evaluated Derek? Clearly, Rollo was attempting to depict Derek as psychopath. He specifically asked the boy if he had a fascination with fire, had problems lying, or felt resentment toward his family; all issues that Rollo could use to imply the boy was a killer in the making. However, the child who had broken down and openly sobbed on the stand did not seem like an unfeeling psychopath; instead he seemed to be compassionate, defending his father and grieving his loss.

Mollye thought that if the good doctor had never interviewed the child, the insinuation that Derek was a monster was unfair, if not unethical. She expressed her concerns to another reporter after Rollo finished his questioning and the court called for a short break. "Do you know if this guy ever talked to Derek?" she asked as they stepped into the crowded stream of people trying to leave the courtroom.

"I have no idea, but I was wondering the same thing," the other reporter replied.

"I think it's unfair if Dr. Larson is being allowed to ramble on about psychopathic children if he's not even a head-shrinker in the case," Mollye said.

They emerged into the open hallway, and Mollye felt a tap on her shoulder. She turned around and found herself face-to-face with Dr. Larson. She was momentarily embarrassed that he had apparently overheard her comment. The psychologist told her that he had not evaluated Derek, Alex, or anyone else involved in the trial. He was merely an expert witness. He seemed disturbed that anyone might think he was speaking about a particular person. He said he intended to let everyone in the courtroom know it as soon as he got a chance.

A few minutes later Dr. Larson was back on the stand, this time before David Rimmer.

"Dr. Larson, you talked about these studies that have been done regarding children who kill their parents, correct?" Rimmer asked.

"That's correct," the psychologist replied.

"In most of these cases, wasn't the parent who was killed by the child a parent who had been sexually abusing the child or had been physically abusive to the child?"

"Mr. Rimmer, before I answer that question, I have an ethical obligation to make something clear to the jury and the court," Larson said earnestly.

"I was going to get to that," Rimmer said quickly. Apparently, the prosecutor knew what Larson planned to say but had not been in a hurry to correct the misunderstanding.

"I've never evaluated any parties in this case," Larson said.

"That was going to be my question," Rimmer said quickly.

"I'm sorry?" The psychologist seemed confused.

"I was going to ask you," Rimmer said, "you have not evaluated Derek or Alex King?"

"That's correct. I have not evaluated any party to this case," Larson explained. "I am simply here as a forensic expert who evaluates many criminals and who has an understanding of the scientific literature on people who kill."

Rimmer continued the questioning, although he had access to the testimony of a psychologist, Dr. Ron Yarbrough, who had actually interviewed Derek. However, he did not call this counselor. The child psychologist believed Derek lacked the capacity for murder.

Yarbrough's evaluation of Derek was never presented in court, either in the Chavis trial or later in the King trial. Sharon Potter considered calling the psychologist to the stand when the boys were tried but opted against it, since she felt Rimmer would respond by having a different State-friendly psychologist examine and testify against the boy. Instead, she hoped in vain that Rollo's next witness would speak up for Derek.

Frank Lay looked every bit the high school principal. He was dressed in a suit and tie, his thin mustache neatly trimmed. He was uncomfortable with the media attention this case brought his family, but he took his seat in the witness box with the intention of answering honestly, his attitude kind but firm.

He gave a brief history on his family's relationship with Derek King and how the boy came to live with them for so many years. He said they hoped to provide the orphaned child with a nurturing and loving home, while his father struggled for financial stability. Sharon Potter sat in the back of the courtroom and took in Frank's testimony with more than a grain of salt. She believed Frank and Nancy Lay were more concerned with giving the appearance of helping others than in actually doing it. There was a lot of prestige in being the principal of Pace High School, and they were well-known in the community, a position the attorney knew was important to the couple. However, she tried to listen objectively as he continued.

Rollo emphasized the comfortable life the Lays had provided for Derek for nearly seven years. Frank eagerly agreed, reciting the "resources" that were available to Derek like a grocery list, but he admitted they were just a substitute family for the boy, who longed for his own parents and siblings.

"We were doing the best we could and he was doing the best he could, as well," Frank explained. He described Derek as a friendly, outgoing child who willingly helped out around the home, but he said the family had trouble bonding with the boy. He directed the blame at Derek, saying his problems with lying and occasionally stealing small things had created a rift.

"We loved him, cared about him, and he cared about us and loved us. But, at the same time, you know, if you're not truthful, it's very difficult to establish trust and a real solid bond."

Hoping to remind jurors of Larson's characteristics of a psychopath, Rollo asked Frank if Derek had a fascination with fire; the principal admitted that he did. Although he tempered his assessments, Lay painted his foster son as a problem child who had a difficult time controlling himself and showed no remorse for his misbehavior.

"Did he ever develop a conscience?" Rollo asked.

"Well, that would be difficult for me to answer," Frank replied. "It would be a shallow type answer. I don't know. I couldn't answer that truthfully."

Many in the courtroom were surprised at what little loyalty Frank Lay seemed to show for Derek, and even more stunned when he inelegantly compared his home to Terry King's stating that Derek "was going from the penthouse to the outhouse." Sharon Potter was not surprised. She remembered her first meeting with Nancy Lay, shortly after she took Derek's case. Nancy arrived for their appointment with a book called *Children Without a Conscience*, proclaiming, "That's Derek!" Nancy insisted the attorney should read it, but Sharon never did. Nancy spent the next several hours describing the terrible things Derek had done. Expecting horrific descriptions of animal abuse and violence, Sharon was amazed when Nancy said, almost in a whisper, "He bought pornography in school last year."

She also mentioned that they had found firecrackers under his bed, and Derek would sometimes plop down at the head of the table when they went out to dinner, usurping his foster father's spot. As Nancy continued, Sharon kept waiting to hear something genuinely "terrible," but none of the events mentioned seemed out of the ordinary for a teenaged boy. When Sharon finally asked Nancy to tell her something good about Derek, she replied, "I can't think of anything."

Nancy walked to the witness box wearing a conservative dress, her blond hair neatly styled. She appeared reluctant, and spoke so quietly the judge prompted her to move closer to the microphone.

Rollo encouraged Nancy to talk about Derek's behavior problems growing up. She described him as an active child who was into everything, "like a little Dennis the menace." Nancy told the jury he was constantly in trouble at home and school. She said he was better behaved when he was with the immediate family because they could keep him under control, but when they had company Derek stayed "in trouble" because he couldn't resist talking with visitors and refused to go outside with the other children.

"Would you find that he would be manipulative in his relationships with others and you perhaps?" Rollo asked.

Nancy agreed that he was. "He was never intentionally mean to anybody. He's a very gentle person. But he would manipulate people to get what he wanted. He would use his situation with his family to try to get teachers to feel sorry for him and other people, that's how he manipulated." Although Nancy testified that Derek loved being around people, she agreed with Rollo that he was a "con man" who only enjoyed being with others until they "got his number."

When Rollo questioned her about the evening they got the call he was in Pace she said Derek was very agitated, and despite the fact he desperately did not want to go home, they refused to let him spend the night in their home.

"Did he tell you that he had a plan with Alex to kill his father, Terry King?" Nancy nodded, her blond hair bobbing. "He said, 'You can't send us back, because my brother is going to kill him. We already have a plan.'"

Mollye was surprised. This was the first she had heard Nancy speak of a "plan." She wondered if the statement was true or an embellishment. However, Rimmer didn't appear to be as curious. Neither he or Rollo had any further questions for Mrs. Lay. Instead the jurors were left with the impact of her last statement.

Mike Chavis gave Ricky a small half smile as he prepared to testify. The smaller, more soft-spoken Chavis brother was adept at blending unnoticed into the background. He was uncomfortable coming out of the shadows, but he could not escape his importance as a witness. He was there the night Ricky allegedly heard the fire call go out over the scanner. He was there when Ricky brought the boys back to the Chavis trailer. His testimony was vital.

Mike's world revolved around Ricky. Mike didn't work; he made money selling his plasma at a local blood blank, and Ricky made it possible for him to survive on that small income, providing him with a home, food, and a car. The investigators and David Rimmer were convinced he wouldn't lie for his older brother on a charge as serious as murder, but Mollye was not. Love and loyalty were powerful emotions, and Mike was short on neither.

He testified he never saw any inappropriate behavior between his brother and the King boys, although he said Terry would punish his children by forcing them to stare at each other for hours. He said the boys enjoyed being with Ricky because he was not as strict as their father and he allowed them to watch television and play video games. Mike continued to quietly defend his brother and the testimony was uneventful until Rollo asked what Mollye thought was an odd question.

"Now, let me ask you this: is there any such thing as a trapdoor at your residence?"

Mike answered quickly, "No, there's no secret trapdoor."

Mollye wrote *Trapdoor* in her notebook along with a big question mark. But the remainder of Mike's testimony was neither strange nor surprising to the reporter. He stuck to his brother's story that Ricky was never involved in Terry's murder.

Later that afternoon the attorneys were preparing for closing arguments. Rimmer had two options since the judge had dismissed the principal theory: he could either drop the charges or argue that Ricky was the murderer. He intended to do neither. The prosecutor stepped before the jury box, firm in his belief that he was on the side of right.

"Good afternoon, ladies and gentleman," he began, his voice booming with confidence. "We're finally at the end of all of the evidence, and we're just about at the end of this trial." He paused. The jurors and the courtroom waited expectantly. David took full advantage of their attention.

"We're here because the King brothers lied. That's why we're here. We're here because they lied. They either lied to the police or they lied to you." The ringing indictment was clear.

"I'm presenting this case to you. I'm going to let you decide what the truth is. I don't have a dog in this fight. My job is to do justice," Rimmer said proudly. "My job is to seek the truth. And what I want to do is present this evidence to you, this case to you, and let you decide whether or not you think the King boys lied to the police to protect Chavis, or were they lying when they testified here. That's going to be up to you to decide."

Rimmer wrapped up his closing statements ten minutes later. Mollye was amazed. As a seeker of "justice," the State has a responsibility to find and present the facts. The prosecutor told the jury he wasn't taking a stand, but clearly he had. Rimmer never even asked the jurors for a conviction. The reporter questioned why he had continued, why would he try a man he obviously believed was innocent? How he could halfheartedly prosecute a man for murder and then ethically ask jurors to ferret out the truth?

Rollo vehemently described Derek as a sophisticated liar and "psychopathic" killer who was motivated by his brother. He admitted his client wanted Alex King, but he declared that Ricky wouldn't kill for the relationship—unlike Alex, Rollo said, whose powerful affection for Ricky was the catalyst that set the murderous chain of events into motion. Addressing the testimony of the brothers that Ricky actually killed their father, Rollo said that "little" story was "unsophisticated." Like the investigators, Rollo wanted it both ways. The children were brilliant masterminds one minute, devising an intricate plot to end their father's life, but as soon as they contradicted their confessions, they instantly became silly, naive boys.

All the while, Ricky sat and watched, managing to escape blame. He looked as though he wanted to cry when the jurors left to begin their deliberations. He swallowed hard against the hot tears of self-pity. He would have to wait a full week before the verdict would be unsealed, along with the results of the brothers' trial.

Chapter 23

Tuesday, September 3, 2002, promised to be another scorcher. Although it was early morning, reporters and photographers were sweating as they set up television equipment and tents outside the M.C. Blanchard Judicial Building. Mollye counted the small army of satellite trucks lining the curb, all preparing to broadcast the events of Alex and Derek King's murder trial to the country. There were even more media crews than during the Chavis trial the previous week.

She squeezed onto the crowded media bench, directly behind prosecutor David Rimmer. Here, she had a good view of the jury and the witness stand, as well as the King boys and their attorneys seated at tables on the opposite side of the room.

Alex wore a tan, long-sleeve, button-down shirt, a yellow tie, and starched khakis with a brown belt. Derek looked ready for a school recital, wearing a light blue dress shirt, tie, and navy blue pants. He rocked back and forth in his chair, talking to his attorneys and glancing at the crowd behind him to smile at his family. Alex also swiveled in his chair, but he appeared to remain cool, occasionally chancing a shy glance to survey the room. He often leaned over to talk to James Stokes and pluck a mint from one of the multiple tin boxes stacked on his table.

"All rise," the court security guard bellowed. The courtroom obeyed as Judge Frank Bell made his way to the bench. Ricky Chavis was the first order of business. David Rimmer wanted to get it on record that Ricky planned to invoke his Fifth Amendment right not to testify in the brothers' trial.

A court security officer retrieved Ricky from a side door and brought him before the court. He looked awkward shuffling his big frame through the courtroom, wearing a prison jumper and handcuffs. He quickly stated for the court that he had no intention of testifying in this trial or the others that were pending against him. Ricky was escorted out of the room before the jurors took their seats.

The packed courtroom was anxious for the main event to begin. There was a sense of anticipation as the attorneys prepared their opening arguments. Ricky Chavis's trial had merely been a warm-up for the State's pursuit of justice in the murder of Terry King. As Rimmer had said, "he didn't have a dog" in the previous fight against Chavis, as a southerner might put it, but he intended to unleash the dogs of war in the trial against the brothers. James Stokes and Sharon Potter were ready for the battle.

All ten jurors settled into their chairs and watched attentively as Rimmer approached them. Tall and confident, his tone implied that his words were no less than the untainted truth and anyone who thought otherwise was a fool. He outlined his case in his straightforward style.

"Good morning, ladies and gentlemen. My name is David Rimmer. I'm the prosecutor in this case and I represent the people of the State of Florida, in which these two defendants, Alex King and Derek King, are charged with first degree murder and arson." The jurors listened, their eyes following the prosecutor as he paced before the jury box. He described the fiery and bloody scene in which Terry King's body had been found, pausing to allow the image of his words to take shape in the minds of the jurors.

"There was something else that was unusual about the situation," Rimmer continued. "His two sons, Alex and Derek, were missing." The prosecutor said the children were eventually turned in by Ricky Chavis, and the boys freely admitted they killed their father, claiming he abused them.

"You'll hear testimony that they confessed with details to the crime, that Derek acknowledged that he went into the room while his father was asleep, beat him over the head numerous times with a baseball bat. These blows fractured his skull, causing his death. He died where he lay sleeping," Rimmer said dramatically. He paused again, stopping to look at the jury. He told them the evidence would show Alex King was the principal. He was the one who wanted his father dead, and Derek, the perpetrator, was the one who carried out his brother's plan.

"After you've heard all of the evidence, I will ask you to find them both guilty of first degree murder and arson. Thank you very much."

David slid into his chair as James Stokes rose from his. "Thank you, Your Honor. May it please the court." With a few long strides, Stokes crossed the room and took a place before the jury box. "Ladies and gentlemen of the jury, you're going to hear a lot more evidence than that."

Moments earlier the courtroom had been attentive; now, spectators were riveted. The prosecutor's position and presentation of the case came as no surprise to the journalists and family members who had followed Chavis's trial. The next day's headlines would be drawn from the defense's plan to prove the children were innocent. Heads lifted a little higher to see above the crowd in the back. Court TV's camera rolled, while the small army of reporters waited with pens poised over their notepads. Stokes would give them plenty to publish.

"What you're going to hear is a number of years ago, Terry King, the victim in this case, was befriended by a man named Ricky Chavis, and from their first meeting Ricky Chavis was introduced to Alex." Stokes spoke Ricky's name as if spitting out a bad taste in his mouth. "In the years following, while Ricky Chavis pretended and acted as a friend to Terry King, what Ricky Chavis did was insinuate himself between father and son. A year before Terry King was murdered, Ricky Chavis began a sexual relationship with the then eleven-year-old child, named Alex King."

Stokes paused and turned to look at his young client, stretching his arm toward the boy. "Alex, stand up." All eyes were on Alex as he rose to his feet, standing straight, his arms by his side. Stokes turned back to the jurors. "This is Alex King. He is my client. It is my pleasure to represent him." Then casually, as if to an old friend, Stokes waved Alex back into his chair. "Go ahead and have a seat, Alex." The boy's expression remained solemn as he sat down.

Stokes continued, the words pouring out as if he couldn't wait to share them. He told the jury Ricky had a history of molesting children and had used his well-worn skill of manipulation to convince Alex that his father was mentally abusive and didn't love or care for him as much as Ricky himself did.

"'We're both gay, only we can understand this love.'" Stokes spoke the words in disgust as he described what Ricky had said to his impressionable young client. He revealed that Derek's return to the King family gave Ricky more ammunition. He convinced the boy that Terry loved Derek more and that Alex would be happier with him. Alex ran away when Ricky called.

Terry King realized Ricky was probably involved in his

children's disappearance, Stokes said, and once the boys were back in his safekeeping, he barred Ricky Chavis from their lives.

Stokes then outlined the last days leading up to Terry King's murder. He described that Derek and Mike, Ricky's brother, watched as the forty-year-old Chavis French-kissed Alex while the boy sat on his lap. Stokes described Ricky's desperation when he learned that Derek had been picked up by the police while visiting his friend in Pace. Stokes told the jury Ricky feared that his relationship with Alex was about to be exposed, which could lead to another prison sentence for the convicted child molester. Ricky put his own plan in place to prevent that, Stokes said, and that plan included keeping both boys. Ricky convinced Alex they could make that happen; all Alex had to do was open the back door Sunday night, and Ricky would come and get them.

Stokes described the boys' confessions as the "Chavis story," saying Ricky coached them to lie in order to protect himself. "They confess to the police because they've been told by Ricky Chavis that you are juveniles and you will get off and we will claim self-defense and I have friends that are cops and I will back you up."

Stokes told jurors the investigators didn't bother to test the validity of the brothers' statements because their confessions were convenient. The defense attorney hoped the jury would see that these boys were not killers, but the pawns of a master manipulator.

"I am confident that after you've listened to this evidence, after you see the manipulations of Ricky Chavis, after you see the flaws in the 'Chavis story,' that if you do your duty as jurors and you follow the law as the judge explains it to you, you will find Alex King not guilty of murder. Because he is not."

Stokes quickly strode back to the desk and sat beside

Alex. The young boy leaned over to whisper to his litigator, covering his mouth with his hand. The exchange made them both smile. Sharon Potter then moved to the forefront. Conservatively dressed and soft-spoken, her quiet delivery contrasted with Stokes's outpouring of injustice. What Sharon lacked in flamboyance, however, she made up for with solid arguments based on legal logic.

"Ladies and gentlemen, I represent Derek King," Sharon began. "The defense contends in this case the facts did not happen the way the prosecutor described it, and on the contrary we contend that the facts will show an entirely different version of what occurred and that Derek King did not do what the prosecution contends that he did."

Sharon emphasized that much of the boys' statements to police were wrong and that Derek had no motive to kill his father, but Ricky Chavis did. "All we ask is that you keep your minds open, and I'm certain that after you listen to all the believable evidence you will say in your mind that the prosecutor has not met his task of proving Derek King guilty beyond a reasonable doubt."

The State's first witness was Derek's former foster mother, Nancy Lay. She again described Derek as an unruly child who was impossible to handle.

After Nancy came the same string of witnesses who had also taken the stand in Ricky's murder trial. When Rimmer put Escambia crime scene investigator Jan Johnson on the stand, the defense was eager to pounce. There was no physical evidence that connected the boys with their father's murder and the attorneys intended to hammer that point home, at Jan Johnson's expense.

The officer took the stand, her thick, curly red hair brushing the shoulders of her conservative black suit. She wore a white blouse buttoned to the throat. A five-star Escambia

Sheriff's Office emblem was pinned to her jacket. A former blood spatter expert with the Florida Department of Law Enforcement, Johnson had recently left her position with the state to take a $53,000 a year job as the head of the sheriff's new crime scene unit.

"Would you tell the jury what you found as you examined the scene?" Rimmer asked.

Years of testifying for FDLE had taught Jan Johnson to be a jury-friendly witness. She turned to them as she answered, her voice soft and polite. She answered the prosecutor's questions with confidence, describing the position of Terry's body and the amount of blood spatter around it.

"In your opinion, was the victim attacked where his body was found?"

"Yes," she answered firmly.

"Is that where all the bloodshed was?" Rimmer asked for emphasis.

"That is correct."

The prosecutor walked back to his table and picked up a large white board covered with pictures. He made a special effort to turn the pictures away from the curious eyes of the press and courtroom spectators, some of whom were craning their necks to get a look at them. He placed the board on a stand facing the jury. Jan Johnson stepped down from the witness box and the two stood on either side of the graphic array of photos, like teachers in a classroom with students.

Pointing to the pictures, Johnson testified about the condition of Terry King's beaten body as well as the evidence deputies found at the scene, specifically what appeared to be damage on the nearby lamp. The point was an important one to the prosecution. In their confessions, Derek and Alex described Derek hitting the lamp once as he attempted to kill his father. They also said they saw brain tissue on the wall.

Investigators were looking for evidence to corroborate his account of the brutal beating.

"There was a defect to the right side of the lamp shade," Johnson said, motioning to the photo depicting a small tear on the shade. As she testified, Derek was rocking and leaning casually in his chair, his chin propped up on his hand. Alex fidgeted with a pen.

The crime scene expert testified she also observed a substance on the walls that was consistent with brain tissue. The substance was photographed, but never collected into evidence. She also testified that the boys' shoes were collected, along with several cans of what appeared to be flammable liquid. David Rimmer thanked her.

Stokes, who had been busy taking notes during her testimony, rose to his feet with energy. She seemed to stiffen on the stand, as if bracing for an unpleasant confrontation.

"There is a considerable amount of spatter at the crime scene, on the lamp, the walls, nearly twelve feet away on the ceiling," Stokes said. "Can you determine the height of the individual who did this?"

"No," she said, her previously warm demeanor cooling fast.

Stokes nodded and looked at the floor as if in thought. "Can you, with your training and expertise," he said deferentially, "determine the direction which the bat had to have swung?"

There was a moment of silence before she answered. "Looking at the spatter . . . um . . . if you're facing the victim, it would be from right to left, the direction of the spatter in which it was traveling."

Stokes stepped around the podium to stand closer to her and the jury. "So—I don't mean to be graphic here—if Terry King is sitting in the chair, the bat would have had to have come down like this, correct, hitting him in the head?" With his left hand in his pants pocket, Stokes casually demonstrated the swing with his free hand, using a pen.

"I thought you were asking the direction of the travel of the spattering," Johnson responded, tightly. "That's two different things."

"Okay," Stokes said. "What would have been the direction of the blunt object that caused the spatter that you've indicated?"

"From right to left."

"Okay, so it would have been coming pretty much down the long axis of his body, correct?"

"It could have. . . ." She paused, looking off to the side as if picturing the murderous swing. She picked up the imaginary weapon to illustrate her point. "He could also have . . . it could have been swung sideways, as well." She dropped her hands and finished quickly. "So, I mean . . . from right to left is all I'm saying."

Stokes stepped closer to the poster board stand still propped before the jury. "If it was swung sideways, assume for a minute this is the lamp shade here, Terry King's head is approximately here, correct?" He gestured to the stand, substituting it for the dead father's head. "So in order to avoid hitting the lamp, we can assume, can't we, that the bat had to come up in a direction about like that." Stokes bent his arm straight up and down, not the left to right movement she had suggested.

She paused, as if trying to think of an explanation that a child might grasp. "I'm not certain," she said finally. She had long since stopped directing her answers to the jury.

Stokes moved on to another line of questioning. "Is it possible Terry King could have been attacked in another part of the house then beaten in the chair?"

Johnson replied that they did not find blood anywhere else in the King home.

"What did you use to determine that there was no blood underneath the soot in the hallway?" he asked.

She waited a moment, then answered, "Just visual examinations."

"We didn't use the magic lights or whatever that we have that will show fluids?" Stokes asked dryly. "None of that was taken to Mr. King's house?"

"There would have been no other examination that we could have used at that scene that we did not use," she said firmly.

Stokes nodded and changed tack again. "You were shown a picture and asked if it was consistent with brains, I believe." Stokes turned to Rimmer. "Could I have that?" he asked, gesturing to the picture board.

"Sure." The prosecutor handed it to him.

Stokes stepped up to the witness box. "And you can identify exactly what you're calling brains in that," he said, glancing at the photograph.

"It would be the large—" Johnson began.

"Mr. Stokes," the judge interrupted, "show it to the jury, so they can see it."

"Sure," Stokes said as Johnson got up to stand before the jury box.

This time she put on her glasses to examine the photo, peering at it before responding. "It would be the large matter, and you'll see some white material within that stain, the larger, clear stain." After pointing it out for the jurors, she took her seat at the witness stand.

"Ma'am, did you collect that sample?" Stokes said.

"We may have." She shrugged. "I'm not sure, no one's asked me that until right now."

"Did anybody send off anything from you to the medical examiner from those walls that was identified as matter, gray matter, brain tissue?"

"No, sir, nothing was actually analyzed."

"Let me ask you this: you've had the opportunity to view your close-up picture with a magnifying glass. If you were in a dimly lit room and you were a twelve-year-old child and you looked up and you saw that, would you have described that as brains?"

Rimmer rose to his feet. "Objection, Your Honor."

"Sustained," Judge Bell agreed.

Stokes rephrased his question. "Would you, looking at that in a dimly lit room, describe that as brain tissue?"

"If I were a twelve-year-old child?" Johnson asked.

"No, if you were you," Stokes said. "Would you look at that and say it was brain tissue?"

"Based upon my experience, I see brain tissue all the time," she replied.

"When you look at that picture, would you say that was brains?" Stokes repeated.

"I was actually at the scene," she said, as if that fact should leave no room for further questions.

"When you looked at it," Stokes said slowly, deliberately—determined to get a direct answer—"were you under the impression that the matter was brains?"

"Yes," she answered, appearing irritated, "that was my impression."

"Then why was it not collected and sent off?"

"It may have been, sir." The jury swiveled their heads from attorney to witness, watching the exchange like a tennis match.

"But weren't you the person that was doing the collecting?"

The jury's eyes swung back to Johnson expectantly, and she neatly sidestepped the question. "Generally speaking, at the crime scene, we collect a lot of samples of bloodstains and gray material, things of that nature, and it's not always necessary to have every sample analyzed."

Stokes questioned her on a few other details before Derek's defense team took over. Dennis Corder, tall and neatly dressed, walked to the podium.

He questioned Jan Johnson about the visual and physical testing crime scene officers conducted on Ricky's car. She testified that they took samples throughout the car looking for blood evidence. A small sample of a substance that turned up in the trunk using a luminol lamp was sent for testing, but the amount was minute and revealed nothing. Under his questioning, she also revealed that they did not send samples from the front seat or the steering wheel for testing.

Chapter 24

DURING THE TESTIMONY, **C**OURT TV'S CAMERA WOULD occasionally take a break from the stand and pan across the room to the children. Another tiny camera sat on the defense table constantly fixed on Derek, allowing the producers to take the shot at will. Ever rocking in his chair, the camera often captured the fourteen-year-old boy with head turned and smiling at his family or joking mischievously with Sharon Potter or Dennis Corder. Alex and Stokes, their expressions solemn, appeared busy jotting down important tidbits about the case. In fact, they were writing furiously, but not necessarily at note taking. At times they were engaged in a fierce game of tic-tac-toe or Hangman.

Kevin Fiedor wore a navy suit and a red tie. He had thinning blond hair, blue eyes, and appeared to be in his late thirties. The state fire marshal investigator was one of the first to examine the charred ruins of Terry King's home. He told Rimmer he immediately realized the fire had been deliberately set.

"There were obvious accelerant floor patterns in the master bedroom," he explained. "A floor pattern is simply a liquid accelerant being poured in a location, and it creates patterns in that area."

"Now, what temperature does an average house fire reach?" Rimmer continued.

"Average house fire . . ." Fiedor paused for a moment. "The range is different depending on which book you like to read, however, it goes from about twelve hundred degrees all the way up to two thousand degrees, and varies based on what's burning."

"Based on your training and education and experience, do you know at what temperature aluminum melts?" David asked.

"About twelve hundred degrees."

Deputies claimed the unrecognizable glob of aluminum they found in the remnants of Terry King's bed was the bat the King boys confessed to using. However, the public had yet to see what was left of it. The prosecutor would not give the jury a glimpse of the melted metal, showcasing the evidence to substantiate the boys' confessions.

The media didn't realize there was no conclusive evidence that the chunk of aluminum was actually the melted murder weapon. Rimmer and the investigators spoke as if it were a forgone conclusion that the unidentifiable glob was indeed the bat, but a metallurgy test was vague. It showed that the glob contained a metal mixture that was consistent with some aluminum baseball bats, but it was consistent with other aluminum items as well. Rimmer did not present those findings in court. While reporters waited anxiously for information about the melted metal, the defense was not surprised when Rimmer went on to another line of questioning.

"Did you receive some shoes from Jan Johnson at the Escambia Sheriff's Office, two pairs of shoes labeled 'Alex King' and 'Derek King'?" the prosecutor asked Fiedor.

"Yes, I did. I sent them to the arson lab in Quincy, Florida."

"No further questions," Rimmer said.

When Dennis Corder stepped behind the podium, the fire investigator revealed that due to the amount and placement of the accelerant in the bedroom, if the boys had ignited the fire as they claimed, they would have been burned in the process.

Reginald Hurchins knew chemicals. He was a senior crime lab analyst for the State Fire Marshal's Office, and the State's next witness. Hurchins testified he found ignitable liquid on the brothers' shoes, similar to the chemicals used in paint thinners, insecticides, and some degreasers. While David Rimmer abruptly ended his questions there, the defense was eager to get Hurchins talking about chemistry and children's sneakers.

The crime lab analyst tested not only the boys' shoes, but charred debris and burned cans of suspected accelerant. Corder wanted jurors to know exactly what the chemist discovered in his lab. Hurchins explained that the accelerant he found on the boys' shoes was a different one from the chemicals that investigators suspected were used to ignite the fire. In fact, from his testing, Hurchins could not even determine how much accelerant was on the boys' shoes or how long it had been there. They could have picked up a drop of it virtually anywhere—a parking lot, garage, or a puddle.

Corder returned to his client, and Stokes stood up. He wanted to make sure the jury wasn't befuddled by the scientific terms and explanations. He strode to the podium, his dry, resonating tone contrasting with Dennis's carefully planned queries. "Just very briefly, to make sure we covered this, the shoes didn't match anything else that you were asked to test, is that correct?"

"No, they didn't," Hurchins agreed.

"Thank you," Stokes said, heading back to his table. "No further questions."

The lack of physical evidence placing the boys at the scene of their father's murder made their confessions invaluable to the State. David Rimmer made the most of the strongest evidence he had—the brothers' statements to police. They had talked not only to the investigators, but also to a string of other witnesses, and Rimmer paraded them one by one before the jury.

A series of youths incarcerated for various crimes testified that the brothers confessed to them that they had killed their father. In every case, the brothers consistently stuck with what James Stokes called the "Chavis story"—a story designed to convince others that they killed their dad out of fear of abuse. Although the State hoped the statements would be damning, Stokes thought the boys' steadfast commitment to the same lies supported his argument to the jury that the brothers had been convinced this "story" would get them out of trouble. He also believed they weren't the only ones who had lied to investigators about the events surrounding Terry King's murder. His eyes followed the prosecution's next witness as he walked to the stand.

Reggie Jernigan looked as if he had just eaten a meal that disagreed with him. However, Mollye suspected it was probably his strong distaste for the situation. He was back in the spotlight, testifying about the man who had cost him his job. She noted that the deputy's lips were curled with a hint of disgust and he hunched his heavy shoulders defensively. He was wearing a short-sleeve white shirt and dark tie. What appeared to be a pack of cigarettes was outlined in his shirt pocket. As Jernigan shifted his heavy frame in the witness chair, the reporter thought he was making every effort to appear confident and unconcerned, like a good ol' boy who was just doing his job.

"Officer Jernigan," Rimmer began, "do you know a man named Ricky Chavis?"

"Yes, I do," Reggie answered, thrusting his chin out as if

to say "What of it?" It was a move that would characterize his testimony.

"How long have you known him?"

Reggie turned slightly in his chair, away from Rimmer. He blew out a long, loud breath and rolled his eyes upward, counting quietly. "About seventeen years, I guess. Didn't know him that well up until about 'ninety-one or 'ninety-two."

Reggie testified that Ricky called him shortly after Terry King's murder, saying that he had found Alex and Derek in Santa Rosa County. The deputy advised Ricky to immediately call Terry Kilgore. The investigator then asked him to pick up the boys and meet him at the Sheriff's Office. Reggie told the prosecutor he was there for a portion of Derek's interview.

Mollye found it revealing that Reggie knew many personal details about Ricky Chavis, including his work and sleeping habits. She was also amazed that Ricky was so close with the deputy that he had called Reggie from jail on the night that he was arrested. As the deputy talked, he turned so that only his profile was visible to the prosecutor.

Rimmer insisted that Reggie recount the car-beating incident, where the brothers took a small sledgehammer to an old clunker in Ricky's yard. Rimmer was finished with the deputy after he gave the jury a picture of a bat-wielding Derek, viciously pounding away at a junk car.

If Reggie Jernigan had seemed reluctant before, his body language positively screamed discomfort as James Stokes walked to the podium with a pad full of notes. The deputy swiveled his chair until he turned away from the defense attorney, sitting completely in profile.

Stokes asked the officer to identify various telephone numbers. They belonged to both Reggie and Ricky Chavis.

Stokes asked loudly, his voice resonating. "On the day after Terry King was murdered—in particular, that morning and on into the afternoon—Ricky Chavis called you quite often, didn't he?"

Reggie wrinkled his brow. "When was that?"

Stokes made a point of answering slowly and deliberately. "On the day after the murder."

Still no answer. This time, Reggie had swiveled so far from the attorney that he would have to answer over his shoulder. "The day after the murder?" he asked again.

"That would be November twenty-sixth," Stokes said.

"Uh . . ." Reggie stuttered, his forehead a mass of wrinkles, as if he were trying hard to think back to the distant past. He could remember how easily Derek handled a sledgehammer or Ricky's sleeping habits, but the simple details surrounding Terry's murder seemed to elude him. "I'm not sure of the exact date," he said slowly. "I believe it was a Tuesday. I received, to my recollection, one phone call. It was around two-ten, two-fifteen that afternoon that he'd found the boys."

"Did you receive any messages from him?" Stokes asked.

"Uh, when?"

"The day after the murder."

"I can't recall, no sir," Reggie said, shaking his head.

"Let me ask you this: do you recall a seven-minute phone call at approximately 12:37?"

"On the day after the murder? I can't recall."

"Do you recall a phone call about 9:42 P.M.? Lasted about one minute, perhaps it was a machine he'd reached?"

"On that morning?"

"That would be in the evening of that day. It would be 9:42 in the evening."

"And that's the day of the murder?" Reggie asked yet again.

"The murder was committed in the morning, so it would be the day of the murder, but this would be the following evening."

"So it would have been Monday night, then?"

"Yes," Stokes answered patiently, enjoying Reggie's discomfort.

"I don't recall it," Reggie said finally. He was blinking hard.

"Do you recall a sixteen-minute conversation that would be at about 10:22 P.M.?"

"I can't recall it," Reggie said defensively. "At that time I was home taking care of my wife. She had just got out of the hospital from surgery." It appeared that Reggie was leaving delaying tactics behind, now opting for sympathy instead.

"What about a three-minute phone call?" Stokes pushed. "That would be the following day, a Tuesday, at about 11:48, almost noon. Do you recall that?"

"No, sir."

"At about what time did you receive the call from Ricky Chavis that tells you that he has the boys?"

"Approximately two-ten, two-fifteen."

"And how long do you think that conversation took you?"

"Two, three, four, five minutes at the most. It was short."

"Would it surprise you if there were no less than eight phone calls on the day of the murder, that Monday, throughout that day, to you from him?"

"Yes, it would," the deputy answered.

"Do you remember these calls?" Stokes asked.

"On the day of the murder?" Reggie repeated. "No, sir."

His point made, Stokes moved on to another line of questioning. He made it clear to the jury that Reggie was aware of Ricky's record, including the child molestation conviction, when he brought the boys into the Sheriff's Office. A check of Reggie's police computer revealed that he ran a criminal records check on his friend years earlier. However, he didn't share the information he had discovered with investigators.

Mollye glanced over at the boys. Alex had his hands crossed over his stomach as he watched Jernigan testify. Derek was smiling at Dennis Corder behind his hand.

"Did Mr. Chavis express any concern for the boys' well-being?" Stokes asked.

Reggie perked up slightly at the question. "Yes, he did."

"Did he say that he cared for them and he loved them?"

"No." Reggie hunkered down again.

"But he did say he was concerned about them?"

"He was concerned about their well-being." Reggie said, defending his friend. "He wasn't sure, but he had suspicions there was the possibility of abuse."

Stokes pounced. "He told you that?"

"Yes."

"Did he tell you how he thought they were abused?"

"Dad was playing mind games with them, psychological."

"Did he use the word 'psychological' or did he use the word 'mental abuse'?"

"Mind games." Reggie was confirming for the jury that Ricky used the exact terms and descriptions that the boys used.

"Did he talk to you about a stare?"

"Yes, and I'd personally seen Terry stare too," he said in defense of his friend.

Stokes ran down another long list of phone calls that occurred between the two in the days after the murder. Once again Reggie stiffly denied any recollection of the conversations, instead pointing out that he had spent much of that time caring for his invalid wife.

The defense attorneys noted that Ricky's phone records revealed more than just a surprising number of phone calls between Ricky and Reggie Jernigan. They ran background checks on many of the people talking to Ricky and were stunned to find that many were convicted felons. His closest friends had been convicted of burglary, grand theft, assault and battery, and lewd and lascivious assault.

Reggie was dismissed from the witness stand, and he walked out of the courtroom through stares of disgust. Mollye felt he had made every effort to defend himself and his relationship with a convicted child molester, even using his wife's illness as a shield. The deputy should have focused on protecting a desperately worried father and his sons.

The court took a ten-minute recess after the lengthy testimony. The jurors were taken out of the room, and the boys' attorneys also walked away, leaving the children alone at their tables with a court security officer. The boys began joking and talking animatedly with the familiar deputy, as if they were anxious to cut loose. Alex self-consciously hid his childish smile behind his hand, enjoying the short break until the jury returned.

Chapter 25

THE STATE'S NEXT WITNESS WAS MIKE CHAVIS. HE HAD the look of a wary dog afraid of another kick. He kept his head down, like his shoulders, and gingerly took a seat in the witness box. The light blue, plaid shirt and slacks underscored his meek demeanor. The defense wasn't fooled; Mike often hid behind his mild manner. He was certainly not an educated man, but the defense attorneys knew that he was privy to more information than he wanted to admit.

Mike testified that Terry and Alex had often visited their trailer in the past couple of years. While he never saw any physical abuse, Mike said Terry would occasionally stare at Alex. However, he said the two seemed to get along most of the time.

"How did that change when Derek came back?" the prosecutor asked.

"Well, you know, Terry and Derek was laughing, they seemed happy," Mike answered with a thick Southern accent, speaking slowly and quietly. His jaw jutted slightly to the side. "It was like Alex was being ignored."

"Did Alex start leaning toward your brother Ricky?"

"It was, you know, more like a friendship," Mike explained.

"Okay, but you say when Derek came back it seemed like Alex was being ignored by his father?" Rimmer asked.

Mike responded, "Yes," and confirmed that it seemed to bother Alex.

Rimmer didn't want to miss an opportunity to reiterate the sledgehammer pounding of the junk car, so he questioned Mike about it. He also recounted the series of events that took place the night Terry was killed, from the moment the boys allegedly called his brother to the time when they later all returned to the trailer.

Sharon Potter was eager to grill Mike. She knew he was not only Ricky's brother, but an ally who might carefully guard Ricky's secrets. Her calm, quiet questioning was well matched with Mike's timid personality. Prying away the layers of suspected lies would take time, but Sharon was patient.

"Good afternoon, Mr. Chavis," she began. "How long have you lived with your brother, Rick?"

"Probably about four years, I believe." He admitted that he had been unemployed for the past couple of years and Rick supported him. He said his brother was also generous to Terry, allowing him and his children to stay at his home when Terry couldn't afford to pay his power bill.

"And the boys, Derek and Alex, stayed at your house some while Terry was working, is that right?"

"Yes."

"And the boys were at your house when they ran away in November, is that right?"

"Yes," Mike answered reluctantly.

"While the boys were at your house, isn't it true that Rick spent a lot of time with them?" Sharon pressed.

"Yes, you know, he would show them how to work on things, when he would work on things, and let them play the video games and watch cartoons and stuff like that," Mike explained, making Ricky sound like a day care worker.

Sharon paused, pretending to scan her notes. In fact, she

was relishing the moment. Mike was perched on his chair like a clown in a dunking booth, anticipating the next throw. She intended to prove that he was a liar, and she believed she knew just how to knock him off balance. The boys had talked to their attorneys about the "hideout" in Ricky's trailer and the trapdoor concealed under a piece of carpet. Mike had testified in Ricky's trial that it didn't exist. The investigators had missed it entirely when they searched Rick's home, and Sharon Potter was prepared to enlighten them.

"Isn't it true that sometimes the boys would hide in the back bedroom?"

"Yes."

"And isn't it true that there was a space that Rick made underneath the trailer where the boys could hide sometimes?"

Mike hesitated. "I don't know if it was for them," he said slowly, "but he had like an attic, a space underneath for *storage,* because he's an electrical—"

Sharon interrupted. "And the boys could hide down there if they wanted to?"

"There's room enough to hide down there."

"Where was the opening for that space that was underneath the trailer?"

"There's one outside the trailer on the side . . ." Mike's head dropped lower. ". . . and a panel in the laundry room. There's like a . . . like a square piece of wood, nailed down."

"And that's in the floor you're talking about?"

"Yes."

It was Sharon's undeniable "Matlock moment." The hideout that Mike had denied under oath in the last trial, he now confirmed existed. It was testimony that not only corroborated the boys' accounts of the concealed hiding place, but demonstrated Ricky's ability to deceive and Mike's desire to cover for him.

Sharon wasn't quite finished yet. "On November twenty-

sixth, early in the morning, you were at home, and you testified that the phone rang?"

"Yes."

Mike also recounted the same testimony he had given the
prosecutor, repeating that Ricky had picked up the boys and
brought them back to the trailer. He insisted that he was
watching TV when they walked in and didn't get a good
look at the children, but that he did notice they appeared to
be carrying a bundle of clothes in their arms. Sharon discovered that his testimony was wrought with inconsistencies.
Each time she questioned him closely, his story seemed to
fall apart one detail at a time. His memories were clearly
geared toward supporting his brother's story.

"Did you tell Rick to pick up the phone and call the police?" she asked.

"No, it just never entered my mind," he drawled. He also
testified that he thought the boys called Rick a couple of
times shortly after they were arrested.

"You heard Rick make a comment something like, 'everything's the same, nothing has changed,' something like that?"

"He could have said that, I'm not sure," Mike said, his
voice even softer.

"And isn't it true that Rick has mentioned sending letters
to you that you could then turn around and send to the boys
in jail?"

There was a long pause while Mike sat silently in the witness chair, the jury and spectators watching him expectantly.
"I don't think so," he finally answered, his voice barely
above a whisper.

James Stokes wanted the jury to understand just how far
Mike would go to protect his brother. He paced before the
jury box, thoughtfully tapping his pen against his mouth. He
looked more like a lecturing professor than an attorney at the

center of a high profile case. He decided to take the jury into Ricky's makeshift dungeon one more time.

"Did you know that's where the boys were hiding when Terry came over to try and find them?"

"Uh, I think they hid down there a couple of times. I'm not sure," Mike said.

"Did you know that's where the boys were hiding when the police officers came over the morning after the murder?"

"No, I didn't know they were hiding down there then."

"Now, I believe the question you were asked last week was this: 'Is there any such thing as a trapdoor at your residence?' and you said, 'No. There's no way to get under the trailer through a secret door.'"

Mike remained silent, but the implications were loud and clear.

The jury would be forced to wait before they heard from the youngest King. David Rimmer called several witnesses to the stand prior to Alex, including the lead homicide investigator, John Sanderson. He was dressed in a dark suit and tie, his blond hair neatly combed, graying at the temples. His light Southern drawl and easygoing demeanor added to his hardworking cop appeal. Rimmer had known Sanderson for years. They had collaborated on numerous cases in an attempt to put criminals away, and the two had a long friendship. Once a cop himself, Rimmer understood the pressures and difficulties investigators faced. Rimmer relied on the case they gave him, putting his reputation out on the same limb as theirs.

"Tell the jury what happened after Derek and Alex were brought to the Sheriff's Office," Rimmer asked Sanderson.

The investigator testified that they questioned the boy before they taped his statement, the usual protocol with any witness. He said Derek's first version of the events that led to his dad's murder were inconsistent with the crime scene. The boy claimed he became so angry after Terry flung his brother over a table that he attacked his father with a bat.

"I told him, the crime scene tells a story," Sanderson said. "And that based on the crime scene, we know what his father was doing and where his father was at when this happened. And at that time he changed his story."

"How did he change his story, what did he say?"

"He said that Alex and Terry were arguing. They thought they were going to be abused for running away, the two of them. He told Alex that he would take up for him. He said when they got home that night, that Terry threw Alex. They waited until Terry was asleep in his recliner, and then Derek demonstrated how Terry was sitting in his chair that evening. He demonstrated this for us, myself and Officer Kilgore, the other investigator."

"Describe his demonstration," Rimmer said.

"He came around, he was showing Officer Kilgore how his father was sitting. He said that he was sitting in his chair, he had his legs crossed and propped up on a couch in front of him and he had a cup. He had some kind of coffee cup or drinking cup in his right hand, either on his lap or beside his leg, in the way he was describing it."

The investigator said Derek also admitted he and his brother had discussed killing their dad hours before they did it.

The prosecutor propped up a large tape recorder on the stand next to Sanderson. The courtroom was quiet as the familiar recording of Derek's youthful voice echoed through the room. Alex doodled on a piece of paper, while Derek slowly rocked in his chair. The jurors were still, listening carefully to the most important piece of evidence to the State's case.

When the tape ended, Rimmer moved on to Alex's statement. Sanderson testified the door was closed and there was no way Alex could have heard what his older brother said.

"What did Alex tell you before you took a taped statement from him?" Rimmer asked.

"He said they had stayed in the woods in Pace after they first ran away."

Stokes casually propped his elbow on the back of Alex's chair and leaned in protectively while John testified. The blond boy seemed oblivious, still doodling on his pad.

"He said after they got home, that Terry grabbed Alex by his arm and slung him, and Derek came into the room and hit Terry in the head with a baseball bat, knocking him into the chair in that room. At that time, after going through this preliminary part here, I told Alex the same thing, that you know, a crime scene tells a story."

"And you didn't tell him what Derek had told you?" Rimmer asked.

"No," Sanderson said firmly. "Then he changes his statement a little bit. He said that after Terry had pushed him down, that he and Derek went into another room and he told Derek, 'I wish he was dead.' "

A tape recorder was brought in and Alex's childish voice, sounding young and high, began playing for the jury. The details were as disturbing as his efforts to protect Ricky Chavis. When the tape ended, Rimmer continued his cross examination with enthusiasm.

"Officer Sanderson, you went to the crime scene on the morning of September twenty-sixth, you've got Terry King's body inside. His sons are missing. . . ."

"Yes." Sanderson nodded.

"Now, when they were brought in on the twenty-seventh, if they had told you they ran away, they don't know what happened to their father, would they have been arrested?"

"No, they wouldn't," the investigator agreed.

"Would you have had any evidence on them at all if they had not confessed to the murder?"

"No, sir."

"Several months after they gave these statements, did you learn that they had changed their story and we're now claiming that Ricky Chavis did it?"

"Yes."

"During that time has anybody come forward to tell you that Chavis has made any confessions about the murder?"

"No."

Stokes jumped to his feet, "Objection, Your Honor!" He was attempting to curb Rimmer's leading questions.

"I'm going to sustain the objection," Judge Bell agreed.

Rimmer continued unperturbed. "At some point during your investigation and your contact with Chavis, did he ever finally acknowledge that after the murder he went up there and picked them up?"

"Yes."

"Did he volunteer that information to you or did you confront him with the phone records?"

"We confronted him with the phone records."

James Stokes was anxious for his shot with the longtime Escambia investigator. "Did you know that when Ricky Chavis showed up, that he had in fact been convicted of and was a pedophile?" he asked.

"I'm not sure if we had all that information at that time, just yet. I just don't recall," Sanderson answered.

"So this pedophile brings you a twelve- and a thirteen-year-old boy and tells you that, 'I took them home,' which by the way, we now know is a lie, that he didn't pick them up from Pace, correct?"

"Right."

"And that's a lie that Ricky Chavis provided. Who would that lie protect?" Stokes asked the investigator. He stopped pacing and looked directly at Sanderson.

"The lie?" he repeated.

"The lie that the boys told you is a lie that I refer to as the 'Chavis story.' Who did that lie protect?"

"Mr. Chavis," Sanderson replied.

"And we just listened to the tape, and wouldn't you agree with me when I say that when they told that lie, the lie that they had hitchhiked to Pace, as convincingly as anything else we heard on that tape?"

Rimmer stood up quickly. "Objection, Judge. I think that's a question for the jury to decide when they listen to the tape."

"I'll sustain the objection."

"Sorry, Your Honor, thank you. I apologize for getting out of order," Stokes told the court. Then he said to Sanderson, "There is one time when my client, Alex King, tells you that he does not want to answer a question. Do you remember him telling you that?"

"Yes."

"Now, Alex King had come in there and confessed to murdering his father. He had confessed to destruction of evidence in that bed and he confessed to arson, correct?"

"Yes."

"Now, let me ask you this: what was the answer to the *only* question my client didn't want to answer?"

"Ricky Chavis," Sanderson replied.

"Is Ricky Chavis still sitting outside your waiting room at that point?"

"I believe so, yes, sir."

"And before this, before the interview with the boys, you had some concerns about Ricky Chavis, hadn't you?"

"Yes."

"And you went to Ricky Chavis's house, didn't you?"

"Yes, we did."

"And he got there before you?"

"He got there about the same time as Officer Kilgore, then I came up right after that."

"Yet he was allowed to run up to the back to use the bathroom, is that correct?"

"He had told us before he left, he had to go to the bathroom, and that's where he went, yes."

"But now we know is that he was going into the back to hide the boys from you, correct?" Stokes said, as if surprised the deputies had allowed Ricky to slip the move past them.

"Most likely," Sanderson admitted reluctantly.

"And we know now that there is a trapdoor in that residence, correct?" Stokes asked.

"No," Sanderson said adamantly.

"You do not know that?!" Stokes asked, stopping short to emphasize his surprise.

"No, we've asked people and everything and I'm not aware of the trapdoor. We were unable to locate it," Sanderson said.

Stokes relished his next question: "Would you be surprised to learn that Mike Chavis testified yesterday that there was, in fact, a trapdoor back there?"

Sanderson looked stunned. "Yes, I would," he answered stiffly.

"Why were you suspicious of Ricky Chavis when you went over to his house before you knew he had taken the boys?"

"That was after the first interview with him, and just, more than anything, a gut feeling that he might know a little bit more than what he's telling us. Not that he's involved," Sanderson added quickly, "but he might know a little bit more."

"Did your gut feeling lead you to run a background on him?"

"Well, we had a run a . . . I just don't recall when we ran the background check or when we got it, but I'm sure it was early on," Sanderson insisted.

"Wouldn't you agree that the fact that he was a known pedophile would have been of considerable concern to you in your investigation involving a twelve- and a thirteen-year-old boy?"

"Well, that was important to it also, and that's why we pulled any records that we had of that."

Stokes began hammering the investigator on the boys' outlandish description of walking and hitchhiking nearly thirty miles to Pace. Sanderson argued that the story was not necessarily unbelievable.

"And is it your assumption that they came up with this story—the thing that we know is a lie—they came up with that independently or did they come up with that together?"

"They would have had to come up with that together, probably."

"And doesn't—having come up with that together—presuppose that they had rehearsed this story?"

"They may have." The investigator nodded. "They may have."

Sanderson testified he was convinced the boys' confessions were true because they were so similar. Stokes pounced on it.

"They almost sounded *rehearsed*, didn't they?"

"No," Sanderson insisted.

"They didn't?"

"Some of it maybe," he conceded, "but the part about what happened, no, not to me."

"So they only rehearsed one part of their story?" Stokes asked.

"Not necessarily," Sanderson replied. "I mean, they come up with this story of what happened and then, separately interviewed, they both change that story."

"But they both change the story in exactly the same way, didn't they?"

"Yes, they did."

Stokes was convinced the investigators just accepted the boys' statements at face value, and he wanted the jury to know it. He grilled Sanderson on other inconsistencies. "And the boys tell you a story of how they stood next to the bed, is that correct, and lit the bed on fire?"

"Yes."

"They said they put the bat on the bed and lit it on fire. We know now, don't we, that if there were accelerants all over and they stood there and attempted to light the bed on fire, they would have burned themselves because they would have ignited exactly what they were standing in, correct?"

"Could be."

"And we know now that the chemicals found on the boys' shoes was not the accelerant that was used in that fire, correct?"

"I do not know that," Sanderson stated.

"You don't?" Stokes asked, playing up his astonishment to the jury. *"You're the lead investigator on this case?"*

"I'm the lead investigator," he replied.

"And you're not aware that those chemicals don't match up?"

"No, I'm not aware of that. I'm just aware that there were chemicals, that's all I'm aware of," he said flatly.

"Wouldn't you agree with me, that's a rather significant fact that those chemicals don't match up, if in fact the boys were standing in them when they lit it?"

"It's hard to say," Sanderson replied.

Stokes shook his head. "If you're confessing to murder, why lie about something like that?"

"I have no idea."

"Could it be that's part of the story they weren't briefed on?"

"I don't know. I have no idea why they would leave that out. I mean, we did question them about it and we didn't get anything from that."

Sanderson also testified that he did not think it was odd that the boys had asked for Ricky Chavis instead of family when they gave their statements to investigators. The deputy said he was under the impression the brothers weren't close with their family. However, the boys' uncle, Greg King, had told reporters that the investigators barred him from attending the interrogation when he discovered, by chance, that his nephews were in custody.

An officer who knew Greg from the college campus where they both worked overheard the news on his police scanner. Greg immediately called the Sheriff's Office and spoke to a dispatcher, telling her he was family and he needed to speak with Investigator Sanderson. The dispatcher put him on hold and returned a few minutes later saying the deputy was busy interviewing the children, but Greg need not worry because a "friend" was with his nephews. Concerned, Greg drove to the Sheriff's Office and banged on locked doors, but no one came.

Stokes believed the investigators made every effort to protect what appeared to be an open and shut case. He implied that the deputies stopped their investigation after they "put the quarter in the slot and got the Chavis story." Sanderson insisted the confessions were sincere and not coached.

"I felt like there was too much as far as how much they knew and where he was sitting and every little detail," he said. "I felt it was too much for them to have known all this."

"But with all these inconsistencies, with all these inconsistencies, and we're charging juveniles with first degree murder," Stokes said, as if to remind him, "you did not feel compelled to compare the two stories, go back out and pick them apart on their differences?"

"To me, we didn't have inconsistencies," Sanderson explained, pressing down on the railing before him as he spoke. "I felt the statements were very accurate to our crime scene, and that's what I was using. That's what I was going by. As far as some little small things that may be a little different, that can happen. Everybody's not going to be exactly perfect in everything that they say in a statement. So some of these things can happen."

"How many lies did Ricky Chavis tell you about this? Did you keep count? If you didn't, that's fine, but how many lies and how many different stories did Ricky Chavis tell you about this incident?" Stokes asked.

"I couldn't tell you," the investigator answered, almost wearily. "We interviewed him at least nine times, I believe it was."

"And there were preinterviews to all of these interviews?"

"Yes, sir."

"And one could assume that the reason you interviewed him nine times, whereas you only interviewed my client once," Stokes pointed out, "was because his story kept evolving, is that correct?"

"Well, there were some differences each time that we interviewed him—not every time, but a lot of times when we interviewed him—and yes, we continued to interview as long as we possibly could, but didn't have enough to charge him early on."

Stokes turned and walked away, dismissing the lead investigator with a look of disgust.

* * *

Dr. Gary Cumberland, the district medical examiner, was short, with a head full of brown hair and a full beard. After more than a thousand autopsies over the past two decades, the coroner was matter-of-fact about his work and adept at simplifying it for jurors.

Cumberland testified that Terry died in a matter of minutes from his massive head injuries. Gesturing to his own face, he detailed the damage, down to the individual fractures and bruises. The medical examiner also described four bruises that extended across Terry's chest, a pattern he said was consistent with being struck two times by a rounded object of some sort.

Once those brutal facts were established, Rimmer continued with a different line of questioning for the doctor. The prosecutor had provided him with a written transcript of the boys' confessions.

"Alex is describing the sound of the bat as it hit the head. In your opinion, is that description consistent with the types of injuries inflicted on this victim with a baseball bat?"

"Yes, sir, they are," Cumberland agreed.

"He gave the description of Terry King's response in reaction to the trauma that's being inflicted upon him. What is your impression of that?"

Cumberland leaned forward, his hands folded together on the witness stand. "Those are the types of responses that I would expect to see."

"How would you describe this process that Alex is describing? Where he says 'by the time he got done he was still trying to breathe, made sort of a sound like a person who has a slightly stopped-up nose.' He goes on to say the skin on his face sort of puffed out from the air. Is there some sort of a medical term for that type of situation?" Rimmer asked.

"Yes," Cumberland answered. "That's referred to as the death rattle."

The Court TV camera zoomed in for a close up of the coroner as reporters began scribbling furiously on their notepads. "Death rattle" would be making headlines before the last witness testified on the stand that day. Dennis Corder would have the task of attempting to undo the damage, but he had anticipated this line of questioning and was ready. Cumberland admitted it was possible someone could have described the injuries to Alex that the boy claimed to have seen.

"And he could have been told about a death rattle, if indeed there was one?"

"Yes, sir," the doctor agreed.

"As a matter of fact, you cannot tell medically if there was a death rattle in this case or not, can you?"

"No, sir, I can't."

The medical examiner also said he could only definitively say there were at least three blows to Terry's head and two to his chest. He testified that the blows to Terry's chest would have made it unlikely the man could have kept his legs crossed or that the cup of coffee beside his leg would have remained undisturbed.

"You indicated there were at least three blows to the skull, is that correct?" Corder asked. The point was important. Derek initially claimed to have hit his father over the head ten times, but the coroner said he could find evidence of only three blows. While more blows were possible, the remaining seven, if they existed, they would have had to be almost perfectly superimposed on the first three fractures.

While Cumberland finished testifying, Mollye hurried downstairs for her midday live report. She had more to cover than just the day's details of the trial. The case was under a national media microscope, and questions were mounting among reporters and analysts about the legality of trying more than one person for the same crime. Mollye briefly interviewed District State Attorney Curtis Golden over the phone, addressing the issue and the possibility that all three defendants could be convicted of the murder. She stepped before the camera in the sweltering late morning heat and recapped the testimony, including the State Attorney's comments.

"Mollye, what will the State do if all three of them are convicted?" the anchor asked from the newsroom.

"State Attorney Curtis Golden says the judge will have to determine which verdict the evidence supports. The State wants to let jurors decide who's guilty of the murder, although prosecutor David Rimmer has said all along he doesn't believe Chavis committed the crime, but that he helped the boys instead. The defense has questioned the legality of that position, but so far the court is taking a wait-and-see approach. All three verdicts will remain sealed until after the boys' trial is over."

When the reporter returned to the courtroom, David Rimmer announced that the State of Florida had rested its case against Alex and Derek King. Dennis Corder made an impassioned appeal for acquittal. Although the appeal was previously discussed behind closed doors, the defense wanted to get it on the record and before the public. Citing several different cases, Corder insisted the State was guilty of prosecutorial misconduct on the basis that David Rimmer tried all three defendants for the same crime.

"The prosecution has a duty to be fair and seek the truth," Corder pleaded, "not just prosecute until he seeks a conviction," he said, gesturing toward Rimmer. "That's what's happening here, first one, then another. He uses one story to prosecute one defendant and another story to prosecute a different defendant. You can't prosecute until you find the right person."

The argument was another curious twist, and the press was absorbing every detail. The controversial case was no longer just about who killed Terry King, but whether the State was pursuing justice responsibly and legally. The defense lobbied against Rimmer's handling of the case.

"The prosecution has been coy," Corder continued. "He indicated that it's not inconsistent theories, because in the first trial he didn't ask for a conviction. All he did was say, 'Jury, find out whatever you want.' But that is not what they've done in this trial. I do not expect that Mr. Rimmer's going to stand here tomorrow in closing and say, 'Jury, believe whoever you want, come up with whatever result you want.' I believe he's going to argue very consistently and strongly that jurors should believe the boys' first story and not the later version we presented in court.

"It will be inconsistent with what he argued just last week in this very courtroom," Corder continued. "Where he said, 'We don't know what happened, you come up with the right result.' The bottom line is, last week someone sat in this chair," he motioned at Derek, "and was prosecuted for this *same* murder, by saying his hands were on the *same* bat as Derek King's, and at that time the prosecution subjected Ricky Chavis to the second most horrible criminal punishment, and that is, mandatory life in prison without parole. This week he's subjecting Derek and Alex King to the exact same thing, for the exact same murder, and we contend that violates their due process."

Rimmer sat calmly stroking the small white goatee covering his chin, confident of what the court's ruling would be. Judge Bell turned to the prosecutor for a response, and he stood immediately, adamant he had done nothing wrong.

"Judge, I feel like the defense counsel's arguments are without merit. The argument I made to the jury, the court is aware of, you were here, there's a transcript of it. You can look at it, it's not even close to what these cases they've cited refer to. And the only reason Mr. Chavis ever got indicted was because of what these King boys did," he emphasized. "That's the only evidence, and I left that up to the jury. There's a lot of other evidence in this case as to their guilt. And I'm certainly not guilty of any kind of misconduct, and as a matter of fact I was proceeding on a principal theory, but the court ruled against me and I respect that. So I left the is-sue of, as to whether he was the perpetrator, up to the jury, based on what these kids said under oath on the witness stand. As to Alex, as the court knows, I'm proceeding on a principal theory, and as to Derek, the perpetrator. So these cases they cited are not even close. The argument is without merit. The motion should be denied." Rimmer remained standing as he finished, comfortable with his argument.

Judge Bell listened, his knee still propped on the bench. He denied the motion with a brief explanation.

"These matters have been discussed at a case manage-ment conference and some other related issues. We had a court reporter up there, the clerk was up there, and there's going to be a transcript of what occurred at this case man-agement hearing. This is the same, in addition to what's been stated in this motion for acquittal, there were other things that were discussed and dealt with that involves these trials. That transcript is going to be available and filed with the court when these cases are over."

James Stokes refocused his attention on the only witness he intended to call.

Chapter 26

STOKES LACKED HIS TYPICAL IRREVERENCE WHEN HE called Alex King to the stand. He was confident the boy could handle himself. Derek, however, had opted not to testify. Derek's attorneys were concerned that he would fall apart on the stand. Although the decision was his, the boy followed Sharon Potter's advice.

The room was silent as the small boy walked toward the stand, looking more like a child marching to his place for school pictures than a teenage murder defendant. He took a seat and a court security officer adjusted the microphones to reach his mouth. The stand hit Alex around mid-chest, making it easy for him to prop his arms along it. He was a tiny figure in his light blue shirt and tie, his blond hair parted neatly to the side. He spoke quietly, stating his name and establishing the fact that he lived at the Escambia County Jail.

"When did you first meet Ricky Chavis?" Stokes began, his demeanor respectful and as close to gentle as the former Marine could display.

Alex responded that his dad had introduced him to Ricky Chavis. "Early on we were just friends. I'd watch him work on things, things and stuff."

"How did Ricky Chavis treat you?" Stokes asked.

Alex looked at his hands. "He always treated me good. He

let me do things, like play on his game machine, watch TV, and stuff."

"Now, did your relationship with Ricky Chavis evolve?"

"Yes, sir, it did." As in the previous trial, Alex's quiet voice dropped to a near whisper when he discussed the personal details of his relationship with Ricky.

"How did it change?" Stokes asked, standing with his shoulders stooped and his hands behind his back.

"Well, I don't really know when, but we had . . ." Alex faltered for words, squirming in his chair. "We had like a relationship, of some sort. Not . . . not sexual, just like, well, we had a relationship. And I don't really know when that happened, but . . ."

"When you say you don't really know when that happened, you're referring to when it became a physical, sexual relationship, is that correct?"

"Yes, sir. I do know it was before my brother came to live with us."

"How did Ricky Chavis convince you to engage in a sexual relationship with him?"

Alex dropped his arms from the stand to his lap, then placed them back on the stand again, all the while staring at the floor. "Well, he . . . he'd like tell me about previous relationships with—I can remember three names, David, Steven, and Tommy." The court was straining to hear him. "He would like . . . we would always spend time together and, well, like . . . one time, I was out on the patio sitting in his lap and stuff and he was . . . we were talking about, he was saying things, like my dad . . . We were on the subject of my dad, like saying he didn't appreciate me and stuff. And we'd talked before about this, about different punishments and stuff that my dad did. He said he shouldn't do that and stuff. He said he didn't really understand me. And he said that he loved me, he said we were different and we were gay and stuff."

"Did he tell you that he loved you?"

"Yes, sir."

"Were you in love with Ricky Chavis?"

"At that time, yes."

"And did you willingly engage in sex with Ricky Chavis?"

"Yes, sir, I did." Alex looked as though he'd like to drop through the floor.

He continued responding to questions, saying the relationship was kept secret from his father and, in fact, everyone. Sometimes Mike would be in the trailer while he and Ricky would spend a long time in Ricky's bedroom.

The jurors also heard Alex describe Ricky's systematic attempts to convince Alex that Terry was mentally abusing him, abuse he never noticed until Ricky told him about it. Ricky also persuaded Alex that Terry was not his biological father and that he only had a special bond with Derek. However, Terry soon suspected that Ricky was attempting to undermine his relationship with his children and he cut off contact between Ricky and his sons. In response, Ricky gave Alex money and keys to his home. The children soon ran away.

"Did Ricky Chavis ever say anything concerning killing your father?" Stokes asked.

"Yes, he did. He said that . . . he said that at one point—I do not know when—but he said that if things ever got so bad as we had to kill our dad, then he would have a place for us."

"Did you think things were that bad between your father and you?"

"No. I thought . . . they were pretty good. We spent a lot of time together. We had a lot of fun," Alex said quietly. He described the good times he enjoyed with his father; doing yard work, planting flower beds, painting and remodeling their house, and going to work with him, where they sometimes talked.

"And yet you ran away from your father?" Stokes asked.

"Yes, sir. I had . . . like since he . . . I really don't know how or why I ran away, but I wanted to be with him and I loved him. But he kept telling me that my dad was staring us down, and like he didn't really appreciate me or understand me and stuff, and he said that . . . he kept talking about punishments and spankings and things. I only remember three spankings in my life, but he kept talking about them."

Alex also described the trapdoor in Ricky's trailer where he and Derek would hide from their father and other visitors. Alex said Ricky provided them with a lamp, marijuana, and a smoking pipe while they were down there.

During the time they stayed at Ricky's home, Alex said he and Ricky made no attempt to hide their physical relationship. Stokes wanted to make sure jurors understood the significance of Ricky's dirty little secret and how it was directly related to the murderous chain of events that followed Derek's return to his father.

"How did Rick react to the news that your brother had been caught?"

"Rick was worried about Derek telling my dad what had been going on that week, like what we had been doing, smoking weed, and our relationship. Rick was worried Derek might not stick to the story about us being in Pace in the woods during that week."

"What did Rick decide to do to correct this problem?"

"He wanted me to go back to Derek. So me and Rick drove out to Pace and went to a Tom Thumb and my grandmother showed up. Before my dad showed up, me and Rick went over to a McDonald's and he told me to make sure we were home at midnight and he would pick us up. He said to make sure the back door was unlocked."

Alex said his father was happy they returned and did not threaten or punish them in any way, even after they returned to their own house later that night. The jurors were leaning forward in their seats, glued to the testimony.

"Did your father go to sleep?" James asked.

"I believe so, yes, sir. We went inside and I believe he went to the green room. Me and Derek went into our room and played board games or something, we were just burning time. Then, I said that I was going to go to the rest room and I went down the hallway and unlocked the back door and used the rest room and came back to our room. I believe my dad was asleep then."

"Then what happened?"

"Then Derek fell asleep, I believe, and Rick came in the back door. Well, he showed up at our door and he told us, well, he shook Derek awake, then he told us to be quiet and we were like, let's go."

"What did Ricky Chavis tell you to do at that point after he awakened your brother?"

"He told us to be quiet and told us to . . . We went out of the house and got in his car and were supposed to get in the trunk. We went into the back door and through the backseat into the trunk."

Alex revealed that this is commonly how they rode with Rick when they were runaways, folding the backseats down and climbing into the trunk. He couldn't remember how long they waited before Ricky returned, but he said they didn't get out of the trunk until they arrived at Ricky's house.

"What happened once you got inside Rick's house?" Stokes asked.

"He told us that there had been . . . said that there had

been a fight between my dad, him and my dad. And he said that my dad was dead, said that he had killed my dad to protect us. He was saying that he had done it for us. He said my dad would never have let us live with him and never let us go. He . . . he said my dad would have killed us before he would have let us go. And he said that . . . he said that it was horrible."

"How did you react to this news?"

"I was crying and I was upset and stuff. I was kind of angry at him, but he kept saying he loved me and that he had done it for me and stuff. He was saying things like, you know how bad your dad was with the abuse."

Alex testified that Ricky was worried when he realized Terry's home had not been consumed in the fire.

"He was saying that he couldn't go to prison. Like, if we went to prison, then if he went to prison, we'd all go because I was involved because I opened the door and stuff," Alex continued in his low voice, his eyes downcast. "He said that we could say that Derek had done it because he was like stronger and stuff and they would believe that, we'd get off on self-defense because of saying that we know all the abuse that he was doing to us. He said that he had cop friends that could back us up on it."

Alex testified it was some time before he and Derek agreed to take the blame for Ricky, but eventually they complied and began rehearsing the story they would tell the investigators. Once Ricky was satisfied, he called Deputy Reggie Jernigan to pick them up. Alex said Ricky specifically told him that Reggie would help them out. The boy believed their plan was working, even after he and Derek were arrested, so they continued to tell the story to other juveniles in detention.

"While you were at the Juvenile Justice Center, were you allowed to make phone calls?" Stokes asked.

"Yes, sir."

"Were you allowed to call Ricky Chavis?"

"Yes, sir."

"Did you and Ricky Chavis have a code word between you?"

"Yes, sir. It was 'everything's still the same,' or something like that."

"And what did that mean?"

"It was just between me and him, it would be like everything is still the same as far as the relationship goes and the story."

"When did things start to go different than Ricky Chavis told you they would?"

"Whenever we went over to the adult jail I started to doubt that. Also, whenever Derek had told me that Rick offered to have sex with him, then I started to doubt our relationship then."

David Rimmer was not convinced the child had rejected the older man. The prosecutor immediately paraded the same series of love letters Alex wrote Ricky, asking the boy, one by one, if he wrote them. By the eighth letter, Alex had locked his eyes on the floor.

Rimmer wanted to show the jurors that the boy had a motive for wanting his father killed. He wanted to be with Ricky, instead of his much stricter parent.

"Did Rick treat you better than your dad did?" the prosecutor asked.

"Yes, sir. Well, as far as like everything that we were doing, like the freedom and stuff, he would let us do a lot of things that my dad didn't."

"And because of that, did you care more for Rick than you did your dad?"

"Well, as far as that goes, yeah, I believe so."

"Did you ever say that you wanted your dad dead?"

"No, sir, I loved my dad. I didn't want anything to happen to him."

"Are you saying that you know for a fact you never said that?"

"Yes, sir."

Rimmer also attempted to pin down other inconsistencies in the boy's testimony—the fact that Alex lied to the investigators when he said his father inflicted scratches on his arm. He reminded the boy that after he was sent to Juvenile Detention, he told his grandmother he "lost his head by what he saw" the night his father died.

The prosecutor also asked Alex how he called Ricky while he was incarcerated in detention. Alex answered that he used the phones provided for juvenile inmates, but Rimmer pressed him about using a cell phone. James Stokes had, in fact, allowed the boy to call Ricky from his personal cell phone. At the time, Stokes hoped to learn more about Ricky's relationship with Alex. However, the investigators were none too pleased when they discovered what the defense attorney had done. As a result, Juvenile Detention instituted a new policy called the "Stokes Rule," which required visitors to surrender all cell phones. Alex said he did not remember if someone gave him a phone with the purpose of calling Ricky.

The second day of the King murder trial closed with Alex's testimony. The defense expected to rest its case the following day. In a matter of hours, the brothers would know if the jury believed they were murderers.

The M.C. Blanchard Judicial Building was a hub of media madness by the third day. With the possibility that a verdict was close at hand, the number of journalists continued to multiply.

Sharon Potter and Dennis Corder decided against calling Dr. Ronald Yarborough, the child psychologist who had evaluated Derek. Although he didn't believe Derek was capable of committing the crime, Derek's attorneys realized that the prosecution would just call another psychologist to refute Yarbrough's evaluation. Instead, they presented witnesses who would support the idea that Ricky was behind the murder and the cops overlooked him because of a shoddy investigation.

Linda Walker revealed on the stand that Ricky and Reggie had been friends for years. She worked as a clerk at the Sac 'N Save where Ricky shopped and Reggie worked off-duty security. She said Ricky would often come there to "hang out" with the deputy. Linda also testified that Ricky called her numerous times in the days before Terry's death, claiming that Terry was abusing her grandsons. She said the last call she received from him was shortly before the murder. Ricky told her he and Terry had argued over the boys and he was going to Terry's house to try and resolve it. She claimed Chavis warned her, "When I get ready to do something, nobody will know that it was me."

Greg King testified that he was concerned about the way the Sheriff's Office handled the crime scene. He told jurors he was surprised to find the doors open shortly after the murder and various people simply coming and going as they pleased through the house. He noted that forensic investigators had removed pieces of the ceiling, the floor, and the wall, but the chair where Terry's body was found remained untouched. He called investigators, worried they had overlooked an important piece of evidence, but he was met with a lukewarm response. Investigators gave the go-ahead to bulldoze the house a couple of months later, and Greg was alarmed that any remaining evidence was now permanently lost.

The jury heard testimony from the Escambia corrections officer who found Ricky huddled in the jail recreation yard, scratching a message into a layer of dirt atop a cement slab. It read, "Alex, don't trust," before the officer wiped it away, obliterating the message. The defense offered the message to demonstrate Ricky's desperation to contact Alex and control the truth.

The remaining witness was perhaps one of the most compelling. Escambia Sheriff's Deputy Glenn Gowitzke was a computer crimes investigator with special fire and arson training. The deputy was a hulking man, the size of a linebacker. He was bald, but kept a thick, well-trimmed mustache that curved around his mouth.

Gowitzke testified that he found child pornography on the computer deputies seized from Chavis's home. He said the pictures depicted boys involved in sexual acts. These findings weren't surprising to many in the courtroom, but his analysis of the alleged murder weapon was shocking. Investigators insisted the glob of melted metal found in Terry's ruined bed was the murder weapon, all that remained of the aluminum bat the boys claimed to have thrown on the bed. However, the unrecognizable glob wasn't entered into evidence and jurors never got a chance to evaluate it themselves. Deputy Gowitzke testified that the warped aluminum was consistent with a window frame and in fact wasn't a bat at all.

"I would have expected to find an identifiable portion of the bat," Gowitzke told the jury. "I've never seen one completely consumed or completely melted."

He explained that in his opinion the fire did not burn hot enough to destroy the bat. He said after such an extensive search, investigators would have found the bat, had it been there.

Dennis Corder made sure the jury got the point. "In your opinion, there are still no signs of a baseball bat?"

"No, the bat was not in the fire. No."

"The globs of melted metal that you found, were any of those consistent with an aluminum baseball bat?"

"It was aluminum. It's a cheap grade aluminum, but it's consistent with the window frame which was aluminum."

"If a baseball bat melted, would it become just a little glob, or what would you expect from your training and experience?"

"Based on no more damage than was in that house, I would have expected to at least have found an identifiable portion of the bat and not a complete melted glob."

When Dennis finished, David Rimmer hammered Gowitzke. "What does an aluminum bat look like when it's melted?" the prosecutor asked, practically sneering.

"If it's completely melted, just a big sheet of molten metal, silver," the deputy replied.

"When did you see one like that?"

"I've seen them over the years, working fires. I've seen partially burned bats. I've never seen one completely consumed or completely melted."

The deputy was the last of the defense witnesses. There was a sense of anticipation among the courtroom spectators as the attorneys prepared for their last chance to argue guilt or innocence.

Outwardly, they appeared calm, but there was no denying the intense scrutiny. Reporters clung to their cell phones, letting the outside world know the case was wrapping up and a verdict could be coming soon. During a short break before closing arguments began, a friend of Sharon Potter's called to let her know CNN would be broadcasting their closing statements live.

Potter pushed the podium to the center of the room. She and Stokes had previously agreed to this arrangement. She would close first, systematically laying out the facts with cool logic, David Rimmer would follow, and Stokes would have the last word, aiming to strike an emotional chord within the jurors.

Potter's job was to systematically discredit the boys' statements by showing the obvious coaching. She reminded jurors of the boys' absurd inconsistencies and their use of terms like "flammable material" and "wooden structure" as well as identical verbiage. Then she ticked off each one of the lies they told to protect Ricky Chavis, lies the investigators simply accepted without question.

David Rimmer gathered a few papers and stepped before the jury, ready to state his case. However, one of his most convincing tools was not in his hands—he carried it in his attitude. His long-held tactic was core deep confidence, and he portrayed it in his walk, his gestures, and his casual "let me break it down for you" slang. More important, it coated his every word. He addressed many of the defense's arguments point by point, saying not only were they inaccurate but implying only an imbecile would believe such folly.

Rimmer emanated empathy for the jury when he discussed Rick "the motivator" Chavis. "Now there isn't any doubt about it all, Rick Chavis *is* a child molester. Rick Chavis was molesting Alex. Rick Chavis did have a motive to want to be with Alex." But he insisted that Ricky knew he was better served by remaining friends with Terry than by killing him, since he realized there was no possibility he could ever gain custody of Alex.

The prosecutor crouched before the jurors like a predator stalking his prey, describing the graphic details Alex told investigators. He drew out every gruesome word. "It doesn't make sense Alex would get all the grisly details from Rick Chavis. Every detail down to the *brains* on the wall, the *hole* in the head, the *sound* that the bat made when it hit the skull and cracked the skull, the sounds that his father made as he was experiencing what Dr. Cumberland called the '*death rattle*.'"

Alex and Stokes had been writing on a pad, half listening to the prosecutor until his dramatic recounting of Alex's words. The boy began staring across the room, rocking in his chair and slowly, almost imperceptibly, shaking his head. Stokes gently squeezed his small shoulder, but Alex gave no reaction and his compulsive actions continued. The former Marine then leaned in protectively, dropping his elbow on the back of Alex's chair. The boy immediately moved closer to Stokes, as if desperate for shelter, and only then did he sit still.

Rimmer continued his closing argument for an hour and a half, a striking contrast to the ten minutes he delivered to the Chavis jury. These were the defendants he wanted to convict. He and John Sanderson were convinced in their hearts these children were guilty, and if the jury agreed, they hoped to have justice in the eyes of the court and vindication in the court of public opinion.

"A wise king once said, even a child is known by his doings, whether his work be pure or whether it be right," Rimmer concluded. "Ladies and gentlemen, on November the twenty-sixth the work of Derek and Alex was not pure and it was not right. You should judge them by their actions, not their ages; by their intent, not by your emotions. I'm asking you to find them both guilty as charged because they are guilty as charged. Thank you very much."

In his gray suit, James Stokes looked especially somber. He paced slowly before the jury, one hand in his pocket, the other earnestly gesturing to make his points. He spoke slowly and deliberately, as if carrying the weight of a heavy burden. The irreverent tone that sometimes lingered just beneath the surface was gone, replaced with a solemn manner. He never allowed the jury to forget the gravity of their decision.

Stokes recapped much of the testimony for nearly an hour, reminding jurors of the lack of physical evidence and pleading with passion. The thirteen-year-old boy who had been his client for almost a year sat across the room, swiveling in his chair and doodling on a pad, seemingly oblivious to the drama unfolding around him. Stokes was not oblivious. He had an inkling of the damage that had already been done to his client. In his final moments of the battle, he still dared hope that he might be able to prevent Alex from spending the rest of his life in prison.

"Your decision is on one issue and one issue only," Stokes said quietly, holding up one finger. "Did the State prove beyond to the exclusion of every reasonable doubt that my client, the then-twelve-year-old Alex King, is principal to murder? And did the State prove that he committed arson?" He paused and stared at them directly. "Ladies and gentlemen of the jury, they haven't even come close."

Stokes turned back to the table, his head slightly bowed by the weight of his responsibility. He glanced at Alex, who looked strangely mischievous, hiding the hint of a smile behind his hand. As Stokes dropped into his seat he realized why. Alex had written *Mr. Stokes is old! Mr. Stokes is old!* over and over on a large piece of paper. While the lawyer had been fighting for the child's life, proclaiming his innocence to the nation, Alex had been preparing a practical joke. James Stokes just shook his head.

The lengthy arguments left little time for the jury to deliberate that day, and the court decided to let them begin the following morning. The boys would spend another night in jail, wondering if this would be their last evening behind bars or their home for the rest of their lives.

Chapter 27

THE JURY BEGAN DELIBERATING AT NINE-THIRTY THE next morning. Every major news network in the country and others from around the world had crews on standby, waiting to report the verdict. Not only would jurors decide the fate of the children, but the outcome of Ricky Chavis's trial would also be revealed. People swarmed the courthouse waiting for word, all speculating on the verdicts. Mollye waited with her photographer at the live truck. Once the jury returned, Channel 3 planned to break into programming with a special report and broadcast the verdicts live. The boys' family remained huddled in the hall, praying they would be taking the brothers home that afternoon. The investigators wanted the spotlight off their work and shone on the children they called murderers. Two weeks worth of testimony and more than a year's worth of wondering and worrying seemed brief compared to the wait that stretched before all of them now. About five hours later, the jury reached a verdict.

There was a mad rush to the courtroom as family, press, and spectators hurried to their seats. Kelly sat with a friend and Lisa French, clinging to their hands. She had already made arrangements to have her mother, Linda, take the children home if the jury delivered a not guilty verdict, since she did not want to take the boys back to Kentucky with her. Linda was ready with open arms. Derek was excited about the prospect of having his own room and inviting girls over to the house. Alex was thrilled with the idea of having his own space, away from his hyperactive brother. However, the jail director intended to release the boys to their attorneys, if they were acquitted, in the hopes of avoiding a family custody squabble.

James Stokes had arranged for a friend who owned a car dealership to bring a shiny new Corvette convertible to the courthouse, in the event that Alex was released. As soon as they could go, Stokes planned to whisk Alex away in the Corvette, the boy's favorite car, and allow him the freedom of being outdoors and away from the media hype. However, he did not reveal his plan to Alex. Instead, he prepared him for the worst, fearing the boy would be crushed with disappointment if he was convicted.

Derek and Alex exchanged nervous smiles, then Alex briefly pressed his hands together and looked upward as if in prayer. Then the deputy announced the arrival of the jury and they all stood. Mollye tried to read the jurors' faces as they marched in, but they looked straight ahead, their expressions blank. The forewoman handed an envelope to court security, who passed it along to Judge Bell. All eyes were on the white piece of paper he read silently, then gave to the clerk.

"Clerk's Office would publish those two verdicts, please," Bell said.

The young woman sitting behind the bench alongside Bell stood. "Clerk in Circuit Court and in for Escambia County, Florida," she began. "State of Florida, plaintiff, versus Derek King, defendant. We the jury find as follows as to count one of the indictment . . ."

Derek stood between Sharon Potter and Dennis Corder,

looking nervous and hopeful. Sharon placed her hand on the small of his back.

"*Guilty* of second degree murder, a lesser included offense, without a weapon."

The silent courtroom erupted into a low hum. Derek dropped his head, then looked back up as the clerk continued reading. His expression was neutral.

"We the jury find as follows to count two of the indictment, *guilty* of arson as charged. So say we all this sixth day of September 2002, foreperson Lynne Schwarz."

Alex stood next to James Stokes, appearing shell-shocked. He slouched against the table as his hope for freedom was replaced with dread.

"State of Florida, plaintiff, versus Alex King, defendant. We the jury find as follows as to count one of the indictment, *guilty* of second degree murder without a weapon. *Guilty* of arson, as charged."

Their mother buried her face in her hands. Lisa French wrapped her arm around Kelly Marino, wiping away tears of her own. Derek rocked in his chair, his head in his hand. The plans for a celebration party, a room of his own, and most important, being with a family who loved and wanted him, vanished. He was faced with a life behind bars, and the isolation that would accompany his term was almost more than he could bear. Judge Bell set sentencing for October 17. They faced a possible twenty-two years to life in prison without parole.

Now seated, Alex's expressionless face began to crack. Tears poured down his cheeks and he threw a small hand over his face to hide them. James Stokes whispered to Alex as the boy quickly wiped away more tears, trying to get them under control. Although Stokes had wisely warned Alex this moment might come, he appeared as much in need of comforting as his client. They all stood once more as the jury left the room. Once the jurors had disappeared through a side door, Alex put his tiny hand in Stokes's and shook it.

"Thank you," Alex told him quietly. "It will be okay." Stokes wondered if Alex really understood the bleak reality stretching before him.

An hour after the children were gone, Ricky Chavis was seated in the chair where Derek had sat, waiting for his jury to arrive. He looked worried in his black suit and maroon tie, his hands folded in his lap. Across from him, David Rimmer was leaning back casually in his chair as if worry was the furthest thing from his mind. Within a few minutes the jurors from the previous week's trial returned to their seats.

Judge Bell looked sternly at the crowded courtroom, "I would like to ask some of the folks in the courtroom, I wish no one would get overly excited once the court publishes this verdict. It would be appreciated."

He pulled the verdict from a manila envelope, opened and reviewed it before once again passing it to the clerk. The courtroom was silent. The boys' devastated families were hoping for a small miracle, that Ricky would also be held accountable for Terry King's murder. They held hands tightly, believing that although the boys had been sacrificed, perhaps Ricky Chavis would go down too.

"Clerk's Office, publish that verdict, please," Bell said.

Ricky and Mike Rollo stood. Ricky nervously adjusted his tie.

"We the jury find as follows as to count one of the indictment, *not guilty*." Ricky heaved a huge sigh. Rollo reached an arm around his back and shook his hand with the other.

"We the jury find as follows as to count two of the indictment, *not guilty*. So say we all this thirtieth day of August 2002."

Ricky braced his hand on the table and squeezed his eyes against the tears of relief. He dropped to his seat, unable to stop crying. The courtroom remained eerily quiet. At the announcement of the verdict, the boys' family dropped their heads. The disappointment was unbearable and they stared at the floor.

After the jury was dismissed, Ricky turned and shook Mike Rollo's hand with both of his. Although he was free of the murder and arson charges, he was still headed back to jail pending the disposition of his remaining cases. This victory encouraged him, and there was a bounce in his step when the court security officers led him away. Ricky now believed he had every reason to hope he would beat the other charges too.

The press was pooling on the lawn of the judicial building, waiting to interview the attorneys. Mollye was just finishing her live report.

"The prosecution says the second degree without a weapon verdicts are what's called a 'jury pardon,' meaning jurors likely sympathized with the children and did not want to hand down a first degree murder conviction. We're about to hear more from the attorneys in this case in just a few minutes. The court also revealed they already knew the outcome of Chavis's trial because they had unsealed the verdict prior to the start of the King trial. They were concerned two guilty verdicts would be unfair. Back to you."

The photographer turned his camera toward the podium, where more than two dozen people with cameras, lights, and microphones had gathered.

David Rimmer stepped up first, flanked by John Sanderson and Terry Kilgore. He called the case sad, saying there were no winners, but he believed the jury made the right choice. Although he conceded Ricky may have influenced the children to such an extent that they killed their father, they were still responsible for swinging the bat. The prosecutor insisted he gave jurors and the public an opportunity to hear both sides of the high profile case, but in the end the boys' credibility was at issue.

Investigators Sanderson and Kilgore were silent at Rimmer's side, the image of solidarity. He turned to his longtime friends and motioned for them to step closer. The prosecutor commended the investigators for an outstanding job, despite the heavy criticism they received for their handling of the case. Rimmer announced he was proud to work with them and said the jury's verdict not only brought justice for Terry King, but "vindicated" the hard work of the Escambia Sheriff's Office.

As Mollye jotted down the prosecutor's comments, she underlined the word *vindication*. It had long since replaced justice in the search for Terry's killer.

PART FIVE
THE FINAL MOVES

"Once the game is over, the king and the pawns go back to the same box."
Italian Proverb

Chapter 28

AFTER THE KING BROTHERS' JURY HANDED DOWN THEIR guilty verdicts, Sharon Potter left for the jail to comfort Derek. After visiting with her young client, she saw his family arriving and asked Linda Walker if Kelly was coming.

"No, she had to go back to Kentucky," Linda told her. "She wasn't feeling good."

Sharon was livid. Derek was upset, depressed in his jail cell, and she saw that his mother had put her needs above those of her children again. "It's not about her," Sharon practically shouted. "When will she learn it's not about her?" The pressure was taking a toll on her normally reserved nature.

The next morning, James Stokes awoke to incessant ringing. The screeching phone jolted him to reality and he remembered what he wanted to forget—the boys had been convicted. James cared deeply for Alex and the devastating drama that had become the child's life. He had even gone to the jail to comfort him after the verdict, worried that Alex needed his support. Instead, Alex was more concerned about consoling his attorney and insisted that James contact his friends and family and tell them, "I'm mad, but I'm okay." James had spent a good part of the night on the phone, eventually collapsing into bed, emotionally and physically exhausted. The phone would not stop ringing, and he snatched it off the hook.

"Hello!" he answered irritably.

"Have you seen today's paper yet? Have you read it?" a friend asked excitedly.

"No, and I don't want to."

"James, you *have* to see it," she exclaimed. "Go get it! You'll be glad you did. Just go!"

Relenting, he stumbled outside and pulled the *Pensacola News Journal* from its plastic sheath. He stared at the bold headline, KING BOYS GUILTY, and mentally cursed his friend. The attorney turned and was walking back inside when he flipped the paper open and read the headline below the fold: KING JURORS BELIEVED CHAVIS SWUNG THE BAT. He stopped in mid-step, a huge smile spreading across his face.

The article revealed that all six jurors believed Ricky Chavis actually killed Terry King, but they convicted the brothers of second degree murder without a weapon because they thought the children had opened the door and let the killer in the house.

The jury, led by forewoman Lynne Schwarz, didn't entirely believe either version of events—the boys' taped confessions or Alex's testimony on the stand. The jurors believed the statements to investigators were rehearsed and incredible and they doubted children their age would use terms like "flammable material" or "wooden structure."

"When they asked Alex about something he wasn't coached in, his voice changed, his demeanor changed," juror Glenda Berg told the *Pensacola News Journal* reporter. "It was almost like two different people."

However, they were convinced that Alex had seen his father die, pointing to the boy's graphic description of the "death rattle" and the sound the bat made as it crushed Terry's skull. They felt the truth was a combination of what the boys told police and the court. The jurors had been stunned when they learned that Chavis had been acquitted of the murder.

"I was so shocked I just couldn't believe it," Schwarz said. "It's disturbing that twelve people could see it one way and six people another. But I don't blame that jury. They saw a different presentation and a different interpretation. It's too bad they couldn't have all been tried together. That would have been a fairer trial."

Schwarz, fifty-one, blamed some of the confusion on the investigators, who she believed handled the case poorly. "Just as common men, we were sitting there and listening to the confessions. There were so many discrepancies between one boy and another. And then there were some places where they were exactly the same, the same verbiage. The investigators should have immediately said, 'There's a problem here and we've got to look into this more, go back to the scene and try to corroborate some of this.' But they didn't. It's like they just stopped their investigations with the confessions."

David Rimmer was shocked by the jurors' comments. He disagreed with their theory and told the paper it essentially would make no difference if the boys appealed. "You cannot appeal based on why the jury did what they did, only if there was something improper, like improper evidence was taken back or something procedural."

The jurors felt Chavis had swung the bat, but they weren't certain if Terry's murder was actually planned or if the truth would ever be revealed.

"There are so many things that are left unanswered that I would like to find out, but I don't think anybody will," said twenty-nine-year-old Mary Lupton. "Only they know truthfully what events really took place. Only them and God, and that will be their final judgment."

To make matters worse for the State, some of the jurors in the Chavis murder trial were now coming forward saying they would have convicted Rick Chavis had they seen the same evidence that had been presented at the King trial.

The jurors weren't the only ones criticizing the way investigators and the prosecution approached the case. The entire country was discussing it. The satisfaction David Rimmer felt after the verdict was short-lived. Now, he found himself in the unfamiliar position of defense. National legal critics took aim at the Assistant State Attorney, denouncing what they called two prosecutions on identical charges. Rimmer defended his decision, making more than half a dozen television appearances and a number of newspaper and magazine interviews, but the critics showed no mercy. He was crucified for pursuing what many saw as two conflicting theories and providing a basis for the boys' verdicts to be overturned.

The Ricky Chavis jury was eager to convict him on the principal charges because they believed he was certainly involved in the gruesome murder, but they felt the prosecution didn't present the evidence or give them the direction they needed for a conviction. State Attorney Curtis Golden decided to weigh in on the issue, making a statement that shocked many in the judicial system and the community: "If Chavis had been convicted, we probably would have requested that the judge set aside his conviction."

National reporters who had spent careers chronicling shocking stories were dumbfounded by the multilayered tale. Booking agents from California and New York touched down in Pensacola and hit the ground running.

As an ABC affiliate reporter, Mollye's connections with the family gave her an opportunity to appear on *Good Morning America*. The producers, hoping for an exclusive with some members of the family, asked her to interview the boy's maternal grandparents and an aunt to discuss their feelings on the case. She found the experience both exciting and frustrating. She enjoyed the national exposure, but found she had little input over the content of the story.

The television interview became the first of many for the Walkers and the Kings. For weeks, producers from *The John Walsh Show* besieged family members with phone calls. They were preparing a segment featuring Alex and Derek King. They were amazingly persistent, sending flowers to some family members and flying them to New York to appear on the show.

The show was a lightning rod for the dramatic case, drawing millions of viewers who had followed the trials via Court TV coverage. On stage, Sharon Potter and James Stokes squared off against generic prosecutors, unrelated to the case but brought in to balance the debate. At issue was the State's prosecution of two people for the same crime. Potter was relaxed and articulate, but Stokes shook with anger as he pointed out how the prosecution had not even tried to convict Ricky Chavis. The audience shared his view, exploding into applause as he demanded, "My client deserves a new trial!"

Jury forewoman Lynne Schwarz had also been flown in for the show. She wore a lapel microphone and was seated in the audience. John Walsh sought her out numerous times, questioning how the jury had arrived at the verdict. As she passionately explained that they wanted their own decision to be set aside, Walsh was moved by her words. He told Lynne Schwarz how much he respected her for having the courage to fight for a new trial for Alex and Derek.

Media attention became commonplace for those embroiled in the case. Some of the biggest names in television were calling Stokes, Potter, and Corder almost daily. James

Stokes was at a disadvantage since he rarely watched television and didn't know who many of them were. At one point he mistook Leslie Stahl for a client. The famed broadcaster called his cell phone, introduced herself, and quickly launched into a conversation. After a moment he interrupted and asked her, "What are you charged with?" and she dissolved in laughter. He got a chuckle each time he retold the story.

Sharon Potter flew to New York to meet with Barbara Walters. The renowned journalist was hoping to arrange an exclusive interview with the King brothers, but Sharon was not impressed. She was unconvinced that an interview would benefit her client. Sharon believed *the ratings* would be the real winners.

The question of the King brothers' guilt became a local, national, even worldwide debate. Letters and e-mails poured into the *Pensacola News Journal*. The boys' case struck a nerve with people from all walks of life, and it seemed everyone had something to say. The majority of responses were critical of the State and Ricky Chavis.

People who had followed the trials took to the Internet to express their outrage. A website called "derekandalexking.org" sprang to life and thousands logged on, debating the issues of trying children as adults, analyzing the minute details of the trials and seeking to help straighten out what they saw as a legal mess. The website attracted people from the legal community who offered free advice and guidance. Donna Gallegos, a Pensacola businesswoman, put her own life on hold and devoted herself to pulling these people together and guiding them to the site. It provided people with an outlet to air their views and offered the contact information they needed. Almost instantly, thousands of letters, faxes, e-mails, and phone calls from all over the world flooded into the M.C. Blanchard Judicial Building and the governor's office.

Mollye was also receiving e-mails from across the globe through her station e-mail account. She sifted through dozens a day. Some were people venting to her as the reporter they associated with case. Many were e-mails that were copied to David Rimmer and Florida Governor Jeb Bush.

One such e-mail read, "The King trial is so sensationalistic that it is making a laughingstock of the judicial system in Pensacola. Regardless of what these 12- and 13-year-olds are being accused of, children in this country should not be tried in adult court on national television. The whole spectacle reveals nothing more than a callous and ignorant state legislature which legally allows children this young to be tried in adult court, a grandstanding prosecutor who is media- and politically hungry, and a community which obviously lets them get away with treating 12-year-olds like hardened criminals. Regardless of the outcome, which will likely be overturned in an appeals court, I hope Pensacola will turn out of office prosecutors and legislators who persecute young children as adults in the name of protecting the community against crime. This case should clearly have remained in juvenile court.—James Farrow, MD, Professor, Adolescent Medicine, Tulane University, New Orleans.

Another wrote, "It is with sadness and disbelief that I have been following the trial. Whether Alex and Derek are guilty of killing their father or not, the fact remains, they are kids and should not be tried as adults and sentenced to life in adult prison! This case is absolutely heartbreaking as well as horrifying!" Kerstin Haavimb, San Francisco.

The media only saw a small sampling of the e-mails and phone calls David Rimmer was receiving. The prosecutor had been fielding calls and letters since the boys were first indicted as adults. Those numbers skyrocketed after the trial, some supportive, many critical, and others even included death threats. The Assistant State Attorney was one of the most respected by his peers within the local judicial system. He had lost less than a handful of cases during his twenty-year career with the State Attorney's Office. He was used to winning, and the constant barrage of criticism from armchair quarterbacks must have been frustrating when he so firmly believed he was right.

The jurors in the King trial were also feeling the pressure. National media news organizations were clamoring for them. Lynne Schwarz was a natural born leader, and through her dogged determination she convinced two of the other jurors—Glenda Berg and Mary Lupton—to speak out about the case.

Some analysts and those in the viewing public ridiculed their verdict, saying they unfairly convicted the young brothers. The jurors were desperate to correct what they viewed as a "mistake" and somehow prevent the children from spending their lives in prison. They stood by their belief that the boys were responsible for opening the door, but had come to realize they should have checked "not guilty" instead of "guilty." After all, the jury was not being asked if the boys were principal to Ricky. That was not one of their choices.

They knew they couldn't fix things alone. Lynne Schwarz and the others wanted to sit down with the boys' lawyers to discuss their options. When they discovered legal ethics prevented the attorneys from reaching out to them, the jurors wrote a statement of their findings: "We believe Alex and Derek King opened the door allowing Ricky Chavis to enter Terry King's house. We believe that Ricky Chavis then beat Terry King to death." The jurors had the statement notarized and sent it to James Stokes.

Next, Schwarz focused her sights on Frank Bell. She

wrote a letter to the judge requesting a meeting, and stated that the jury believed Ricky Chavis was the perpetrator while Alex and Derek were principals. Bell politely refused their offer in his own letter.

David Rimmer steadfastly argued that the juror's feelings on the issue had no legal standing, only their verdict. However, the defense insisted the jury's verdict was so uncertain that it appeared they never intended to convict the King boys of their father's murder.

Meanwhile, the Internet interest in the plight of the King boys had surged out of the computers and into the phones. A conference call among nineteen people from California to New York resulted in the formation of a grassroots group called "Under Our Wings." It was led by Bishop Thomas Masters, an articulate and passionate South Florida minister who tried to dissuade legislators and prosecutors from trying children as adults. The group's goal was to give concerned citizens the opportunity to express their outrage, in the hope of change. They helped organize candlelight vigils, peaceful protests, and online petitions, gathering thousands of signatures. When the court set a hearing to discuss the case on October 17, the group's organizer, Donna Gallegos, promised a rally and invited Bishop Masters to speak.

The King boys were scheduled to be sentenced, but the public outcry was reaching a fever pitch. The boys' attorneys had filed motions and were prepared to ask the court for a new trial or to throw out the verdicts. Under Our Wings was hoping for a massive show of support that morning.

Upon learning of the protest, David Rimmer told the *Pensacola News Journal*, "That's their right if they want to protest. Personally, I don't have time to argue with every little yellow dog that barks along the highway." He went on to conclude how Judge Bell would react to the protesters. "I think the judge is going to base his ruling on the law," he said. "I don't think he's going to be influenced by what any angry mob might want to tell him to do."

As the courthouse lawn began to fill up with the "little yellow dogs," the leader of the pack spoke with reporters.

"Clearly these boys have already been through so much in their lives," Donna Gallegos said. "I feel the state has done an incredible amount of additional damage. The rally is just going to be a lot of concerned parents, grandparents, and others from across the country."

Kelly Marino flew in from Kentucky to attend the rally and thanked the protesters for their support of her sons. The crowd was smaller than predicted, but television coverage wasn't. The footage aired on CNN that evening. The group protested quietly, but carried signs that screamed for attention. Lisa French held a poster that read: PENSACOLA: THE PEDOPHILE'S PARADISE!

Bishop Masters led the protesters in asking Judge Bell to grant a new trial for the Kings. "Judge Bell and Governor Bush, let me remind you that the whole world is watching Pensacola today; they are not just watching how we treat our children, but they are watching the entire American judicial system." As he spoke, the audience began to murmur its approval. Before long each remark the charismatic minister made was followed by a shout of accord from the audience.

Lynne Schwarz was among the guest speakers. The middle-age mother broke into tears as she tried to explain the jury's decision and their desire to help the children get the support they needed to lead normal lives. The rally ended just as the hearing upstairs in the judicial center was about to begin. The group formed a circle, held hands, and prayed tearfully for justice.

* * *

The King brothers walked into the courtroom wearing green jail jumpsuits. Their dapper appearance from the previous trials was gone. Derek's hair was longer and in need of a cut, and Alex bore the unfortunate acne signs of the onset of puberty. Both boys seemed depressed. The press was allowed to sit in the jury box to make room for the crowds trying to find a seat.

The defense argued its motions to have the verdicts thrown out or to grant the Kings a new trial. Both defense teams had feverishly researched the rare case law on trying two people for the same crime. They had made the same arguments twice previously, but in September, after the boys had been convicted, a new Florida case came out with similar facts in which two people had been prosecuted for the same crime. That judge had frowned upon it and reversed the convictions. Now the defense had a solid precedent on which to base their motions. David Rimmer was ready to argue that such a decision would be a miscarriage of justice. Judge Bell had already made up his mind and would read from his prepared notes.

The judge marched into the packed courtroom like a man on a mission. He began by praising Rimmer's twenty-year career with the State Attorney's Office. He called him one of the finest prosecutors in the system, saying that he had personally worked with Rimmer on many cases and believed he would never act unethically. But despite the prosecutor's past conduct, Bell said his handling of the King case was "unusual and bizarre."

David Rimmer's expression never changed, but he seemed to brace himself in his chair. Across the room, James Stokes exchanged a quick glance with Sharon Potter.

Bell said he did not understand why Rimmer prosecuted Chavis as a principal to the crime when Derek and Alex King said, "He did it. We didn't do it." The judge questioned

Rimmer's decision to pursue the principal case against Chavis and put the brothers on the stand, even though their testimony contradicted the prosecutor's theory.

The judge speculated that Rimmer had allowed the brothers to testify in the Chavis trial in order to get a preview of what he could expect the following week in their murder trial.

Judge Bell also chastised David Rimmer for his decision not to put Chavis on the stand. He said that Ricky could have been granted immunity for his testimony, as the brothers had been.

"He would have certainly been a good witness," Bell admonished. "Where's the logic?"

Judge Bell continued his scathing review. Although the court had agreed prior to the start of the trials to seal the verdicts, Bell explained that the decision posed a problem. What if there had been three guilty verdicts? Judge Bell remembered that when he asked about it, Rimmer had said he would ask the court to set aside Chavis's verdict.

"What?" Bell blared, recalling the moment. "I'm going to set Ricky Chavis's first degree murder conviction aside because they've all been convicted?" Bell tossed a hand first at the defense, then the prosecution. "Why not set the King brothers' case aside? Why not set them all aside?"

The judge paused, knowing the words he was about to speak would rock the world.

"There's no question in my mind that they did not receive a fair trial," Bell stated slowly and clearly. "If everybody in this courtroom is not committed to a fair and legal process, they should not be in here," he said firmly. Bell told the excited gathering that he was granting the motion and throwing out the verdicts.

The room was stunned. The boys were confused but saw a huge smile light the face of James Stokes. Kelly Marino began crying and laughing, wiping her eyes with a tissue. The jurors from the King trial relished the moment of victory.

Judge Bell was not finished with his surprises. In another twist, he ended the hearing by ordering the case to mediation. This was an option often used for family law or petty crimes in which a mediator, acting as a liaison, tried to hammer out a deal between all parties. Mediation in a murder trial was unprecedented.

Bell assigned fifty-six-year-old Bill Eddins to the position of mediating the King case. Eddins had practiced law in the Panhandle for nearly thirty years, as a mediator, former prosecutor, and defense attorney. His dark hair, glasses, and conservative suit gave Eddins the kindly appearance of a family member. Lynne Schwarz hoped the result of mediation would be punishment coupled with rehabilitation. The boys' family just wanted to see them come home.

Chapter 29

THE SMALL CROWD GATHERED AFTER DUSK, PULLING jackets and scarves tight against the cold night air. Fall temperatures were finally cutting through the stubborn heat that had smothered the Florida Panhandle throughout the summer months. The cooler temperatures were a welcome relief, but the biting wind swept across the candles, causing some to flicker and blow out.

The normally bustling courtyard outside the M.C. Blanchard Judicial Building was a virtual ghost town after dark. Only the parking meters were vigilant as the group held hands beside the empty street, heads bowed.

"Heavenly Father," one woman prayed, "we ask for your grace and wisdom. You know what's best for these children, Lord, and we pray that your will be done."

Less than two weeks had passed since the court tossed out the King brothers' convictions and ordered the case into mediation. Donna Gallegos, the local leader for Under Our Wings, rallied friends, family, and supporters for a candlelight vigil. She also invited the local press, hoping the group's message of justice and leniency for the King brothers would be broadcast to the community. Mollye was there with a cameraman to cover the event for the late newscast.

* * *

James Stokes was amazed. Two of the most respected criminal attorneys in the State had appeared on his doorstep, offering their services. They had called shortly after the boys' trial, ready to help with an appeal, but James had been concerned; Jayne Weintraub and Ben Kuehne came with a hefty price tag. Knowing the family had little money for attorneys' fees, James thought perhaps the high-priced litigators only wanted a piece of the free press surrounding the notorious case. He soon learned who was picking up their tab.

"Rosie O'Donnell?" he said incredulously. "You've got to be kidding me."

The attorney assured him they were sincere, and so was the popular comedian. Organizers from derekandalexking.org had contacted a number of celebrities who called Florida home, petitioning them for help. O'Donnell had opened her heart and her checkbook because she felt "it was the right thing to do." James welcomed their input with open arms, and soon after their conversation, the lawyers were on a flight from Miami to Pensacola, ready to meet the brothers.

James introduced them to Alex with enthusiasm, but since Derek was Sharon Potter's client, he knew he shouldn't allow his newly found cocounsel to interview the older King brother without her permission. But his excitement over the prospect of high-powered help got the better of James, and he quickly pulled Derek into the meeting. Weintraub and Kuehne were convinced they could win the brothers' freedom in a new trial. In their opinion, the case and the prosecution was riddled with enough holes to create reasonable doubt for another jury. Sharon learned the Miami lawyers had talked to her client outside of her presence, and felt it was a serious ethical breach. But she knew they couldn't represent both boys anyway. It would be a conflict of interest to represent both of them.

* * *

When Jayne Weintraub appeared on *Good Morning America* following the court's ruling, Stokes wondered if he had made a mistake. During the interview, he felt that she attempted to take credit for the judge's decision and the implication was a thorn in his side. Afterward, he began distancing himself from the so-called celebrity attorney. Now, with mediation looming over their heads, Stokes was becoming more adamant that he, Sharon Potter, and Dennis Corder did not need the assistance of the two South Florida litigators.

Kelly Marino, the boys' mother, disagreed. She was convinced her children were innocent, and was as unimpressed with Sharon's and James's performances in the courtroom as they were with her parenting skills. Having retained the rights of being the boy's legal guardian, she began working closely with the new hired guns, insisting that Sharon and James include her in the mediation process.

Mollye sat in the courthouse, chatting with Barbara Walters's producer and another producer from *Good Morning America*. They were sitting on benches that stretched along a wide hall, waiting patiently while the attorneys and the boys met behind closed doors for the first day of mediation. David Rimmer was seated in a small room at the far end of the hall. Alex and Derek and the lawyers were in a room near the small group of reporters and family who awaited word of the outcome. Bill Eddins, the mediator, would emerge from one door and walk quickly down the hall to disappear behind another one. Several minutes later Stokes or Corder would materialize and stride solemn-faced to their opponent's quarters. The secretive nature of the discussion lent a film noir feel to the scene, as if they were all aboard the Orient Express with everyone scurrying from one room to the other on a furtive mission. Each time a door opened and footsteps fell, all conversation stopped in the hall. Observers could only speculate about the negotiations; the details of the mediation process would never be revealed to the public.

Six hours later the group was still sitting there when Bill Eddins emerged for the last time and told everyone to go home, no agreement had been reached. Kelly Marino was worried. She did not want her boys to plead to a crime they didn't commit, but she was concerned that David Rimmer would insist on it. She was right.

"I'm told that he's wanting adult sanctions," she told Mollye. "Just have them plead to a lesser charge. That will ruin the rest of their lives. It will be with them forever." Kelly was publicly thankful for the "caring" support Sharon and James had given her children, but she made it abundantly clear that in the event of a retrial or a mediation agreement she did not support, she intended to fire them and retain the Miami attorneys hired by Rosie O'Donnell. Sharon Potter disregarded Kelly's words with her usual disdain for the woman, but Stokes was increasingly annoyed with Kelly's threats and with what he viewed as unneeded interference from the South Florida outsiders.

The second round of mediation began a week later. Confident the case would go back to trial, Stokes didn't even a bring a notepad to the courthouse. Potter had her reservations. Initially, she thought Judge Bell's decision to throw out the verdicts was a miracle, a second chance to secure an acquittal and get the boys' lives back on track. However, there was no guarantee a second jury would acquit them. In fact, the only absolute that remained was the State's determination to send the boys to prison. She was prepared for a fight, but found herself embroiled in a grueling battle.

The boys seemed oblivious to the heated discussions, and made a remarkable discovery that diverted their attention from the possibility of life in prison: latex gloves. The gloves were part of a fingerprinting kit, and they begged James to let them fill the latex with water, a request he firmly denied. Noticing their disappointment, he suggested they use air instead, and the boys proceeded to inflate the gloves into five-fingered volleyballs. They were thrilled to play outside the confines of their jail cells, even if they were still under the close watch of court security.

Eddins presented their mediation agreement to the judge after nightfall. Derek, Alex, their attorneys, and David Rimmer were all there, ready to sign off on the deal.

"We have come to an agreement that we believe is in the best interest of the children," Eddins told Bell. "I believe I say that for everybody in the room."

The agreement specified that the brothers would plead guilty to third degree murder and each would provide a statement of guilt. David Rimmer had been adamant that any plea bargain had to contain a written confession. In exchange, Alex received seven years in prison, Derek faced eight years. Bell didn't think the penalties were harsh enough, but finally compromised.

The deal also promised that Alex would testify in Ricky Chavis's upcoming trials, including the lewd and lascivious charges Ricky faced for molesting the boy. The thought of describing the humiliating acts was a painful prospect, but Alex gladly accepted the agreement. He felt a new trial just wasn't worth risking the possibility of a lifetime behind bars, and although James said he would likely win his freedom in court, Alex didn't want to take the chance. James told Bell he was "firmly convinced" the boys knew exactly what they signed.

James, Sharon, and Dennis were amused by the obvious gesture of defiance in Alex's statement. The poorly written account was entirely out of character for the bright boy. An avid reader, Alex was fanatical about grammar and spelling. In fact, he even corrected the attorneys, much to Sharon's chagrin. She had once mailed Derek some legal documents while he was incarcerated with his brother. She carefully wrote "Priviledged" on the envelope, warning prying eyes away from the contents. A constant reader with a sharp wit, Alex immediately noticed the extra *d* in the misspelled word and relished each opportunity to remind Sharon of her mistake. During a phone conversation with Derek, Sharon heard Alex in the background teasingly yell a variety of words she should spell for practice. Amused, Sharon directed Derek to ask Alex if he knew how to spell "hospital." Giggling, Alex stopped tormenting her.

James thought that Alex's entire confession would be sent back for revisions because it was so ridiculously written, but to his surprise, the court eagerly accepted both boys' statements.

Satisfied with the pleas, Judge Bell agreed that a morning press conference would be the best opportunity to reveal the results to the voracious press. The attorneys hoped the overnight delay would give the brothers enough time to discuss their decisions with their families and, as Dennis Corder said, "head off the criticism that we sold the boys down the river," which they fully expected to hear from some family members. Sharon also wanted to make sure the family supported the boys in their decision. The boys agreed they wanted to talk to their mother, both pairs of grandparents, as well as their uncle.

Kelly Marino was furious. She met with her sons at the jail that evening and was horrified at the deal their attorneys had arranged. She couldn't call the media because the court had asked her and other members of the family to sign a confidentiality agreement, stating they wouldn't go public with the details of the plea agreement right away. The attorneys knew that the confidentiality agreement wasn't binding, but hoped the family would abide by it long enough for them to enter the pleas in court. Kelly immediately turned to her newfound allies, hoping Jayne Weintraub could somehow undo the damage. The Miami attorney was on a plane to Pensacola within hours.

National and local press were also converging on the M.C. Blanchard Judicial Building. Many were positioning cameras and equipment on the front lawn, preparing for live coverage of the hearing as well as the courtyard press conference that was to follow. The November day was cool, and many returning journalists thankfully noted that the unbearable heat they endured on their last visit was finally gone. The brothers' family barely noticed the chill as they went upstairs for the mediation hearing. They were too heartbroken.

Derek and Alex appeared in their green jumpsuits, smiling and joking with their attorneys. Everyone seemed relaxed, as if they were meeting to socialize instead of to settle the outcome of a criminal case that had riveted the nation. As Judge Bell took his seat, the crowd leaned forward, eager for the hearing to begin. But there would be yet another delay. Jayne Weintraub presented a motion that said the boys might not be competent to make a deal with the State and they needed a psychiatric evaluation before entering their pleas. Kelly Marino sat with her friends and family, clutching their hands in the hope that Bell would grant the motion. A delay could give them time to pursue a new trial, but Judge Bell had other plans. He peered down from his bench, irate at the outsider's presumptuous interference. He was on the verge of ridding Escambia County of this media circus and putting Terry King's killers—or so he believed—behind bars. He had no intention of letting this Miami attorney interfere, and denied the motion. Kelly sat in the gallery, her back rigid with anger.

The boys, their attorneys, David Rimmer, and Bill Eddins walked to the bench, lining up before Judge Bell like a loose formation of battle weary soldiers, ready to surrender. Bell was more than ready to accept a truce. He announced the details of the brothers' plea agreement to the packed courtroom, reading the confessions aloud in his casual Southern style. He immediately began stumbling over the numerous misspellings, grammatical errors, and sloppy sentence structure that plagued Alex's statement. "Derek got bat and hit dad hed," it read. "After wile dad didn't mov."

The judge also thoroughly questioned the boys' lawyers about the brothers' competency, attempting to further debunk the previous request for a psychiatric evaluation. They insisted the boys knew exactly what they were doing.

"They're children, but they're very intelligent children," Dennis Corder explained to the court. "They're much more intelligent than many adults we deal with on a day-to-day basis."

Stokes agreed. "There is a need for counseling, and I'm afraid that may have been confused in that person's mind with the need for a competency evaluation."

Bell respectfully asked Rimmer for his input on the fairness of the plea. "I know this is a concern of yours, because I've had too many years of experience with you to know that is not something you take lightly," Bell said, offering a verbal pat on the back to the prosecutor he had publicly chastised a few weeks earlier.

Rimmer stood at attention, his hands behind his back. "What I wanted in this case is what I got," he stated with absolute confidence. "I wanted the truth. I wanted them to tell the truth, to take responsibility, because I think that's the first step toward any kind of rehabilitation."

However, prosecutors aren't generally in the business of rehabilitation, and David Rimmer had fought vigorously against juvenile sanctions for the brothers. He insisted they face imprisonment within an adult facility, where punishment was key and "rehabilitation"—a word that sounds gracious in a courtroom—is lost in the wasteland of career criminals. When Judge Bell sentenced the brothers, effectively slamming down the gavel on their case, the court did not expect that the children would be cradled in the nurturing arms of well-intended juvenile workers who, through counseling, discipline, and education, would attempt to prepare them for a successful return to society. Rehabilitation was not the goal; only retribution for the man who was beaten to death on a cold, November night and the children who recanted their confessions.

As Kelly stormed out of the courtroom, her sons walked with childish reluctance to the far end, where a deputy waited to fingerprint them. Derek went first, his smile fading as he watched each of his fingers being rolled over an inkpad and pressed firmly on an identification card. He stepped aside for his brother and stood carefully wiping the ink off his hands until Sharon put an arm around her client's shoulders. With his usual irreverence, James fondly teased the boys until smiles returned to their faces, but the smiles lost their joy as deputies escorted the young prisoners from the courtroom.

Outside, the press was mobbed around a podium, waiting for the key players to make their statements. An indignant Kelly Marino and her attorneys spoke first. They insisted the agreement was illegal because Kelly was barred from participating in the mediation process. The outraged mother declared her children were too young to understand the consequences of their decisions.

"I talked to my boys," she cried. "I know the story they

told me. They are one hundred percent innocent and they were told there is no way out of here!"

David Rimmer planted his feet behind the podium, ready to take on any reporter, any question. He had endured professional and personal attacks for his handling of the case. The man who won the majority of his cases and successfully took center stage in the Pensacola criminal arena had become the object of ridicule and criticism. His hard-earned reputation was the trite fodder for late night talk shows and news magazines, all due to one case and two young suspects—the King brothers. The angelic young faces that captured the hearts and loyalty of people across the world were just a facade, in the prosecutor's eyes, and he was convinced that everyone would realize his pursuit of truth had prevailed, that he was right and those who believed the boys to be innocent were wrong. He summed it all up in one word.

"I feel totally *vindicated*," he said. "I feel like the Sheriff's Department's totally *vindicated*."

Investigators John Sanderson and Terry Kilgore had also been catapulted from virtual obscurity to subjects of local and national spite. The longtime homicide investigators resented the criticism, and they eagerly gave interviews following the mediation hearing.

"I think they liked it when they killed him," Kilgore told reporters. He relished this moment, even wallowed in it. "I think they're going to do it again. I think they're going to kill again!"

Sanderson tempered his comments with professionalism. "We felt all along that Derek swung the bat and Alex talked to him about it, pretty much masterminded it."

While Rimmer and the sheriff's investigators savored the moment, Alex and Derek sat in their jail cells, their home for the past year, wondering when they would depart. It happened at midnight. They were placed on a bus and whisked away for the long journey across the state to the North Florida Reception Center in Lake Butler, Florida. There, they would be evaluated by the Department of Corrections, which would recommend the best facility for their placement.

The process took nearly a month. Rimmer and Judge Bell both supported placing the boys in an adult prison. The brothers' family and attorneys wanted juvenile sanctions. State prison officials allowed the Department of Juvenile Justice to decide. Sharon, Dennis, and James visited the children at Lake Butler. During one visit, Derek's attorneys were pleasantly surprised to see that at least one aspect of the boy's personality had not changed—his appetite. While he talked animatedly about his adventures at the facility, Derek spent ten dollars of Dennis's money on the snack machines, devouring chips, candy bars, hot wings, and sodas. Sharon and Dennis were happy to accommodate him. Both attorneys had made the deal because they felt it was in the brothers' best interests. Their decision was based on circumstances, not guilt.

"It was a compromise, and obviously we would have been happy to see the boys walk out of the jail," Sharon Potter said. She believed Derek's situation stemmed from a family that had simply let him down and she felt a responsibility not to do the same. This was a child who often called her three or four times a day, even at night, to talk for hours. Sometimes he phoned out of loneliness, other times to keep her posted on her favorite soap operas. She was forced to give them up years ago in favor of a career, and Derek had enjoyed keeping her updated.

The world saw two people accused of a heinous crime. Sharon just saw two children. The first night they were in adult jail, the boys had only a mattress, blanket, and toilet. There had been no TV to keep them occupied, so they had wet toilet paper and made pictures on the wall. Another time, they put soap on the floor and skated until they had holes in their socks.

Supporters of the Kings were thrilled to learn that the Department of Corrections was considering sending both boys to juvenile facilities. Judge Bell and David Rimmer were outraged and fired off letters seeking to keep the boys in the adult prison system.

"Give me a break!" Rimmer wrote in a letter to the Department of Juvenile Justice. He said that transferring the boys would be an "outrageous decision" and a travesty of justice. "If this request is granted, in my opinion, it will be the moral equivalent of sending them to their room without letting them watch *The Sopranos*," he said sarcastically. But his angry words fell on deaf ears as the boys were transferred into the juvenile system.

"The lady of justice has been beaten, gang-raped and left for dead!" Rimmer vented furiously. His mention of "rehabilitation" in the mediation hearing was long forgotten, replaced now with a hunger for punishment. He also discussed the unfairness of the decision on *The O'Reilly Factor*. When asked by the host, who appeared to share the prosecutor's outrage, what physical evidence linked the boys to the crime, Rimmer pointed to the accelerant on their shoes, knowing tests showed the accelerant was different from the one used to set the fire.

The transfer was based largely on the boys' ages. The department had educational and treatment programs that would better prepare Alex and Derek for success when they were released. The community saw it that way too, and expressed its views in the *Pensacola News Journal*. One man wrote that although he had always been a fan of David Rimmer's, he was now disappointed.

"I was dismayed to read Rimmer's response to the King

brothers being placed in juvenile facilities, 'The lady of Justice has been beaten, gang-raped, and left for dead.' I thought it went, 'Vengeance is mine, saith the Lord.' I believe Rimmer should pay a bit more attention to his King James Bible and a bit less to his Black's Law Dictionary." In the upcoming months, the Lord's vengeance would be usurped once again by the angry prosecutor.

Chapter 30

ALEX KING KNEW HARDSHIP. HIS YOUNG LIFE HAD NEVER been easy, but past events, including his murder trial, were minor compared to the misery that was to come.

The State was preparing to try Ricky Chavis for kidnapping and molesting the boy. The kidnapping charge was based on a law stating that a person is guilty if he confines a victim under thirteen without the consent of his or her legal guardian, with the purpose of committing a crime. Even if the child consented to be there, it was still a crime. Derek was thirteen at the time, and could not be included in the charges. However, they applied to twelve-year-old Alex.

In order to make the kidnapping charge stick, the prosecutor had to convince jurors that Alex had been molested. If he failed, the kidnapping charge would disappear since the law required that Ricky confined Alex "for the purpose of committing a crime," in this case, sexual molestation.

Alex was key to making the State's case against Chavis, and David Rimmer deposed him prior to the trial. The deposition was embarrassing, but James Stokes did what he could to reduce the trauma. He kept things matter of fact and unemotional, attempting to lighten the depressing mood with humor.

At one point in the deposition, Mike Rollo asked Alex if

Ricky Chavis was a circumcised male, a point that would verify Alex's credibility.

"I do not know," Alex responded.

"You don't?" Rollo asked excitedly. The case against Chavis could collapse.

Alex looked at his attorney questioningly. "I don't know what that means," he said.

But Rollo knew the importance of controlling the moment. "Are *you* circumcised or do you know?" Rollo tried.

"I don't know what *circumcised* is," Alex responded.

There was an awkward moment of silence as the adults in the room looked at each other beseechingly. "Okay, let's go off the record," Rollo directed. Unable to suppress a smile, James suggested that he take Alex aside and explain it to him. The two huddled together while James drew a picture of a circumcised penis and another of one uncircumcised. Alex soon understood the difference.

"Are we pretty clear on the definition here?" Rollo asked.

James nodded and suggested they substitute the word "circumcision" for "flap of skin."

"All right," Rollo began. "Alex, you took a little break here and you've had a chance to discuss this with Mr. Stokes. So let me ask you, do you have an understanding of what circumcision is now?" He chose not to use the "flap of skin" reference.

"Yes, I do."

"Is Mr. Chavis a circumcised male?" he asked. Everyone leaned forward in anticipation.

"Yes," he answered simply. And, in fact, Ricky Chavis was. The case could go forward.

Alex told them the abuse began one summer night on Ricky's screened porch, where they sat together on an overstuffed chair. The forty-year-old child molester got him stoned. He fondled the boy, then moved him to a sofa in the same room and introduced his latest victim to oral sex. Alex told of oral sex that took place in a number of strange places, including one that focused even more suspicion on Ricky's close friend, Deputy Reggie Jernigan.

Alex wasn't the only one being deposed. Mollye Barrows had received a subpoena from Mike Rollo to give a deposition in the latest Chavis trial. Throughout the past year, Mollye had interviewed many people in her coverage of the case, including Ricky Chavis, and Rollo wanted to know if his client told her anything that could come back to haunt him in this latest trial.

Since Ricky was first incarcerated, Mike Rollo had fought a losing battle to keep his client quiet. Ricky had confided in several jailhouse snitches, and at one point Rollo sent Ricky copies of police reports that included their statements. In spite of Rollo's constant admonitions, Ricky was either unable or unwilling to zip his lip.

Mollye arrived at the court reporter's office carrying a small leather portfolio. She had meticulously transcribed notes of all of her interviews and brought copies to the deposition. The office was located in a charming wooden cottage in downtown Pensacola. Stepping inside, she smelled a pot of fresh coffee and noted the informal feel of the room. Many people found depositions intimidating, but this lovely setting did much to help those who were nervous to feel more at home and relaxed.

She was greeted by Mike Rollo and David Rimmer. Rollo smiled and thanked Mollye for coming, gesturing her to a chair at the conference table. He seated himself directly across from her, with David Rimmer at the far end of the table. The court reporter was at the other end and seemed happy to meet the local celebrity; the two women chatted warmly for a moment before beginning the deposition. The court reporter then turned on a tape recorder, punched the keys on her transcription machine, and they were off and running.

Mike Rollo began asking Mollye questions about the time she had spent visiting Ricky Chavis at the Escambia County Jail. She told him what they had discussed, including his upbringing, the King boys, and the fact that he had never admitted guilt to her about any past or present charges.

After ten minutes it was David Rimmer's turn. He asked Mollye if she had come across anyone who claimed to have been molested by Ricky Chavis. Mollye mentioned Herb Helton, and Rimmer asked her to contact him. Mollye stepped out of the room and called Herb on her cell phone. She explained to him that the judge had agreed to allow previous victims of Ricky Chavis to testify in his current case and then gingerly asked him if he wanted to talk. Herb seemed nervous about being pulled into the case, but he agreed Mollye could give the authorities his number, and she supplied it to the two attorneys. The deposition ended after only fifteen minutes.

As Mollye headed to the station on that Friday morning, she felt uneasy. The trial was scheduled to begin on Monday. Rimmer had brought the molesting charge against Chavis almost a year ago, and with the trial only two days away, he was just now locating witnesses? She felt his philosophy of "less is more" might simply be "too little, too late."

David Rimmer's image had taken a huge beating in the last year. Legal analysts across the country had condemned what they called "bizarre" choices the prosecutor's office made in handling Terry King's murder case. He was under investigation by the Florida Bar for charges ranging from withholding exculpatory evidence to submission of perjured testimony and false evidence. Further complicating matters, Rimmer had thrown his name into the hat for a vacant position on the judicial bench, and it was clear that the negative publicity could hurt his chances.

Mail, faxes, and e-mails from across the world indicated that many people still believed Ricky Chavis was responsible for Terry King's death, and that Alex and Derek had simply accepted the safest way out by taking a guilty plea and receiving a light sentence. Rimmer seemed desperate to repair his damaged image and convince the public that he had been right all along, that the brothers were responsible for their father's death. His insistence became a concern to some in the legal community. They murmured that he was taking the case too personally; he'd been unable to leave this one at the office.

The day before Ricky's trial concerning lewd and lascivious behavior began, Rimmer spoke to reporters again. Instead of recounting the child molester's horrible deeds or the need to protect innocent children from sexual predators, he chose to focus on the King brothers.

He told the *Pensacola News Journal*, "Anyone who doesn't think Alex and Derek killed Terry King thinks Elvis is still alive." The comment spoke volumes about the prosecutor's fixation on the case. Many readers were also alarmed that Rimmer was more intent on being "right" than he was on convicting Ricky Chavis of molesting Alex King.

Many were also skeptical that the convicted child molester could receive a fair trial in Pensacola. After all, the notorious inmate had often been front page news for a year. When defense attorney Mike Rollo argued that a change of venue was necessary, Judge Bell declined the motion, stating his belief that with some effort, unbiased jurors could be found.

One hundred potential jurors were assembled for a long and tedious day of questioning. Some were dismissed after revealing they would be inclined to find Ricky Chavis guilty because of his prior conviction for a similar crime. Others said they felt the allegations against Chavis were equal if not *worse* than terrorism. But by the end of the day, a jury of three men and three women had been picked. They would decide if Ricky Chavis would live the remainder of his life in prison.

While courtroom 407 was bustling with jury selection, Herb Helton was wrestling with a gut-wrenching decision. His instinct for self-preservation told him to lie low; let the other victims of Ricky Chavis tell their stories and put the pedophile away. He had only been out of jail a few months on DUI charges, and he never wanted to see cops or court-rooms again. But when Investigator John Sanderson showed up at his house and asked him to testify, he nervously agreed. Since Sanderson had neglected to bring a subpoena, Herb was free to change his mind. If he failed to show up the court could do nothing about it.

He dreaded the coming ordeal. The thought of facing Ricky for the first time in years and recounting the humiliating details of his abuse was bad enough, but knowing that the courtroom would be packed with spectators and reporters was almost more than he could stand. He desperately wanted to keep his name out of the press. The day before the trial Herb tacked a note on his front door addressed to Investigator John Sanderson and David Rimmer, the prosecutor: "Don't try to find me. I will not testify."

On February 11, 2003, Ricky Chavis found himself back in the courtroom. The strain of spending more than a year in solitary confinement had taken a toll on his appearance. His hairline had crept back farther on his head, and he made little effort to brush the remaining stubble. He wore the same olive suit of his previous court appearances, but it was rumpled and loose on his tall, gaunt frame.

Many believed the kidnapping and sexual battery case was open and shut; one newspaper columnist jokingly recommended that Ricky Chavis give up travel plans for Lent. If convicted, he could receive life in prison plus an additional 170 years. Ricky had recently discussed the grim outlook with his brother. He told Mike that if he were to receive more than thirty-five years, he would hang himself. Mike could handle having his brother in prison, but the thought of suicide was unbearable. The younger Chavis knew there was nothing he could say to stop him.

James Stokes tried to protect Alex from the unmerciful media attention that would accompany the humiliating trial. Judge Bell denied Court TV's request to provide live coverage and instead allowed Mollye's station, WEAR, to control the videotaping and give copies to the other media. Stokes wanted the court to take it a step further. A week before the trial, he phoned Judge Bell's office asking him to clear the courtroom and turn off the television camera during Alex's testimony. Bell's secretary informed him the judge thought it was the prosecutor's responsibility to make that request, explaining that Rimmer was Alex's advocate in this case. Stokes made it clear to Rimmer and the local press how Alex felt.

"My client is thirteen years old, and he's going to talk about intimate details of a sexual relationship with an old guy," Stokes told the *Pensacola News Journal*. "Of course I'm going to try to clear the courtroom. The older and more mature he gets, the more this sexual stuff becomes embarrassing. I think the more it dawns on Alex how bad he was used by Ricky and how manipulated he was, the more consternation he has of testifying."

Clearly, Alex was nervous, and providing a comfortable courtroom setting could make it easier to discuss the graphic details, bolster his testimony, and increase the chances for a conviction. David Rimmer could have elected to have Alex testify by closed circuit video, but he didn't. He told Alex that live testimony was generally more persuasive, but the courtroom could be cleared of unnecessary spectators, which would thin the crowd. Florida law states that when the victim of a sex crime is testifying, the court *shall* clear the courtroom upon victim's request, regardless of age or mental capacity.

In fact, moments before the trial was set to begin, Alex told the court that he would prefer to have the courtroom cleared. Kelly Marino also spoke on her son's behalf, but Bell denied their request. In frustration, he pointed out that no one had filed a motion to that effect. Stokes's attempts to intercede had been rebuffed, and Rimmer had not filed the necessary motion. Cameras would be rolling when the trial got under way.

David Rimmer had a difficult choice. Alex's testimony was crucial to convict Ricky Chavis, and letting the child molester skate out of the charges was unthinkable. But if he forced Alex to testify under the terms of his plea agreement—that he had a role in his father's death—the boy's own words would destroy the credibility needed to convince jurors Ricky was guilty. However, a courtroom confession could be the prosecutor's moment of triumph and vindication. Would he malign the credibility of Alex King to repair his own damaged image, or would he be able to set aside his ego to keep a pedophile off the streets?

Alex entered the courtroom wearing orange pants and a blue juvenile detention shirt. His hands were free, but the dragging chains around his ankles punctuated each step he took. The effect made the ninety-pound boy appear less like a victim and more like a criminal. Like Ricky, he had also changed in the months since the trial. His blond hair was now in a buzz cut and he had dark circles under his eyes. His voice had begun to deepen and he looked much more like a teenager than the child Ricky Chavis had abused. He no longer appeared to be the kid who could face whatever the court threw at him; he seemed self-conscious and filled with dread.

The prosecutor didn't appear to be sympathetic toward the victim he was charged with protecting. Only a few months ago Rimmer had stood before another jury, condemning the boy as a murdering liar. His opinion had not changed, and Alex knew it. The boy was unable to view Rimmer as a friend and the prosecutor did little to help him. He made little effort to encourage Alex to relax, nor did he attempt to soften the humiliation the boy might feel.

The problems were immediately apparent. Alex's speech was stilted and hesitant. He had trouble with even the simplest questions. When asked to identify Ricky Chavis, he looked over but didn't meet his eyes. He did manage to point at Ricky and describe his clothes.

The prosecutor wasted no time getting to the point. Rather than easing his witness into the embarrassing details, he began with a jolt. "When you met Ricky Chavis, did he tell you whether or not he was *gay*?" Rimmer asked. Alex fought an internal battle to stay focused. The boy who testified clearly and confidently in the past now looked and spoke like a victim. Rimmer realized he was going to have to keep it simple to make any progress.

He walked Alex through the litany of allegations, from the mental abuse to numerous sexual assaults. Some family members were infuriated when Rimmer asked, "Sometime after your twelfth birthday, did Ricky Chavis start a sexual relationship with you?" The word "relationship" implied the child could be an equal partner of a consensual couple and ignored the difference in maturity levels, as if children should assume responsibility for being manipulated into sex. The term implied an attitude that blamed Alex for the sex abuse and diminished the crime.

Alex began to withdraw as the testimony dragged on. He was forced to recount in graphic detail the times and places where the oral sex had taken place. Perhaps no one should have been surprised to learn Reggie Jernigan's rental home was among the locations, but the testimony caused spectators to turn to each other in wide-eyed shock.

The torment continued when David Rimmer saw his chance for vindication and seized it. He forced his own witness—the victim—to rehash lies and details of the murder.

"Did you testify in your own trial?" he asked Alex crisply.

"Yes sir," Alex answered.

"Did you tell your jury that it was Rick Chavis that killed your dad?" he demanded. He needed to shore up Alex's credibility if he hoped for a conviction against Chavis. Instead, he destroyed it, demonstrating for the jury that his own star witness was a liar and a killer.

"Yes sir," Alex responded.

Rimmer seemed to relish this long-awaited moment. "Alex, how do you feel now about blaming Rick Chavis for this murder?" he asked.

Many courtroom observers were stunned. Was the victim being asked to show remorse to the perpetrator? This line of questioning would only hurt the prosecution's case. Mike Rollo spoke before Alex could answer.

"Objection," he said firmly. "Relevance." The prosecutor had no legal grounds for asking Alex about the murder. Under the rules of evidence, the only permissible questions about the slaying were if Alex had ever been convicted of a felony, and if so, how many times. Any other questions related to the homicide were simply irrelevant. James Stokes and Sharon Potter were dumbfounded.

"I'll withdraw it," Rimmer told the judge, but he had sunk his teeth into Alex King and seemed fiercely unwilling to let go. "What would you have done, Alex, if Rick Chavis had been found guilty and you and Derek had been found not guilty?" he continued.

"Speculation," Mike Rollo insisted.

"All right," Rimmer said quickly. "I'll withdraw."

The judge was losing patience. "Don't ask questions that you're going to withdraw just because there's an objection," he lectured Rimmer. "Ask questions that are relevant, that have not been asked before, as opposed to asking a question, having objection, and withdrawing it."

Rimmer attempted to defend his position. "I think it's relevant to the state of mind."

"Then, *sir*, don't withdraw your question!" Judge Bell insisted. "Give me a chance to make a ruling. Ask questions that are relevant and let's go forward."

But Rimmer refused to be derailed. "Alex, what would you say now to those people who believed you when you said Rick Chavis killed your dad?" His voice rose insistently. "What would you say to those people who *believed* you?"

The gallery was incredulous. Rimmer was trying desperately to shame his own witness. Again, Mike Rollo spoke up. "Same objection."

"How is it relevant?" Bell demanded.

"I think it's relevant to his credibility in the eyes of the jury," the prosecutor offered weakly. However, there was simply no answer that could enhance Alex's credibility. To most in the courtroom, the questioning was nothing more than a thinly veiled attempt to scold and embarrass the boy.

It had absolutely no bearing on the child molestation case. The judge agreed the question was irrelevant and Rimmer finally surrendered: "No further questions."

Alex appeared physically and emotionally drained as he awaited the next round of questioning. He had expected to be grilled by the defense, but not the prosecution too. Rimmer had decimated his own key witness on the stand. The jurors could hardly be expected to trust the boy when it was clear the prosecutor didn't. A conviction seemed unlikely, and the defense hadn't even taken to the field.

All Mike Rollo had to do was reinforce the prosecution's efforts to discredit the boy. The defense attorney spent much of his time highlighting discrepancies in Alex's testimony, then insisting that his client had never molested the boy. During the second tedious hour, Rollo prodded the child to describe Ricky's penis and cite the dates of the sexual abuse. The deck was now stacked against the prosecution, and it would take a mountain of corroborating evidence to prove Alex had been molested.

The solemn-faced boy finally stepped down from the witness box, and the seat was still warm when his brother took it. Derek also looked years older. He appeared medicated and fought to keep his eyes open. He shivered in his short sleeves and blew on his hands to generate warmth, although the courtroom climate was comfortable.

As if reliving the murder trial, Rimmer instructed Derek to describe the night his father was killed. This was his chance to discredit the second King brother. Derek's anguish was palpable. He sat for nearly a minute, moving his mouth, but the words wouldn't come. Rimmer finally asked if he wanted a break. The boy nodded sorrowfully, and a deputy led him from the courtroom. Sharon Potter went after them.

With Alex and Derek's testimony reduced to ashes, Rimmer would have to scramble to rebuild the case. The best hope was to present a string of credible witnesses who had also suffered at Ricky Chavis's hands. Rimmer scanned the gallery and headed toward a woman who knew Herb Helton.

"We really need Herb to testify. Can you try to find him?" he asked, stressing that he was uneasy about the outcome of the trial. She quickly disappeared in search of the reluctant witness. Time was running out. The trial was expected to end the following day. Rimmer then turned his attention back to Derek. He found Sharon attempting to comfort the distraught boy. Contrary to his statement moments earlier, the prosecutor told Sharon that he thought the trial was going well and that he expected Chavis would be convicted. Sharon was not convinced.

Fifteen minutes later Derek resumed his place in the witness box. He told jurors that Ricky often gave him and Alex marijuana, and he described seeing Ricky take Alex on his lap and French-kiss him. Rimmer attempted to validate the boy's testimony with physical evidence. He marched before the jurors waving a picture of Alex that had been torn from a newspaper and carefully wrapped with transparent tape. An officer at the jail had found the treasured photo in the breast pocket of Ricky's jumpsuit, pressed close to his heart. Rimmer also showed them a picture of Alex that had been taped to the headboard of Ricky's bed, along with a letter found in his nightstand that read, "I love Ricky Chavis so, so much." The evidence pointed to a man obsessed, and Rimmer bolstered that image with testimony that Ricky was caught scratching a letter to Alex in the jail yard.

The State's next witness also had firsthand knowledge of Ricky's insidious ways, but when Mark Watkins took the stand, Rimmer did little to paint a vivid picture of the events. Instead he fired clipped questions and ran him through a dry, matter-of-fact line of questioning in less than three minutes. Mark testified that he met Ricky in 1984 at the age of thirteen. He and Tommy Penton, had run away from a juvenile facility and gone to Ricky Chavis's house. Once there, Chavis had given them pot and slept with them in the same bed. Mark said he spent two nights with Rick and awoke twice to find Rick's mouth on his penis. But Rimmer's questioning lacked passion and did little to illustrate the destruction Chavis had wrought in their young lives.

Then twenty-two, Ricky was sent to prison for the crime, but Rollo tried to minimize his client's guilt, saying, "He was a much younger man. In fact, he was an older boy." Ricky instantly took the cue, dropped his hands into his lap and sat looking wide-eyed and naive.

David Rimmer was just wrapping up the long day in the courtroom when his secretary passed him a note saying that the elusive Herb Helton had been found and had agreed to testify. Herb was upset to learn the case against Chavis was going badly. He empathized with Alex, having been the boy's age when Ricky first molested him. The thought that Chavis could go free to assault other children motivated Herb to take the stand despite his reservations.

Rimmer and Rollo spent their evening deposing the last-minute witness in order for him to testify the following day. His story of betrayed trust and molestation was shockingly similar to Alex's. But would his testimony be enough to convince the jury Chavis was guilty? Herb hardly slept that night, praying it would.

Herb was the first witness to be called the next morning. He looked handsome and confident in his new, perfectly starched outfit. He wanted jurors to see, hear, and feel his sincerity as he shared his most personal experiences with the world. He stepped into the witness box and swore to tell

the whole truth. Mollye sat on the front bench next to her
cameraman and gave Herb a smile of encouragement.

"How old were you when you met Ricky Chavis?" the
prosecutor began.

"Thirteen," Herb answered.

"After you met Ricky Chavis, did he ever perform oral sex
on you?"

"Yes, sir."

"Approximately how many times?"

"Over twenty-five times over five years," Herb stated.

"When is the last time that Ricky Chavis performed oral
sex on you?" Rimmer asked.

"Nineteen eighty-five," Herb stated.

"Where did that take place?"

"In his vehicle." Ricky had a history of using cars for his
trysts.

"Have you ever been convicted of a felony?" Rimmer
asked. He knew that Rollo would ask this if he didn't, and it
would be better coming from him.

"Yes, sir. Just one," Herb admitted.

"No further questions," the prosecutor concluded. He
turned and walked away.

Herb was stunned. Why was Rimmer finished? The
lawyer hadn't asked him about the wild times he spent with
Ricky Chavis. He hadn't asked if Ricky had given him marijuana. He had come prepared to tell the world how Ricky
Chavis had "groomed" him, breaking him down little by little, building his trust, getting him stoned, showing him
pornography, pushing him to masturbate, and then pressur-
ing him into sex. He was ready to share the details of the
psychological therapy he had sought to repair the damage
done by the child molester. He was sure his experiences
would convince even the most skeptical juror that Ricky
Chavis was a remorseless pedophile. But after a few short

minutes of dry, unemotional questioning, Rimmer was finished with him. The door was open for Rollo's attempt to discredit him.

"It's true, isn't it, that you began writing Mollye Barrows, the news reporter for Channel 3, while you were in jail?" he began.

Mollye was startled to hear her name spoken by the defense attorney. She looked up from her notes and felt all eyes on her.

"Yes, sir," Herb said.

"How many letters did you write her?" Rollo continued.

"Probably around ten." Herb had no idea how many letters he had written from the jail, but there had been plenty. With little else to do, he had poured his heart out to the reporter, and she had often returned his letters with kind but professional notes of her own.

"Is it fair to say that you had sort of a *crush* on Ms. Barrows?" Rollo queried. Mollye couldn't believe what she was hearing. The question seemed better suited for a middle school slumber party than a court of law. She suppressed a smile at the mental image of Mike Rollo in curlers and baby-doll pajamas.

"Yes, I did," he admitted. The insinuation implied Herb was driven to testify not by his past experiences, but by his desire to impress the television reporter. Having made the point, Rollo moved on. "The contact that you claim happened began in 1980? About eighteen years ago?" Rollo asked.

"Give or take."

Rollo wrapped up his questioning and Herb was released.

Despite his seeming eagerness to put Herb on the stand, the prosecutor had squandered the opportunity. Here was a man who could also tell the Ricky Chavis story, and the defense attorney had succeeded in making him look like a lovesick school boy. Herb stepped out of the box and took a seat in the gallery, feeling crestfallen.

The prosecutor also called Alex's two grandmothers. Joyce testified that she saw hickeys on her grandson's neck shortly after he returned from a visit to Ricky's. Linda Walker also described Ricky's systematic attempts to convince her the children were being abused.

However, the convicted child molester did not appear to be worried. Ricky was relaxed and chatty while the jury was on break. Cameras caught him chuckling with courtroom deputies, leaning back in his chair, flipping his foot back and forth like an overgrown kid. Mike Rollo, who was standing, glanced at him, and Ricky smiled broadly. Mike refused to engage and looked away. He would only invest time and effort straightening Ricky's tie or putting an arm around his shoulder if the jury was present. When Rollo didn't respond to his charm, Ricky abandoned the effort.

During the trial, members of the King, Walker, and Chavis families often sat close together. They were respectful and not unkind to one another. Those who were well-acquainted with Ricky's history were surprised to see Steve Bell among Chavis's supporters. Many expected him to testify. After all, he was Ricky's ultimate victim. Thirty-two-year-old Chavis had taken in the fourteen-year-old runaway and molested him for six years. By the age of twenty, Steve had filed a restraining order against Ricky and fled. The experience left him with only a sixth grade education and the clothes on his back. Steve had eventually made his peace with Ricky. If he had simply been physically forced into sex, he might have found some comfort in confronting the offender, but Ricky was an accomplished pedophile with decades of experience. Like many victims of the master manipulator, Steve was convinced that the sex that had occurred between him and Chavis was his fault. He sat on the bench next to his young pregnant wife and cried often throughout the trial.

If called to testify, it was likely he would have taken responsibility for the crimes, but the jury might have recognized the value of Steve Bell's story, as in fact the press did. The local paper ran a lengthy article describing the sordid details. He could have also shown jurors that Ricky was still actively seducing children as recently as 1998, progressing beyond the 1980s when he had molested Herb Helton and Michael Walker. Without a more recent victim, the jury might conclude that Chavis was a reformed child molester. But Rimmer never gave jurors a chance to hear Steve Bell's testimony.

Instead, the witnesses continued to focus on Terry King's murder. The defense called Mike Chavis, who recounted the night of the murder and told the court that while his brother had expressed an interest in having a "relationship" with Alex when the boy turned sixteen, he had not seen any sexual encounters.

Lead investigator John Sanderson took the stand looking confident and put the final nail in the State's coffin. Sporting a tan and an impeccably tidy goatee, Sanderson said that he had always believed that the boys killed their father. When questioned about the lump of metal found on the bed, he stated, "One part of the aluminum looked like maybe *the end* of an aluminum bat." This was particularly amazing since the police had ripped the house apart searching for the bat long after "the lump" had been found and its validity as the murder weapon questioned.

Sanderson questioned Alex's allegations that Chavis had molested him. He believed Mike Chavis's claims that Ricky wanted to have sex with Alex but intended to wait. He took the word of the convicted felon's brother over the testimony of two of Ricky's past victims, a grandmother who saw hickeys, and the evidence his own department collected. Many questioned his refusal to call for an investigation of the child molester who had concealed children beneath a secret trapdoor, kept them from their frantic father, lied repeatedly to the police, collected child pornography, stored childish love letters and tiny underpants in his nightstand, glued the boy's picture to his mirrored headboard, carried another in his breast pocket, and composed adoring messages on cell walls and sidewalks and in the dirt. So much corroborating evidence in a sexual battery case was unusual. Often such cases were simply the victim's word against the accused. Opinions were split on who killed Terry King, but people everywhere were convinced that Ricky Chavis had molested Alex. The thought that the lead investigator might have turned a blind eye to Chavis's guilt invited suspicion.

In his closing statement, Mike Rollo strode before the jury quoting from the book of Amos, then tossed in his own quirky interpretations. "Hate evil, love good," he lectured. "Maintain justice in the courts. Perhaps the Lord God Almighty will have mercy because the Lord God says I despise your feasts. I can't stand your assemblies. Even though you burn offerings and all that, I don't want 'em. Get them out of here! Away with your music and praises and all that. I'm not going to listen to it. But let justice roll on like a river and let righteousness fall like an everlasting stream."

David Rimmer, always quick with a comeback, told jurors, "Justice does roll like a river. In this case, it rolls like a river and it overflows its banks and it washes away all reasonable doubt. And the only thing left standing is the guilt of Ricky Chavis."

After brief instructions, the jury left to deliberate and the gallery quickly emptied. Everyone hoped to grab a quick dinner and hurry back, in case the jurors were not long at their task. Most had barely finished eating when cell phones began to ring. The jury had a verdict after just three hours. Abandoning restaurants en masse, everyone rushed back to the courtroom. Ricky searched for his family but found they were gone in his moment of need.

He stood grim-faced, on the verge of tears. When "not guilty" on both counts of kidnapping and molestation rang through the courtroom, a photographer snapped a picture of Ricky clapping his hands like a delighted child. The photograph would accompany the stunning headlines. He had successfully avoided life in prison. But the jury agreed that Ricky had hidden the children while their father desperately searched. He was convicted on a lesser charge of false imprisonment, and could receive a maximum of only five years.

Ricky would be sentenced immediately. Judge Bell invited the boys' family members to speak. Kelly Marino was instantly on her feet. She was anxious to stand before the judge and let him know Ricky Chavis could never pay a high enough price for the destruction he had wrought in the lives of her children. She asked for the longest sentence possible for him. When she turned away from the judge and headed for her seat, she noticed a line of infuriated family members had formed eager to slap Chavis with the highest possible penalty.

Linda Walker approached the bench and said, "I think Chavis ought to get the maximum amount of time for what he did to Terry King. He kept those kids while Terry was going crazy looking for them." Judge Bell seemed to appreciate her comments. Terry King often seemed to be forgotten in the flurry surrounding the trials. The last weeks of his life were torturous, but the irony of Linda Walker's comments were lost on most. Few knew that Terry had suspected her of hiding his children during those agonizing weeks.

After the family spoke, Bell turned to Ricky. Ever conniving, Ricky told the judge he wouldn't mind the longer sentence except that he feared for his safety in prison and thought the shorter one would be better. Someone in the back of the courtroom groaned. Judge Bell looked exasperated and said sharply that "safety" wasn't his responsibility.

"Five years is very easy for me to impose," Bell said curtly. "*Extremely* easy." He reminded the packed courtroom of how Terry King had frantically searched for his sons. "His friend, Mr. Chavis, is helping him, but instead of helping him he's the one that's got them," he recounted. "That's a little hard to swallow. By falsely imprisoning these two runaways, hiding them from their father and lying to him, that's unconscionable," he chastised Chavis. "That's lacking conscience."

A full conviction on the kidnapping and sexual battery charges carried "life in prison plus 170 years." All Bell could do was give Ricky five. With more than one year of time served under his belt, Chavis would be out in a little more than three.

The moment the gavel dropped and court was adjourned, family members burst angrily from the courtroom. Bright lights flooded the hallway and cameras rolled. Reporters instantly encircled Alex King's mother for her reaction to the verdict.

"This is a sad day for any child who has been sexually abused," Kelly said furiously. "I think Rimmer did a horrible job prosecuting the case. I think he did the bare minimum!" David Rimmer's "less is more" philosophy had crashed and burned.

Rimmer defended his performance and was eager to give interviews. A documentary crew from New York was in town gathering footage for a story on the King case. The prosecutor was relaxed and chatty as they followed him around throughout the next day. The camera caught him stopping to greet another attorney who expressed regret over the outcome of the Chavis trial. The community was united in its shock over the acquittal. Rimmer, however, did not focus on the fact that he had failed to keep the pedophile off the streets. He had shot down Alex King on the stand and didn't seem bothered that the jury focused guilt on the victim, not the child molester.

"You know, in a way it's kind of satisfying to know that they found Alex was the liar he is. So that's a moral victory, know what I mean?" he said and laughed. The film makers froze. They instantly knew the weight of the words. They exchanged wide-eyed looks which silently said, "Please, God, please let us have caught it on tape." Rimmer's infamous words were indeed recorded, and would confirm his attitude decisively to those who held any doubt.

On a bulletin board in David Rimmer's office was a quote from Babe Ruth: "Never let the fear of striking out get in your way." The baseball analogy seemed oddly appropriate in the days after the Chavis trial. *The Independent Florida Sun*, a popular weekly newspaper, dubbed the prosecutor a "Loser" in its high profile column listing local "Winners" and "Losers."

The article declared: "Rimmer lost another big one when Ricky Chavis was acquitted of ten counts of sexually molesting then twelve-year-old Alex King. Some family members and legal experts complained that Rimmer's recent case against Chavis relied too heavily on Alex's testimony. They question why the State Attorney's Office didn't hire an expert who works with child abuse victims to help the jury find their way. Rimmer, who received heaps of criticism last summer from legal analysts for conducting separate trials charging both Chavis and the King brothers of first degree murder, has one more shot in the courtroom. Chavis is looking at thirty-five years max in prison when a February 24 trial begins on charges of accessory after the fact and evidence tampering."

David Rimmer needed to hit the next one out of the ballpark.

Chapter 31

THE TRIAL HAD TAKEN A TERRIBLE TOLL. IN THE ENSU-
ing weeks, Alex was struggling. When a worker in the jail
made friendly conversation with him, he found a suffering
child. "Have you finally settled on what you want to do when
you grow up?" the man asked lightly.

"Yes, I have," Alex responded quietly. "I want to not feel
pain. I could jump off a high place and break my leg and it
wouldn't hurt. So I could break my arms and I wouldn't feel
it." His past dreams were now replaced with the simple desire
to stop life's agony. He no longer pondered the future with
hope. The sexual molestation, the brutal death of his father,
his confinement in adult jail, the murder conviction, the humiliating testimony before cameras in a crowded courtroom,
and the jury's disbelief had shattered the usually resilient boy,

His mother found him close to tears. He told her that he
had just read the newspaper article featuring a huge headline
that screamed, CHAVIS NOT GUILTY OF ABUSING ALEX, and
showed a five-inch picture of Ricky clapping his hands in
celebration.

"I don't care what people say about me," he said. "I
don't care what anybody thinks anymore." He was convinced that the people who heard his testimony would now
think that he and Derek had killed his father and lied about
the molestation.

Alex tried to explain his words in court. He told his mother that he feared that he could receive forty-five additional years in prison for perjury if he didn't stick with his written confession. Kelly had never seen him so anguished, and she began to cry.

"Everyone believes in you, Alex. We all do," she told him. "And we love you so much, honey." His eyes welled up with tears and he hung his head.

Alex had not been told if his testimony would be required at Ricky's third and final trial. David Rimmer would be prosecuting that one too, and most people thought he would now depend solely on Derek. The last jury had not believed Alex's hesitant testimony, and there was no expectation that he would perform better in the upcoming trial.

The trial opened on a perfect Monday afternoon in late February 2003. The sun was shining, and a cool sixty-seven degrees embraced Northwest Florida, but Ricky Chavis had no way of knowing how good it felt outside. He sat in jail hoping Mike Rollo would win his freedom.

The attorney was busy crafting his defense. Rollo was skillful, but this one would be tricky. Chavis had admitted to harboring the boys, washing their clothing, and lying to the police. Rollo needed to convince the jury that his actions weren't the result of evil intent, but that Ricky had acted out of compassion. The "family friend" had simply been worried about the boys and hoped to help them calm down before turning them over to the police.

The State had to prove beyond a reasonable doubt that Ricky had known of Terry King's murder, hidden the boys to help them avoid arrest, and washed their clothes to hide evidence. The final showdown between the State and Ricky Chavis was fast and furious. By the time it began, the prosecutor and the defense attorney could fire off the details of this story from memory, enabling them to quickly sift through myriad details, selecting bits and pieces to create a custom version to fit their particular needs. They had much to choose from. Ricky had told a new story each time he had met with police, and he'd created an entirely different account in his testimony before the grand jury. The story that would work nicely in one trial could be discarded in favor of a completely different one in the next trial.

Mike Rollo decided to draw much of his information from Ricky's grand jury testimony instead of the sworn statements he had made to police. The testimony was riddled with outrageous lies, including Ricky's statement that he lived alone. He had told the grand jury that his brother had moved out and wasn't residing at 607½ Palm Court when Terry King was killed, although Mike had been living there for years. His attorney pieced together choice bits from that testimony, tiptoeing around the lies and, as usual, making his client look like a candidate for sainthood. The defense attorney delivered an emotional opening statement. He took the jury by the hand and led them into the dark depths of the story, describing in chilling detail the brutal death of Terry King and representing his sons as remorseless killers whose gentle features disguised the monsters beneath. He portrayed Ricky Chavis as yet another "victim" of the wicked children who convinced him they killed their father in self-defense.

Unlike the previous three trials, this one fell to Judge Joseph Tarbuck, who was known for the efficiency of his courtroom. He was not a man who struggled with indecision. He assessed and rendered with lightning speed, wearing a pronounced frown while doing so and tolerating no nonsense that slowed the wheels of justice. He was tall, thin, and bespectacled, with sprouts of white hair framing his ears, and his seemingly stern appearance and demeanor did little to allay the fears of defendants in his courtroom.

The majority of Rimmer's case rested with Derek. He entered the courtroom in mismatched prison garb—orange pants and a green v-necked top with long sleeves underneath. He was just recovering from a nasty case of the flu and coughed throughout his testimony. Rimmer was ready to cash in on Derek's plea agreement. The boy knew he couldn't veer far from the words he wrote in mediation or he could face thirty years for perjury. The confession included the statement that he killed his dad and that Rick covered it up.

This time Derek didn't break down on the stand. His voice was dull and flat as he recited, "My dad went to sleep. I killed him with a bat. Put it on the bed. Set it on fire with a lighter." He went on to say that he, Alex, and Rick went to a field in Alabama, where Rick told them to take off their clothes. Then they went to Rick's house, sat down, and smoked a bowl of weed. Rick put the clothes in the washer. Derek said Ricky had spent a day and a half coaching Alex and him on how to confess to police.

He spoke thoughtfully and clearly, owning up to some unpleasant accusations, but refusing to accept the blame for everything Mike Rollo heaped upon him. The defense attorney bombarded him with questions in an attempt to prove that there was great animosity between Derek and his father. Throughout the testimony Derek defended his dad, saying he loved him and liked living with him. He admitted he also enjoyed being at Rick's, but most of all, he wanted to be with his brother, wherever that was.

Rollo needed to convince jurors that Ricky never encouraged the boys to lie to the police, but Derek refuted him. "Rick said to say that Dad beat us, to claim self-defense and we could get off of the murder charge." Now it was Derek's word against Ricky's. However, Ricky wisely decided to let his attorney speak for him.

"When you were with the Lays you had everything. You had a swimming pool, they took you to Washington D.C. But the Lays finally gave up on you, *didn't they*?" Rollo asked cruelly.

"Yes, sir," Derek replied quietly. Rejection was no stranger; he had no trouble believing or admitting that people didn't want him. Mike Rollo was slow to realize that Judge Tarbuck's courtroom bore little resemblance to Judge Bell's. The breaches that were commonplace in Bell's courtroom were not tolerated in Tarbuck's. When Rollo repeated the same question, the judge looked at the prosecutor expectantly. When he heard no objection and saw that Rimmer had no intention of making one, his patience exploded. "I want you to quit repeating the same questions over and over again!" he chided Rollo. The defense attorney persisted, but Tarbuck was firm.

The nightmare never seemed to end for Ricky's reclusive brother. Mike Chavis knew what happened the night Ricky and the boys returned after the murder and was always the best hope of providing the truth. He knew he was teetering dangerously close to the brink of going to prison. After all, Alex and Derek were hidden in his home after the murder, yet when investigators came looking for them, he sat and talked with them pretending the boys weren't there. Had investigators turned up the heat on him, he might have had a lot to say. Ricky obviously realized his brother was a risk to his story; he had told the grand jury that Mike didn't live with him at the time of the murder.

In this trial Mike offered his most creative testimony to date, stating that Ricky hadn't meant to hide Alex and Derek from police. Even more startling was his response when asked if he would lie for his brother.

"If it was something minor," Mike declared, instantly destroying his own credibility.

Ricky Chavis watched as his own duplicity was unveiled

before the court. John Sanderson affirmed that Chavis had told many conflicting stories to police, but Ricky's attorney was ready for that. He stuck to the account Ricky had told the grand jury, as though that version was the real truth.

"Do you have any reason to believe that Rick Chavis's grand jury testimony wasn't truthful?" Rollo asked John Sanderson.

"No," replied the investigator, but his answer ignored the numerous and bizarre lies in that testimony. Ricky had told the grand jury that his brother didn't live with him, and that he had never given marijuana to the King boys or spent time alone with Alex. Ricky's deceit included statements that he only drove one car, had never taken the boys to Thanksgiving dinner, and had never previously kept a runaway juvenile in his home. When describing the night of the murder, Ricky had told Sanderson that Alex had called babbling from the EZ Serve, but told the grand jury that Derek was the one who had made that call. Incredibly, the lead investigator stated that he had no reason to believe that the testimony wasn't true.

The fourth and final trial in the saga concluded without a trial jury ever hearing a single word from Ricky Chavis. He had watched while others sweated, cried, and were severely grilled, secure in the knowledge that he would never have to answer an uncomfortable question.

When the case went to the jurors a short time later, family and spectators were nervous. Mollye stopped Jerry Chavis as he wearily left the courtroom and asked how he felt. "I've just been a nervous wreck," Ricky's father said. "I can't sleep at night. In a way, I think he's not guilty, but I can only hope that they won't give him the maximum if he's found guilty."

The case was hanging almost completely on Derek's testimony. If the jury believed him, they would convict

Ricky. To win an acquittal, Rollo needed to prove that Derek had a strong motivation to lie, but he had little proof to offer. The strange case that had gripped Pensacola for too long was finally moments away from conclusion. The family of Alex and Derek lined up on the same long bench. Mike and Jerry Chavis took a seat in the back, while Judge Tarbuck sat perched high above the courtroom, looking down like a stern grandfather. Above him hung the Great Seal of the State of Florida, reading, "In God We Trust," and depicting a Native American woman and palm trees.

Courtroom security was in full force, prepared for any violent eruptions that Ricky's acquittal might bring. Everyone recognized the very real possibility that the defendant could be back on the streets within little more than three years. The four women and two men of the jury returned looking as though they carried the weight of the world on their collective shoulders. The deliberations had taken six hours, and they were now ready to pass judgment on Ricky Chavis.

The deputy strode across the courtroom with the verdict in hand. Judge Tarbuck rolled his high-back chair hastily over to the officer, took the verdict, and scooted back into place. He grasped a microphone and slid it to his chest. Members of the jury avoided looking at Ricky, choosing instead to focus on Judge Tarbuck as he read their decision without the slightest trace of emotion.

"We the jury finds as follows: As to count one, *guilty* of accessory after the fact to first degree murder. We the jury finds as follows: As to count two, *guilty* of tampering with evidence as charged, so say we all, this fifth day of March 2003."

There was silent jubilation in the front row of the gallery. Tears began to flow and hands were squeezed in an effort to stem the emotions threatening to burst forth in celebration. In the back row, Mike Chavis hung his head while his dad strained to process what the judge was saying. Ricky appeared grief-stricken and his face flushed as if he would cry.

"I would ask the court to impose the maximum penalty on both counts," Rimmer announced. After hearing Ricky's long list of felonies, Tarbuck was eager to comply even over Rollo's adamant protests. Two deputies escorted Ricky to a table. His gaze was unfocused and faraway as his fingers were mashed into the ink pad and rolled over the card.

The families hugged each other in relief and happiness, with little gratitude to spare for the prosecutor who won the victory. They were once again met by the media as the courtroom doors opened. Jimmy Walker had tears of happiness in his eyes as he told reporters how much the verdict meant to his family.

"Now Chavis won't be able to hurt any more little boys," he avowed. The bear of a man embraced Kelly Marino as photographers moved in to capture the moment of celebration they shared.

"This is a happy ending to a very hard year and a half," Kelly said, slowly shaking her head. "My children have suffered so much because of Ricky Chavis. Hopefully he'll be a very old man when he gets out," she added. She quickly excused herself and withdrew from the cheerful chaos. "I've got to see Alex and Derek and tell them the good news!" she said happily, and hurried away.

David Rimmer was the man of the hour, and reporters moved in close so as not to miss a word. They had grown to expect creative quotes from the prosecutor. He told reporters he had always believed that Chavis was heavily involved in the case. "It's like having an eight-hundred-pound gorilla in your living room—kind of hard to ignore." Reporters laughed and scribbled down the quip.

Though he finished on a high note, it wasn't without a price. The prosecutor had not made it onto the short list for the vacant position on the bench and for the time being would remain in the State Attorney's Office. However, he was encouraged months later when his peers on the Florida Bar's Grievance Committee cleared him of ethics violations in the handling of the Chavis and King cases. They found no probable cause to support the complaint, and the prosecutor told the press he felt free to continue his fight for justice regardless of age or circumstance.

Mike Rollo was furious over the lightning speed of Judge Tarbuck's decision. "The jury took five hours deliberating, and the judge took maybe fifteen seconds making up his sentencing decision," he lamented. "That was totally unfair." Ricky Chavis's defender promised to appeal the decision.

As Mollye rushed to get the news on the airwaves, she remembered the prediction Ricky had written in a letter to her nine months earlier: "I already know the murder and arson charges will disappear, but I don't yet know what will happen about the accessory after the fact." Now he does, Mollye thought with a wry smile.

Later that week, Kelly Marino, Linda Walker, and Lisa French shared the good news with Alex and Derek. The boys were happy and relieved. Ricky Chavis would at least pay for some of his crimes. It was a rare full contact visit, so the children hugged their relatives over and over in celebration of the verdict. The brothers had pleaded guilty to third degree murder but privately always maintained their innocence. After their visit, Kelly spoke to reporters who were waiting to hear the boys' reactions. She told them her sons had written confessions during court-ordered mediation in order to get a plea agreement.

"They were happy because they knew this was the last chance," she said. "Derek and Alex both know they were lied to by Rick. He told them, 'If you take the rap, you'll get off because you're juveniles.' "

Chapter 32

ALEX AND DEREK WERE IMMEDIATELY SENT SOUTH, THE long journey to their facilities taking two days. With the boys locked up so far away, their visitors were few. Joyce and Greg King were the first to make the long journey from Pensacola to Central Florida. Kelly Marino was also anxious to visit the boys in their new facilities.

Kelly saw Derek at Omega Juvenile Prison, located in Palmetto, just north of Sarasota on Florida's west coast. Once inside the high security gates, the scene was surprisingly beautiful. The setting was serene and quiet except for a large American flag whipping in the breeze. Weeping willows were scattered across the immaculate grounds and the modern buildings looked more like a college campus than a prison. A large pond highlighted the sanctuary, and a humorous sign posted next to it read: *WARNING: CORRECTIONAL ALLIGATORS ON DUTY*! The only evidence of the facility's serious business were the barbed-wire fences and myriad video cameras surveying every square foot of the grounds.

Derek was in isolation. Omega Juvenile Prison kept incoming boys separated from the others while they systematically set about modifying the boys' way of thinking and behaving. *Omega*, meaning "the end," was the final stop in the juvenile system. Boys who couldn't conform well enough to be housed there could find themselves transferred into the frightening world of the adult prison system. The small boy who had refused to stand up to the bullies in his old middle school found himself among some of the most brutal teenagers in the state.

Although Kelly had traveled from Lexington, Kentucky, to see Derek, she was not permitted to visit except during regular visitation hours. The Omega Juvenile Prison ran smoothly because the rules were simply not bent for anyone, inmates or their families. Kelly had the challenge of scheduling her visits so she would see Derek in Palmetto and then scurry across the state to see Alex at Okeechobee Correctional Institute on the scheduled day.

Derek's program had a boot camp feel to it; the juveniles were stripped of privileges upon entering, and had to earn rewards back slowly. As they progressed up the levels, the boys could receive luxuries such as books and colored pencils. For many months Derek's phone calls to family lasted only five minutes as he waited to move to the next level with longer call times. He remained locked up most of the time, emerging for school classes and then returning to his cell.

He found the isolation unbearable and poured out his loneliness in letters to family and friends. He begged Linda Walker to write to him, but realizing the demands of her work schedule, modified his request, saying, "You don't have to write anything. Just pick out a card and sign your name."

Kelly arrived early for her visit and stood outside the gates in the sweltering sun for a few minutes. Though alone at first, she was soon joined by several others coming to spend an hour with the young inmates. A buzzer sounded precisely on time and the gate popped open. Inside the small lobby, she was greeted by officers in military-style outfits. Multipocket pants were tucked into combat boots, and short-sleeve shirts revealed muscled arms that appeared capable of squelching any trouble the jailed youths might stir up.

Derek was thrilled to see his mother. She spoke to him in loving tones, as though he were still a small child, and he seemed to enjoy her doting over him. After a few minutes of reassurance he said, "Mom, thanks for just talking to me normal and not fussing at me."

"Sweetheart, I didn't come here to fuss at you," Kelly assured him, "I came because I love you. No matter what, my love for you will always be the same. There's nothing you could say that will change that."

Derek was anxious to know how Alex was doing in prison, and Kelly could see how protective he was of his little brother. Family had always been so important to him, and thoughts of his loved ones consumed him.

She was not permitted to bring anything for the boys, although she was allowed to mail hygiene products to Derek. She took great pleasure in shopping for the latest, coolest deodorants, shampoos, and body washes. Alex was allowed to receive shoes. Kelly bought a very hip pair of Nikes, only to learn that his feet had outgrown them before they arrived.

Her visit to Alex was enlightening. When she arrived, she signed in and waited in the lobby to be escorted to him. Moments later, Alex's counselor walked through the door, smiled warmly and extended his hand. Daron Washington, a tall African-American man, could have stepped off of the cover of *Gentlemen's Quarterly* or *Sports Illustrated*. Immaculately dressed, he carried with confidence a muscular frame that still spoke of his years playing college baseball. The counselor invited Kelly back, chatting about the facility and the progress Alex was making there as they walked. He seemed genuinely fond of the boy, and Kelly was anxious to see how they interacted together.

When Alex saw his mother, the delight showed in his young face. His eyes sparkled as he quickly began telling her all about the facility. He spoke enthusiastically of several inmates and told his mom that they had nicknamed him "Anakin," after the famous Star Wars character. Then he recited a mission statement that set forth goals he was expected to accomplish while at the correctional institute. His recitation ran for several minutes, and Kelly was amazed that he never stumbled or paused. Daron Washington smiled when he finished, telling Kelly that Alex had memorized in several days what many of the others failed to do over many weeks. Kelly could see he was genuinely proud of his newest ward.

Alex and Daron Washington shared inside jokes, and Kelly felt that an excellent relationship had developed between the two. He boasted of the boy's intelligence, good attitude, and excellent grades, yet quickly drew the line when Alex's sarcastic wit teetered close to the edge of disrespect. Clearly, the man already knew him well, and Alex had respect and affection for his counselor. Daron Washington invested his heart in this job, combining tough discipline with positive reinforcement. He simply chose not to judge any of the boys in his charge on their past behavior, but focused instead on their futures, preparing them for success when they moved outside of his care.

James Stokes, Sharon Potter, and Dennis Corder stayed in close contact with the boys, speaking to them by phone each week. They were all happy with the progress the boys were making. Florida's Department of Corrections had exercised supreme wisdom by refusing to place Alex and Derek in the harsh, crippling, angry world of adult prison. Transferring them to juvenile facilities had given them a chance to survive, and perhaps to heal.

On May 21, 2003, Mollye reported a new segment in the seemingly never-ending King chronicles. The news package opened with footage of Kelly Marino. "The mother of two Pensacola boys convicted of killing their father is in jail in

Kentucky tonight. According to an arrest warrant, Kelly Marino was arrested in Lexington for social security fraud. She gave false information to the Social Security Administration to get survivor benefits checks. The checks were intended for her sons, Alex and Derek. She cashed four checks worth more than $13,000 and is now charged with four counts of theft by deception."

The story then cut to a sound bite of Sharon Potter stating that she was not surprised at the arrest. She said it was clear from the beginning Kelly Marino was trying to make money off her sons' case. "At this point I think they probably don't have any illusions about whether their mother is ever going to really be a mother. If they did, my inclination would be to leave them with whatever dreams they might have about that, but I think they already know she's never been there for them and never will be."

Kelly spent a week in the county jail awaiting a court date, and got a small hint of what her sons had been through.

The Escambia County Sheriff's office found itself in new hot water well after the high profile trials. While covering a breakfast meeting with Sheriff Ron McNesby, Mollye Barrows asked him why he wanted to host the meeting.

"There are people in the community that have some time available in the morning that could come. People like this group here. You see a lot of ladies here today and that's a good group to reach. And they sometimes don't know, they don't watch the news and read the paper like men do. So it was really a good opportunity."

The comments angered many of the women and one told Mollye on camera that she would like the sheriff to know that women in general are very well read, do watch the news, read the newspaper, and stay up on current events. After the story aired letters from women throughout the county began appearing in the *Pensacola News Journal* saying that not only do they keep up with the news, they also vote, and planned to remember McNesby's statements at election time.

Lord Byron wrote, "*All tragedies end with a death,*" and the Alex and Derek King saga was no exception. On June 11, 2003, their champion, James Stokes, died in an ultralight aircraft accident. James and his best friend, John Johnson, were killed when the plane they had bought two months earlier crashed in a wooded area just outside of Pensacola. Mollye was on vacation that day, but cut it short to hurry to the station and cover the sad news. Scanning through archived footage of James, she found one of his last quotes and watched him spring to life on the screen with his usual fire: "I'll say this until the day I die, that but for Rick Chavis, Terry King would still be alive."

Kelly Marino learned of the accident and thought of Alex; he was scheduled to talk to James by phone that afternoon. She feared that the loss would crush Alex completely. Phoning his facility, she spoke with the psychologist and Daron Washington. They were with him to provide comfort when he learned the heartbreaking news. Derek was not permitted to talk to his mother at unscheduled times, so the news was delivered by the chaplain.

At a funeral home in Pensacola, James Stokes, the proud Marine, wore a helicopter pin in the lapel of his gray suit and had a flag draped neatly across his casket. A beautiful circle of red, white, and blue flowers adorned with a *Semper Fi* banner stood guard as people from all walks of life filed by to pay their respects. Leslie Stahl from CBS News sent a magnificent flower arrangement, and James's family members smiled, recalling how in a phone conversation he had once mistaken her for a client in need.

David Rimmer visited the funeral home, remembering James as a worthy opponent who represented his clients with zeal. Sharon Potter and Dennis Corder stayed with the Stokes family a long time, laughing through their tears and sharing stories of James's memorable antics and good deeds. They talked of how James thrived as defender of the underdog and his generosity to so many who could not pay him. Sharon wrote a touching tribute to her longtime friend in a local Bar Association newsletter.

One client asked James's mother if she could be permitted to put something in the coffin to be buried with him. She left a delicate white handkerchief embroidered with a red satin heart, a poignant reminder of the flood of clients' tears James had wiped away during his career.

Linda and Jimmy Walker also stopped by the funeral home to pay their respects. Jimmy had rushed over after work, without enough time to stop by his house for a shower and clothing change. Fearing the funeral home would be closed before he could arrive, he had borrowed a clean shirt from a coworker. The shirt was too small, had a missing button, and bore the name "Ken" over the pocket, but Jimmy didn't care. Paying his respects to James Stokes and his family was more important than his attire.

At a nearby church, James and the friend he perished with were remembered by a community that loved them. When the six o'clock service began, the church was completely filled, with 150 people still waiting outside on the lawn. Church leaders scrambled to accommodate the overflow, setting up chairs in an adjoining chapel and feeding the service through speakers. The two men were remembered for the joy they brought to others.

Less than eight months after James's funeral, Sharon Potter attended the memorial service of another close friend. Early in the afternoon of December 30, 2003, her law partner, Dennis Corder, took a drive along a beautiful stretch of highway between Navarre and Pensacola Beach. The two-lane road cuts a scenic path between the Gulf of Mexico and Santa Rosa Sound, the gorgeous view accentuated by miles of snow white sand dunes. Surrounded by this panoramic setting, Dennis pulled his Nissan Sentra off the road and parked. Traffic is often light along the leisurely thorough-fare, and there was no one to hear the shotgun blast when Dennis took his own life.

Donna, his wife of nineteen years, was one of the few people aware of Dennis's long-fought battle with depression, but that didn't make losing him any easier. She stood in the foyer of the elegant Pensacola funeral home smiling sadly and offering a warm hug or handshake to those who came to pay their respects. She expresssed her gratitude to a friend, saying that Dennis would have been amazed at the turnout and support. The stream of guests included Judge Frank Bell and David Rimmer as well as several other prominent judges and litigators. Jimmy and Lisa French also attended the service, shaking their heads in disbelief and sorrow at the death of yet another attorney involved in their grandsons' case.

Dennis's closest colleagues were heartbroken by their friend's suicide, shocked that the most intelligent person they had known would end his life at forty-two. They remarked that the man who had made a perfect score on his Law School Admissions Test and could zip through a notoriously difficult *New York Times* crossword puzzle had also been clever enough to hide his suffering from the very people who would have helped him. Many were surprised to learn that Dennis had had his pilot's license and that he had spoken and read French fluently. As with his accomplishments, Dennis had kept his innermost thoughts and anguish from many around him.

Several attorneys who had worked with Dennis at the Public Defender's Office years earlier spoke warmly at his service, remembering a loyal friend and a hardworking attorney with a passion for justice. They told how fellow defense attorneys had nicknamed Dennis the "Burning Bush," the man they had gone to when the final word was needed to settle an argument. As demonstrated by his committment to Derek and Alex King, Dennis had known his work as a defense attorney was important, and he had often given his time and advice to prospective clients at little or no charge. He would put any personal problems aside when he entered the courtroom and fight tenaciously for that often elusive "not guilty" verdict. In fact, a client's acquittal had meant so much to Dennis that during his time at the Public Defender's Office he would hang a black pirate flag, adorned with a grinning skull and cross bones, on the door of his office, or that of a colleague, each time the prosecution lost a case. Wiping away tears, one of Dennis's friends gave that flag to Donna. His friends said that Dennis had told them his marriage to her was the best decision he'd ever made. Their kind words were comforting to her, Sharon, and Dennis's family.

Pictures displayed at his memorial showed Dennis doing what he loved: snow skiing, enjoying his friends, and spending time with his wife and "Mozart," their beloved Himalayan cat. He had joked that the pet was like a child, and Donna asked that in lieu of flowers donations be made to the Humane Society. But in the end, those passions weren't enough to beat back the demons that had haunted Dennis, and he succumbed to the pain he felt he could no longer endure.

Sharon was devastated. She lost not only a talented partner but a dear friend. She struggled through each day after his death, finding solace in her work and friends. She carried in her heart one small comfort, that perhaps Dennis had finally found peace.

* * *

One man, well acquainted with both Dennis Corder and James Stokes, was unable to attend their memorial services. Ricky Chavis had taken a one-way trip to the Jackson Correctional Institute in Malone, Florida, where his notoriety kept him busy avoiding his own funeral. This prison excursion, unlike those from his past, posed a special problem: everyone knew his business. Ricky's greatest fears were now realized.

The high profile trials that had "outed" him exposed Ricky's prior conviction for child molesting and preceded him to his new lodgings. This was a truly dangerous fix. He would be one of those deplorable inmates known as "tree jumpers," a prison phrase used to depict the kind of person who hides in trees or bushes and springs out to seize and brutalize little children. Some of the members of NAMBLA might encourage him to openly embrace his "intergenerational love lifestyle," but doing so behind bars could be hazardous to his health. While isolation from other prisoners would ensure his safety, solitude for thirty years was a gloomy prospect for the man who thrived on the company of others, particularly children.

Reliving his experiences as a "boy-lover" could lift his spirits. Ricky had countless memories with which to entertain himself, but his vivid recollections would fail to capture the crippling humiliation and emotional disability he had inflicted. The memory of his self-serving lust might bring him brief pleasure in the darkness of his mind, but the experiences brought a lifetime of pain to his numerous victims, whose trust and childhood innocence had been destroyed.

Herb Helton still bore the scars, but he was one of the fortunate ones. He had come full circle, confronting Ricky in the courtroom and setting himself free. Afterward, Herb had written a touching letter to David Rimmer, thanking him for the opportunity to testify, finally exorcising the demons of guilt and shame that had dwelled in his soul for so long.

The long years that stretched before Ricky provided him with ample opportunity to ponder how his "devotion" robbed two little boys of the most precious time of their lives and consigned them to the soul-scarring experience of prison. He could always reflect on the personal shame and humiliation he had visited on Alex, and relive the child's torment as he sat for two hours on the witness stand, cameras pushing in for the tight shot as he was forced to describe the distinguishing traits of his assailant's penis. Without his boy-love support group, Ricky might succumb to the "brainwashing" of prison therapy, calling a halt to his ever-evolving self. His best hope was to link up with others who could help elevate his spirits by offering validation of his lifestyle. He knew they were out there. Someone in West Virginia had anonymously deposited a thousand dollars in his prison account. Contact with such supporters would be necessary to preserve his sanity. Without their reinforcement to absolve him from blame, he might have to confront the totality of his deeds and begin to realize that having sex with children is an abomination. Such thoughts, to introspective Ricky, could shatter his peace of mind. He might simply drown in depression.

But the past proved that Ricky was a survivor, adept at using children to escape the consequences of his crimes. He also had faith in his ability to manipulate the legal system, and he believed it was only a matter of time before he would return to Fort Chavis. But it hadn't happened yet and he often cried over his plight. However, Ricky had few tears for the man who had asked only for his friendship.

Terry King had simple achievements. He made no wealth; financial burdens were an anchor around his neck. His unremarkable career centered around a minimum wage job, and a show of hands would reveal only a few loyal friends who claimed to know the shy, reclusive man. Yet the father who passed unnoticed on the street during his life became a household name upon his death. Terry King stood firmly between the pedophile and the object of his debauchery, and paid the ultimate price. The struggling father had lost his children and then his life. His murder was indeed gruesome, but Terry King's legacy is not a violent death. It is a loving heart. Sadly, he would never know that Ricky Chavis was finally prevented from obtaining the treasure he had sought to steal. Though the road was long and the cost dear, in the end, the hearts of Alex and Derek were restored to the father who gave his life for them.

Epilogue

On a bright, warm, summer day, birds circle high above the immaculate grounds where Terry King was laid to rest. The late afternoon sunlight filters through the trees and casts long shadows across the soft carpet of grass.

Though Alex and Derek have yet to visit their father's grave, a message waits for the day they will come. Words of deepest understanding are engraved on a marble headstone, destined to wait nearly a decade before being read by the children for whom they were written. Only then will the message be imparted with the timeless compassion and grace of a gentle father:

"I love you Alex and Derek."